HOME PRESERVING MADE EASY

HOME PRESERVING MADE EASY

· A COMPLETE GUIDE TO ·

Pickling / Smoking / Canning / Drying
Freezing and Jelly-Making

Vera Gewanter & Dorothy Parker

· ILLUSTRATED BY ·
Nancy Tausek

· The Viking Press / New York ·

· *For Sid and Saul* ·

MAY THE SAINTS PRESERVE THEM!

Copyright © 1975 by Dorothy Parker and Vera Gewanter
All rights reserved
First published in 1975 in a hardbound and a paperback edition by
The Viking Press, Inc.
625 Madison Avenue, New York, N.Y. 10022
Published simultaneously in Canada by
The Macmillan Company of Canada Limited

LIBRARY OF CONGRESS CATALOGING IN PUBLICATION DATA
Gewanter, Vera.
Home preserving made easy.

(A Viking compass book; C591)
Includes index.

1. Food—Preservation.   2. Canning and preserving.
I. Parker, Dorothy, 1922-   joint author. II. Title.
TX601.G45 1975   641.4   74-4792
ISBN 0-670-37715-5
ISBN 0-670-00591-6 pbk.

Printed in U.S.A.

CONTENTS

v

CONTENTS

CONTENTS

vii

$$\boxed{\cdot \text{ ACKNOWLEDGMENTS } \cdot}$$

For their help and encouragement in the face of great odds the authors wish to express their deepest gratitude to the following:

Mrs. Elisa Ronchi of Milan, Italy
Mrs. Luciana Alfieri of Rome, Italy
Mrs. Anne Marie Noverraz of Geneva, Switzerland
Mrs. Giorgía Kyriakákis of Chaniá, Crete, Greece
Mrs. Consuelo Torres of Buenos Aires, Argentina
Miss Yvette Foucauld of Paris, France
Mrs. Bibi Jeppesen of Oslo, Norway
Mrs. Kathryn Edwards of Bridgewater, Connecticut
Mrs. Marilyn Fenno of Montpelier, Vermont
Mr. Michael Norman of Bath, Somerset, England
Mr. Robert Parker of Cocoa, Florida

And all the enthusiastic and generous people in the agricultural extension services of the fifty states of the union. Our heartfelt thanks.

Vera Gewanter
Dorothy Parker

HOME PRESERVING MADE EASY

IN PRAISE OF PRESERVING

The idea for this book was born of disaster—an all-night blackout during a siege of skyrocketing inflation and tight money. As your authors bemoaned all the provender going to ruin in their electrically powered Deepfreeze, which slowly but inexorably was defrosting itself into a great puddle, it struck us how unnaturally dependent we moderns have become on freezing as a means of preserving our food; and how, ironically, such power failures always seem to occur just after we have shopped and packed our freezers with perishables. Although freezing is often suggested for storing many foods, there are countless other methods of keeping them fresh and nutritious that work just as well, and some that actually offer far more effective safekeeping of certain comestibles for weeks or even months.

Consider the lowly snap bean. Its splendid flavor when freshly picked is lost almost entirely when frozen, but not when it is canned at home. Compare the last batch of frozen fish you bought at the supermarket with the mouth-watering delight of the seafood you ate at that shore restaurant that serves only the fish running that very day, and your gustatory enjoyment of marinated herring or smoked salmon. If you have been bitterly disappointed in the contrast between those slimy frozen melon balls

3

from the supermarket and the tempting succulence of a country-fresh vine-ripened melon laid open before you, pickling your melon (see Index) will assure you of year-round contentment.

Total dependence on electricity for the functioning of all of one's household is rather a perilous, wasteful, and lazy way to live. We should all welcome the end of this country's superabundance, which is fast giving way to a period of shortages (and possibly rationing) that is bound to last for quite some time. A more natural and independent lifestyle awaits us, one that no longer conforms to the needs and comforts that were dictated to us by a legion of anonymous industries but instead makes us rely on personal inventiveness and accomplishment.

Until a few years ago a return to the earth and to life on a more natural level was considered a somewhat eccentric poetic dream pursued by a rising tide of young people and a small minority of disenchanted middle-aged. Now the very real circumstances that involve all of us are making it an imperative necessity. Perhaps we can look forward to an end of the age of plastic man and a return to the simpler, more healthful life. We can learn much from our ancestors' better understanding of nature and the marvelous chemistry contained in the products of the earth. How our forefathers retained and benefited from it by means of preserving is what we hope to share with you in this book. Their knowledge and expertise, enhanced by the occasional use of the most practical inventions of our age, can help us all create more self-sufficient households, and restore as well some of the sophistication our tastebuds have gradually lost on a diet of foods that are sadly—and often harmfully—tampered with for the sake of efficiency.

We realized on that dark night that our supply of food would not always be at hand, contained in a block of ice. We decided to get rid of our Deepfreeze; we would rely instead on the freezing compartment of the refrigerator for storage of only those foods that keep best when frozen, for some kinds of leftovers, the one-dish meal that is so much trouble to make that it's an economy of time to make several at a time and then freeze them, and the home-baked bread we make at home one day a week. We made plans to preserve more and more and by all the fascinating methods available to us. We moved out our Deepfreeze and gave the space it had occupied to our food-smoking equipment, drying racks, canning kettle, and cartons of fruit jars and jelly glasses, accouterments that take up less space, have a longer life, and, above all, a more stable disposition than most electrical gadgets. Most important of all, they cost next to nothing to operate.

The inflationary spiral that at this writing is still whirling upward strikes every one of us where it hurts the most—nutritionally. The "cost of feeding a family of four" is presently so unbelievably high that a growing number of us have taken to growing as many of our own provisions as we can. But the means are not always available; some of us can only take advantage of any windfall that comes our way in seasonal reductions, wholesale prices, or pick-your-own-and-save specials. Such bonuses, however, usually saddle us with an overabundance of one food all at once. Accustomed as we are to variety in our menus, how can we accept the idea of consuming a bushel of apples before they go bad? How many apple pies in a row can your family eat? How much applesauce can an already bulging refrigerator hold? But store these fruits or transform them into wine, cider, relish, fruit cake, dried cereal, butter, and a number of other delicacies, and the lucky holder of that fabulous bargain in Winesaps or Cortlands will be able to savor them throughout the year, in many different tempting forms.

Furthermore, all of us are becoming increasingly suspicious of the questionable additives in the commercially prepared, prepackaged, plasticized foods. It has been estimated that the average American consumes five pounds of such food additives a year. These dyes and chemicals are far more beneficial to the wholesale shipper and warehouse keeper than to the human anatomy. More than ever, people are scurrying to farmers' markets and taking to the more natural ways of growing, preparing, and preserving their foods.

A few general rules will make our readers' efforts all the more rewarding. Perhaps the most important is a constant awareness of one of Nature's most clever maneuvers: The viand at the very zenith of ripeness and most attractive to behold is the one with the most luscious flavor and the best capacity to nourish. The moment you pick a peach or an ear of corn, its vitamin content (among other things) starts to diminish. If you commence your preserving just as soon after gathering as you can, you will conserve the optimum yield of vitamins and minerals in the foods you preserve. The longer vegetable matter is cut off from *its* source of sustenance, the less nourishing it becomes. For other products, especially pork and fish, the negative possibilities are even more decided.

We digest food by means of enzymes, a special class of substances which control chemical reactions in plants and animals. Fruits and vegetables ripen by means of enzymes. The enzymes in produce make it grow to maturity but will also eventually cause it to rot. Successful preserving depends on inhibiting the action of the enzymes, often with the help of fermenting agents such as vinegar, sugar, yeast, or alcohol. Although inevitably some nourishment is lost when you eat anything but a food fresh from field or bush, much of it is locked in by the very process of preserving.

Not so many years ago, it suddenly became chic to be a good cook. Even baking your own bread became glamorous. In our present times of crisis, the practical art of preserving is growing ever more popular. The methods we offer in this book are relatively simple ones, intended for the small-to-medium-family home preserver, although the recipes are infinitely expandable. You will discover many pleasurable and profitable alternatives to dependence on the freezer and the supermarket, for we have tried to provide various and superior systems of preserving specific foods without damage (indeed often with enhancement) to their nutritional value, texture, and flavorsome goodness. For the home gardener, these wholesome ways of getting the most out of his crop will prove a boon; for the do-it-yourselfer here lies yet another challenge to your spirit of creativity, your ingenuity and self-reliance. The pleasures of preserving, like cooking, increase with imagination and taste, and once you have absorbed the basics of each method of preserving, you will be tempted to improvise. Our divergent backgrounds have permitted us to treat our subject from many angles and, we hope, as completely as possible. Vera Gewanter, born in Italy, brings to the effort her years of living in Europe and in South America; and Dorothy Parker draws extensively from the experience of growing up in New England, and traveling throughout North America and the British Isles. In this book we have noted what comestibles work best for *us*, but if you discover a new treatment for a favorite food, tell us about it. If you invent, let's say, an exciting, exotic preserve we have not included, write. We'd like to hear from you and try it, too.

THE HOUSE YOU LIVE IN AND OTHER USEFUL EQUIPMENT

· SPACE ·

You may have, just beyond the turn of a doorknob, superlative facilities for keeping the foods you preserve. Does your house have an uninsulated, well-ventilated attic? Then you already have the ideal environment for the drying of herbs and certain fruits and vegetables, which you can spread out, hang from rafters, or string and suspend from studs. If you live in an apartment, you may have a closet with just the right degree of heat and dryness to accommodate such drying of foodstuffs. Or, your roof, if you live where the sunlight can be counted on and the air is not heavily polluted, can do the job for you.

If you are a home owner, look around your property. There may still be standing that relic of the old days before the advent of indoor plumbing—a springhouse, a little roofed construction enclosing a source of fresh water. It's an ideal place to store cheese and certain other products that do well with a little humidity.

Is there a cellar under the first floor of your house? Then you probably have a whole spectrum of conditions perfect for preserving foods, and ample space as well for the proper storage of wine, cheese, root vegetables, grains, meals, and flours. Does it have a "cold closet" or are shelves already in place? If not, they can be easily constructed by means of the old brick-and-board method you've been using for books for years. Neatly lined up on your new shelves, those ranks of preserved meals you prepare and store will give you a tremendously satisfying feeling of security as another long, cold, inflationary winter comes on.

If the springhouse is gone, somewhere in your cellar, away from the furnace or boiler, there is surely the dark, cool, dry place that will be so often mentioned in the following pages; you may find as well the warm, dry place you will need occasionally.

If you lack this kind of spacious, all-purpose cellar under your house, it's just possible that you do have a larder or pantry, that utilitarian, marvelous small room that during one period in our architectural history was considered indispensable. It may be *there*—if steam heat has not been piped into it by a previous owner—that you can find the amplitude of cool, dry space you will require. Some older houses offer perfect storage space in what was once called the back hall, that narrow little room between the back porch and the kitchen that sheltered the icebox into which the iceman plunked a cake of ice every few days. Apartment dwellers may be able to provide themselves with cool, dry storage space by adding one or two extra kitchen cabinets.

If you have neither cellar nor pantry but are fortunate enough to have a bit of ground around your house, you can make your own vegetable storage cellar out of a barrel, or some boards; the

only tool you will need is a shovel (see the illustrations on page 9). You will in effect be returning the vegetables to the earth they grew in (or a simulation thereof), but affording them new protection from predators and from the elements. If you live in an area with medium-to-heavy rainfall, or if your ground tends to be quite damp from other sources, you may want to add some plastic sheeting to your homemade storage cellar. Lay the plastic next to the earth, with other layers of wood, straw, or similar material between it and your produce. You can keep any number of hard vegetables and fruits through the fall and winter in such a root cellar.

• TOOLS •

A number of items are indispensable, many of which you can easily make yourself. You will find directions and specifications at the beginnings of the chapters where they come into use. For example, the chapter on sausage-making opens with instructions for constructing your own sausage-making device; that on smoking, with plans for a home-fashioned smoker; and our extensive treatment of canning begins with all the information you will need about canning kettles, special fruit jars, and the pressure canner.

No home preserver should begin without a collection of glass jars in various sizes, and some Mason or Ball jars (see Index). If you are lucky enough to own a good supply of stoneware, be sure that their glazing is entirely free of cracks or holes. (You can always use the cracked ones for potting your plants.) And, if you are dealing with anything acid—fruits, tomatoes, vinegar, wines—be perfectly sure as well that the glazing is of a non-lead variety. Lead glazes are usually, but not always, identifiable by their gray color. Avoid using copper utensils as well as copper pots (even though lined with tin) both for cooking and as temporary containers for acid foods.

You will need tissue paper, the kind that shops use to pack clothes or breakable gifts; even more appropriate will be the tissue you sometimes find wrapped around fruits from the market or wholesaler. You will also need a supply of bags or sacks. Some muslin, too, or cheesecloth, which can be bought very inexpensively (the unbleached variety is recommended) from your dry-goods store, will be useful when making cheese and for other things as well.

Equip yourself with slotted spoons, sieves, strainers, drainers, and colanders in various kinds and sizes. You can make a flat sieve by stapling or nailing a piece of rustproof window screening over the top (or inside, high up toward the top) of the frame of a child's drum or some cylindrical piece of wood such as an old-fashioned hat box (see illustration below).

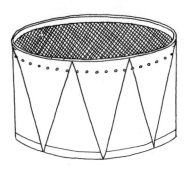

A steamer is another piece of equipment essential to the home preserver, for the steaming of vegetables retains their nutritive value far more effectively than boiling. Fancy French vegetable steamers are efficient and even decorative items to have around the kitchen, but they are hardly necessary when it is so easy to make your own. If you have a good heavy cooking pot with a cover, a cup-shaped strainer of about a quart capacity with a handle, and a pair of those little L-shaped braces that will hold it on top of a pot or pan, then you have a vegetable steamer. Put enough water into the pot to form steam but not so much that it will reach the bottom of the strainer, add your cleaned vegetables to the strainer, put the pot cover on top, and then steam on medium to high heat, checking once or twice to make sure that your water has not all boiled away. You can, if you prefer, substitute for the strainer a French-frying basket, or one of those wire cages for whirling washed salad greens dry.

Some wooden items that you should have on hand are barrels, firkins (those wooden buckets with covers and handles that are especially good for storing sugar, grains, meals, flours, and such), cutting and pressing boards, and spoons; as a matter of fact, as many wooden utensils as you can collect. Except for some special purposes—jelly testing, for example—wood is so much safer and easier to work with than metal. You will want assorted wooden spoons, stirrers (try chopsticks), and spatulas for a hundred different uses—some flattened, others rounded, or perforated.

Metal spoons or utensils should not be used for such acid-containing foods as the fruits in jams, milk, many other comestibles, and when pickling. Metal, especially aluminum, can discolor certain foods or lend a bad taste. And wood, of course, does not scratch the pots. Stainless steel is equally acceptable.

The old-fashioned food grinder of cast iron that clamps onto the edge of the table or counter, fitted with several grills with holes of various sizes, is a wonderful and versatile machine to have. The mortar and pestle, too, is an excellent tool for grinding seeds and for achieving the right degree of pastelike consistency for some kinds of sauces and condiments.

If you have an electric blender, you have no doubt been making your own milk shakes, vegetable or fruit drinks, peanut butter, potato-pancake batter, and a host of other delights for years. But you may have been frustrated by its limitations: It won't grind coffee beans, turn wheat berries into flour, or dried corn kernels into corn meal; and if you put in rather hard nuts you break, scratch, or dent your blender canister. There is now on the market a home-style machine with a heavy-duty motor and several speeds and actions that will purée, pulverize, grind, blend, mash, grate, chop, whip, or liquefy anything at all. Called Nature Blender, it is really a considerable improvement over other blenders and grinders because it combines the features of both machines and simplifies other tasks as well.

Perhaps you can pick up a food scale at a flea market, country auction, or hardware store. If you plan to cure meat and game, you will probably want one that hangs up and hefts by means of a hook or suspender; for jam- or jelly-making, you will find useful the kind of scale on which you can lay a flat-bottomed pot or pan, for you will have to match the fruit you are jellying or preserving with the appropriate weight of sugar, and doing it by volume is less reliable. (*Tip*: If ever you are puzzled about how to weigh a quantity of pulp or juice, just weigh a skillet or pot, then pour in the juice, weigh again, and subtract the weight of the pot to obtain the net weight of the food.)

As for pots and pans, baking dishes, measuring cups, and the like, you probably already have a selection that will prove adequate to all your preserving needs. Who among us doesn't own a shallow rectangular pan and a large platter? Before you go out to buy some utensils especially for preserving, first search through your attic, woodshed, and kitchen cabinets, and consider the various uses you can put a utensil to, so that you won't have to make any unnecessary purchases.

Your own two hands will prove to be the best, most versatile tool that you can possibly have. Don't be afraid to use them in preparing foods for cooking or preserving.

Incidentally, we cannot stress too often the importance of absolute cleanliness in performing all the preserving processes. Clean hands, scrubbed work surfaces, sterilized utensils and containers—all such precautions are imperative and will save you disappointments and possible loss.

• MATERIALS •

Some meats, of course, are better preserved if aged first (see Index), but you will be one step ahead of the game if you work with fresh, unblemished, good-quality raw materials—meat that has been butchered properly, fish straight from the stream, lake, or sea, fruits or vegetables within a few hours of harvesting. Caught early, they may be kept late and their bloom and nourishment preserved intact for weeks or months—sometimes even years.

Naturally ripened tomatoes, melons, and other fruits are so vastly superior to those that have been picked unripe and then aritificially ripened that there is just no comparison. You can tell by the aroma, for an artificially ripened fruit just doesn't have the natural fragrance. And the flavor—the very life of the fruit —is gone, possibly because commercial ripening is often done in gas chambers. Grow your own if you possibly can, and let the sun ripen it for you.

If you can't grow your own produce or buy it from a farm market, chances are that much of what you purchase will have a coating of some kind that either changes its natural color (as on oranges and tangerines) or acts as a temporary preservative (the wax on cucumbers, for example). There's little you can do about this, but try to use only the peels of citrus fruits that have not been dyed. And peel the obviously waxed cucumbers, or at least scrub their surface with a stiff brush. A preliminary scrubbing is a good idea, anyway, for the surfaces of many supermarket-bought fruits and vegetables—the ones that are tough enough to stand it, that is. Citrus fruits, cucumbers, and hard-rind squashes are often treated with a greasy substance of doubtful nature, and a good scrubbing with a hard brush before cooking or eating them is more healthful.

The type of salt you use is another important factor in successful preserving. Don't use free-flowing table salt. Instead, supply yourself with coarse salt—otherwise known as rock salt, pickling salt, dairy salt, sea salt, kosher salt, or flake salt—or any natural salt that has not been iodized or otherwise treated to keep in humid weather. The starch that is sometimes added to table salt is all right for sprinkling on raw salad, but tends to add a cloudiness to preserves. The salt that the water-conditioning man brings to soften very hard house water so that it won't corrode plumbing is usable, for it, too, is just pure coarse salt.

Sugar is another staple ingredient in many kinds of preserving. You will find more about it in a later chapter, but we will mention it briefly here so that you can supply yourself properly. Sweetening comes in many forms, one of which is honey. If you want to substitute honey in every recipe that calls for sugar, you should cut the specified amount to about half or two-thirds. But because honey adds its own taste, this may not be ideal for certain delicately flavored foods. We often compromise by using both together, in varying proportions but most often half sugar and the rest honey.

Many suggestions about preserving come from an earlier time and include the use of lye. We don't recommend it, because it is a dangerous substance to have around if sufficiently caustic. Once lye was prepared by leaching water through wood ashes, a process that produces an acid with burning properties. Today lye has come to mean any solution resulting from leaching, percolating, or the like. Coffee, for example, is a kind of lye. Baking soda (bicarbonate of soda) can often be used in place of lye; it helps preservation and is harmless. We have, however, specified the use of ashes or charcoal in some occasional special ways in the pages that follow.

Lime, incidentally, is an excellent preservative for certain foods, but we never suggest adding it directly to the food. It should be used only as an outer coating or bath that is subsequently discarded before the food is eaten.

• LABELING •

Of course, you will label every food you preserve with the name of the product and the date on which you store it. In most cases, pasting a label on the container will be sufficient, but special labeling instructions are given at the outset of appropriate chapters.

If you plan to preserve considerable quantities of food, or if you make use of storage places, we suggest you keep a log in the kitchen. The readers who intend to repeat their home preserving every year may find it useful to add some comments to their logs as to, let's say, the life and performance of certain foods. The log can then be consulted when the next preserving season approaches.

NATURAL STORING

• THE COOL, DARK PLACE •

One of the easiest, most natural ways to preserve a great variety of edibles is to store them in a cool place where the temperature is above freezing and does not vary much between thirty-five and fifty degrees Fahrenheit. This is not too difficult to effect in most parts of the United States; most foods need to be stored between fall and spring, and by the time summer comes, the larder will contain practically no foods that can spoil easily.

In some cases, however, this storage place should also be dry and airy, and still other foods require a certain amount of humidity. You may wonder how you can find such a spot in or around your home, but with a little ingenuity this can often be accomplished. For some of you, especially if you live in the city or in southern climates, it may prove to be a little more difficult.

Unfortunately, with the advent of refrigeration, the old-fashioned root cellar disappeared from the American home. Actually, many foods can keep much longer, and some (cheese, for example) taste better if stored in a cool place that is neither as cold nor as humid and confined as the refrigerator.

The old-fashioned root cellar, or a similar version, can be reinstated without too much difficulty in many homes. Our basements, peculiarly enough, often serve as game rooms or utilities rooms; the living room is hardly used. It would be more logical and healthier to move back above ground and once again use the underground portion of our homes for its original purpose.

The heating system in the basement makes the utilization of this level of the house a bit problematic, but it is not impossible. A partition from floor to ceiling built with good insulating material can lower the temperature in the section of the basement you plan to use for food storage. The root cellar must have at least one window, for ventilation, and preferably two, for air circulation. Your basement must be sufficiently insulated against water seepage in case of heavy rains. Shelves should then be built at different levels and, whenever possible, the cellar divided into two sections, with a door in between. If you plan to store fruits and vegetables, the odors emanating from one will not penetrate the other. Once in a while open the door and allow the air to circulate for a few hours, perhaps with the help of a fan. However, if a separation of this type is impossible, the foods that exude odors and those that absorb them can be stored separately and under cover.

If your house does not have a basement, or if you cannot adapt any section of your basement successfully, consider the possibility of adding a makeshift cellar or hatch jutting out of the house into your backyard, accessible from the outside. The walls should be at least partly underground (see illustration below).

The floor should be made of packed soil and the door preceded by a few steps, also dug into the ground, and can be placed on a slant, not necessarily vertical. The roof can be either dome-shaped or slanted on one side to reach ground level. The outer walls and roof should be insulated and covered with soil, on which you can plant grass, flowers, or any other ground covering you may prefer.

If you have a tool shed on your grounds, you can reorganize it so that at least a portion of it can double as a cellar in the winter. Move the lawn mower and other bulky tools to the garage or basement to make room in the tool shed for the food you plan to store.

The use of part of your garage as a cellar is not particularly recommended because the fumes from the car may affect the food. However, if the temperature is right, certain foods can be stored in the garage, provided they are well wrapped or covered.

Smaller cellars can either be built or dug into the ground (as illustrated below). A barrel or an old trunk, for example, can be completely or partially buried. The opening should be accessible, but covered with straw and dirt, plus a top sheet of plastic. With a barrel, this is more easily accomplished by placing it on sloping ground and digging from the front of the slope, thereby setting the barrel horizontally into the ground and using the top of the slope as natural covering.

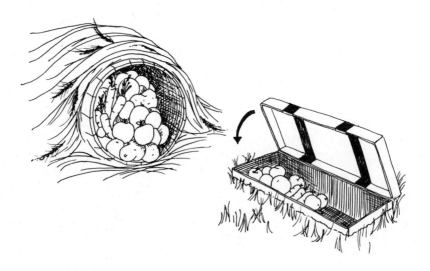

In climates that are fairly cold in winter, mounds can be built above ground, provided they are very well insulated; and, since they are more accessible, protected carefully against rodents or other animals. Such mounds, pits, or trenches can easily be built or dug. You will see later how certain root vegetables, such as celery and cabbage, can be "replanted" in the soil. They cannot, however, endure the frost, and should be housed in trenches with a wooden roof, or with a roof made of tiles or any other hard, protective material (see illustration below).

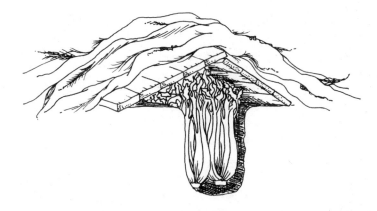

The rule, then, for any container you may use or pit you dig is that it insulates and protects your foodstuffs from the cold and rodents. Remember, though, if you live in an area where it snows a lot during the winter, plant a stick where you have buried your hoard of treasure, or it may be difficult for you to find when you go to dig it out.

The urban dwellers among you may consider it impossible to store any food except by means of refrigeration. But you may be able to do so on a smaller scale. Your need to store food is not as great as that of people who live in the country. Food stores are more accessible to you, and the chances are you will not have the windfalls we have mentioned before. Nor will you have crops to store, unless of course you have a weekend place in the country and plan to take your harvest to the city.

Assess your specific situation. Do you live in an apartment that has a balcony or a terrace? A fire escape? A closet-pantry with a window? A storeroom where you can keep the heat down to a minimum? A backyard, however small? Or, if all else fails, a window you could adapt for this purpose? You can use any of these places for storage of a limited amount of food.

Perhaps you remember the outside "cupboards" that were once kept on kitchen terraces. Those families whose space was limited had at least one or two smaller versions, hanging from the outside walls next to their kitchen windows. These boxes were made of rustproof or painted metal and had slanted roofs with little overhangs on the three sides. They came in all sizes and shapes, but the three sides exposed to the air were made either of metal screen or of stronger metal with small holes. The door was also made of screen and sometimes placed on one side so that the contents would be easily accessible.

Whether you intend to have one of these food cages built or make it yourself, adapt the idea to your particular needs and to the space you have available. Put some shelves in it, preferably adjustable, and pack some soil or sand at the bottom, which you can sprinkle occasionally with water if the weather is too dry and if the foods you store need some humidity. If you have a terrace, build a large, free-standing cupboard; if not, hang a smaller one outside your window or outside wall. The polluted air, however, requires that the city dweller cover or wrap the food he stores in this manner.

Our homes are usually overheated during the winter, so that finding a cool spot indoors is not always easy. But a city dweller can have a special pantry-closet built, if possible with a window, or with the door of the closet built very close to an outer wall and window. Good insulating material should be added to the sides of the closet, with no insulation of course on the side of the outer wall. Make sure first that the walls intended for this closet don't have any hot-water or heating pipes running inside.

The variety of apartments in this country makes it impossible for us to suggest a solution that would serve all our city readers. However, even if the temperatures you can reach are not low enough to permit long-term storage, they will nevertheless be an improvement on those of an overheated apartment, and anything you store will certainly last longer than if you leave it on your kitchen shelves. Flour of any type, rice, pasta, cereals, spices, potatoes, squash, canned food, the jars of any preserve or pickle, onions, garlic, oil, and many other foods will stay fresh much longer, even if you succeed in lowering the temperature to only sixty or sixty-five degrees Fahrenheit.

Man survived for thousands of years without refrigeration. So, while there are optimum temperatures at which certain stored foods can last, most foods can be preserved fresh even if there is some variation in temperature or humidity, so that there are no definite rules you must follow. Basically, one should try to reproduce the conditions of the old-fashioned root cellar; our ancestors perfected it through experience and passed their knowledge on from generation to generation. We have advantages they didn't have: scientific experiments of our local and national agricultural extension services, and our local weather bureaus to cue us in on the best conditions and most suitable foods to store at the time.

While long-term storage of many foods is most successful at temperatures that range between thirty-five and forty-five degrees Fahrenheit, your food won't spoil unless it freezes and thaws. Higher temperatures will not actually spoil the food; they will just shorten the storage time. If you cannot provide such low temperatures, you will have to check your food more often and eat it sooner.

It is advisable to have two thermometers, outdoor and indoor. A humidity gauge is helpful though not essential. The thermometers should be of the kind that records the maximum and minimum temperatures so that you can figure out what happened during the night. The outdoor thermometer will also be very helpful to you in determining when to pull up the last crops, which usually has to be done before frost.

If you grow your own vegetables, plant some rather late in the season, so that you'll be able to store these just before frost and just before they are fully ripe. Freezing does not damage some root vegetables, provided they are properly stored and will not refreeze after thawing. Above-freezing temperatures are, however, imperative for the best end result.

As mentioned previously, fruits and vegetables should be stored separately whenever possible. The products that most affect each other if stored together are cabbage, cauliflower, turnips, potatoes, melons, apples, and pears, so make sure that these are kept separate.

Any fruit or vegetable you decide to store should be harvested on a sunny day and only if it has not rained heavily prior to that day. The crop should be allowed to cool off overnight, either outdoors (after sundown, and if you are sure it will not freeze during the night), or in a cool place, with a few exceptions that we will later call to your attention.

To make it easier for you to store your fruits and vegetables, we have separated them and listed them alphabetically. For other foods, follow this general rule: If they are whole and not in pieces and they have a natural skin of their own, you can retard spoilage by means of a number of insulating materials, indicated under the names of the various foods. Some of the substances specified are interchangeable, although the length of time it will be safe to store your food may vary slightly with your choice of material, in which case the food should be checked and tested more often to make sure it is still edible.

• FRUITS •

— APPLES —

Apples should be harvested when mature but still very firm. The late varieties keep best, but if the weather doesn't turn cold soon after picking, the storage time of apples may be shortened considerably; they thrive in a temperature of fifty degrees Fahrenheit or a little lower. The fruit can be stored in bins or crates, but will last longer and retain more flavor if wrapped individually in non-porous paper such as tissue paper; or if the containers are lined and covered with plastic sheets with several holes in the plastic. Apples can also be stored in smaller plastic bags, a few at a time, but again the bags should have holes. This keeps the humidity high and prevents the apples from absorbing the surrounding air.

— AVOCADOS —

It is becoming more and more difficult to buy ripe avocados. As they bruise easily, the stores sell them unripe and let the consumer do the ripening. This, however, becomes an advantage if you want to preserve a few. Buy them very hard and store them in a cool place, making sure that they don't touch. Check them for ripeness every few days.

— Berries —

An old Swiss way of preserving many types of berries—primarily those that are naturally tart—is to store them slightly unripe, as they are. All berries should be picked when still firm, a few days away from full ripeness. Those that you can store Swiss-fashion are huckleberries and sour varieties of blueberries, gooseberries, and currants. Cranberries can also be stored in this way, but you may wish to first dip them in ascorbic acid (see Index for formula).

Wash and dry the berries thoroughly (not even a drop of water must be left when you store them) and just drop in sterilized bottles or jars. Use self-sealing jars and fill them with the berries to the very top, without crushing the fruit. If you use bottles, tap from the outside with your finger so that the berries will settle, as they should be packed very close together; or tap the bottles on the table a few times. If this does not work, tap them with a hammer covered with a rag until the berries do settle. This must be done while you are filling the bottles and not when the bottles are already full. For best results, very little air should be left in between the berries, and containers must be tightly sealed. Boil bottle corks for three or four minutes and dry completely, then sink the corks into the bottles, and add melted paraffin to the top of the cork.

If stored in a cool place, the berries should last several months.

— Citrus Fruit —

Grapefruit, oranges, and lemons should be packed in open boxes and kept at a temperature as close to thirty-two degrees Fahrenheit as possible; but be careful not to freeze them! They can only be preserved for a few weeks if stored in this way. You can, however, preserve for a much longer time if you coat the rinds with either Vaseline or melted paraffin. Make sure you cover the entire surface. If treated this way, it is best not to use the rinds.

Lemons can also be preserved by submerging them in cold

23

water. Add a flat surface slightly smaller than the top of the container and weigh it down so that the lemons will stay submerged. The water should be changed every two or three days.

You can bury lemons in perfectly dry sand, making sure the fruits don't touch.

Tangerines can also be coated with vaseline or paraffin, but require a slightly higher storage temperature, about forty degrees.

Another good way to preserve citrus fruit is to dissolve two teaspoonfuls of boric acid in one quart of boiling water. When the solution has cooled, submerge the fruit completely for thirty minutes. Then wipe each fruit dry and wrap in tissue paper, and bury in very dry sand, stem side up. The fruits should be totally surrounded by sand and not touch one another. The container in which they are stored should be covered and placed in a cool place.

If after some time the fruit shows a little mold or becomes soft, make another solution, doubling the amount of boric acid, and pour the cooled liquid over the fruits. Leave them completely submerged for five minutes, wipe dry, wrap again with clean paper, and store.

— GRAPES —

If the grapes have been sprayed while on the vine, it is advisable to wash and dry them thoroughly. Remove any overripe fruits that might ruin the bunch, and choose only ripe but firm grapes for storage.

Spread the grapes out in flat boxes or cartons on a bed of straw, sawdust, or similar insulating material, putting more straw in between bunches, then cover with a thick layer of straw. It is best to store grapes in a single layer or two layers at most. They can be preserved for several weeks, but it is advisable to check them once a week in case they begin to spoil.

If you want to preserve grapes for several months, line a container with plastic and spread them on a thick bed of wooden ashes or bran; make sure the bunches don't touch and surround each bunch with the same insulating material. Finish with another thick layer of ashes or bran, then close the container tightly, adding another sheet of plastic at the top before covering.

Another method is to make some cones out of strong paper that has not been torn in any way. Mix water and flour into a paste, not too thick but of some consistency. Join the tips of the cones with either this paste or with some tape, and brush the paste all over the outer surface of the cones. Small paper bags that you can shape into cones with tape can be used, but they too should be thoroughly brushed with the paste.

When the cones are completely dry, insert a cluster of grapes. Now cut as many twelve-inch pieces of string as you have paper cones. Tie one end securely around the stem of each bunch of grapes, and leave the long end to be attached to a pole or stick, then suspend the stick in between two hooks, horizontally. If you open a bag to check if the grapes are still in good condition, use that particular bunch of grapes; do not retie the bag.

For the varieties of grapes whose fruits are not close together but rather separate, there is another, simpler system, although the grapes may stay fresh for only about four or five months.

Cut several pieces of string about ten or twelve inches long and tie a loop at each end of each piece. When all the pieces are ready, pass the tip (or small end) of each bunch of grapes into the loops. This should attach them securely enough. Hang them upside down, so that each bunch is slightly spread out and does not touch the next. Then hang one or more sticks horizontally, and place the grapes astride. Keep for a few days in a cool, dry, well-ventilated room, then suspend the poles in the cellar, away from the walls.

— MELONS —

Choose melons that are not completely ripe and, if possible, that still have a bit of stem attached. Put them in a very dry place in a single layer and with a little space between each fruit. Then bury them in wood ashes, again making sure they don't touch. Cover with more ashes and cover the container. Melons can be preserved in this manner up to three months.

You can instead cover their surface completely with melted paraffin or Vaseline. Wrap separately in tissue paper and lay on a bed of corn husks in a large container or bin. Cover each layer with corn husks, finishing with a thicker layer. They will last three or four months—some varieties longer—if stored in a cool, airy place.

— PEACHES —

Slightly unripe peaches can be laid in a cool place without allow-ing the fruits to touch. Peaches are a soft fruit and may keep only a couple of weeks or a little longer.

Another way to store peaches is the following: Peel them and immediately dip in a strong ascorbic-acid solution (see Index for formula) for a few minutes. Pare and either cut in half, remov-ing the stones, or leave whole and thrust them out with a skewer or similar object, trying not to damage the peaches too much. Store without delay in large self-sealing jars filled to the top, in a dark, cool place.

The fruit must be eaten as soon as the jars are opened. Our nineteenth-century source tells us that "peaches done in this manner have arrived at California from New Jersey in perfect formation."

— PEARS —

Store like apples. Certain varieties of pears ripen soon after pick-ing and cannot be stored for long, so choose late-ripening varie-ties for longer storage. Unlike apples, pears do best without plas-tic; paper covering is here recommended but not essential.

— PERSIMMONS —

Store persimmons like your avocados, but allow to ripen ex-tremely well before eating or preserving in jams. Ripe persim-mons are very soft and dark in color, the skin translucent and almost to the point of splitting.

— QUINCES —

Gently wipe off the fur and follow directions for storing peaches. If the quinces are hard, they may keep for a few months.

— RHUBARB —

Store like berries. Rhubarb's tendency to discolor does not affect its quality, but you may wish to dip it in a strong ascorbic-acid solution before drying completely. Or, you can add ascorbic acid to the amount of water needed to submerge the rhubarb after stuffing it in bottles or jars.

Warning: Use only the stems as rhubarb leaves are poisonous.

• NUTS •

Hard-shelled nuts can last many months in their shells in a cool place, although they become a little dry. For fresher nuts keep them a whole year buried underground in pressed soil or in dry sand. If you bury them outdoors, don't forget to mark the spot or you'll never find your cache. Bury them deep to keep the squirrels away.

— CHESTNUTS —

There are two basic ways to store chestnuts, with their skins on or after peeling them.

To store them with their skins on, place the chestnuts in a wooden box or barrel in alternating layers of sand or bran or sawdust, starting at the bottom with a layer a few inches deep and finishing with a similar layer. A sandy soil can be used instead of sand. Store the container, covered, in the root cellar.

Chestnuts stored in this fashion can be preserved until late spring. If they begin to sprout (which they sometimes do in early spring), just take them out of the container and spread out in a well-ventilated place for a few days, until the sprouts dry out. Very often, airing them out in the spring will keep them in good condition until midsummer.

If you choose to store peeled chestnuts, remove both skins and submerge completely in cold water for at least eight days, changing the water daily. At the end of this period, place them in shallow containers in a cool, dry place, and stir them once in a while, especially during the first few days. They will need to be soaked again for several hours before using.

— PISTACHIO NUTS —

Shell the nuts and place them in a jar with cold water to cover and a pinch of salt, which helps keep their green color.

• VEGETABLES •

— ASPARAGUS —

Asparagus, both wild and cultivated, can be stored successfully for several months and, according to some sources, for a whole year.

If you pick the asparagus yourself, cut the stems very close to the ground, even if they seem woody. Do not wash but instead heat one of your electric burners (if you have an electric stove) or heat a metal plank (even your iron), and immediately after cutting each stem another inch or so, sear the end by pressing it on the hot metal for a few seconds. Do not cut and sear more than three or four asparagus at one time, and keep the metal very hot at all times. This sears in most of the nutrients, which would otherwise be lost during storage.

Now store the asparagus in dry bran to which you will add salt in the proportion of about one cup for each five or six pounds of bran. Make the bottom layer of bran rather thick, then alternate with asparagus, and finish with another thick layer of bran. The asparagus should be placed in large metal boxes that can be closed tightly or in wooden boxes lined with large sheets of plastic. Add another sheet of plastic at the top and cover securely.

Asparagus can also be stored in charcoal, but each stem should be wrapped in tissue paper after searing. These containers, too, should be closed.

— BEANS, SHELL —

Fresh lima and other shell beans can be preserved several months if stored in their pods. But the pods should not be too large and must still be fresh; they should not be hard or dry.

Their container should be waterproof and have a close-fitting cover. Make alternating layers of coarse salt and pods, starting and finishing with a thicker layer of salt. As you fill the container, press down after you spread out each layer of beans. Press again at the top and add a weight inside the cover. (Large pebbles on top of the last layers of salt will do the trick.)

When ready to use the beans, soak the pods in cold water,

changing the water two or three times. Then shell and soak again without pods. Discard any beans that may have shriveled.

Dried beans (see Chapter 3) can be stored in plastic bags or metal containers indefinitely, though any container will do as well provided it cannot be invaded by rodents.

— BEETS —

Harvest beets late as they can take frost, provided the soil is not too dry. Pull them up with their roots but don't disturb the soil around the roots. Leave a couple of inches of beet tops to avoid "bleeding" and help retain nutrients. Store at the bottom of a root cellar or where the humidity is highest, in crates or boxes with insulating layer at the bottom; or, better still, line your containers with a plastic sheet. Alternate layers of slightly moist sand and cover with another plastic sheet. You should punch several holes in the plastic to allow your beets to breathe.

— CABBAGE —

The late variety of cabbage can be harvested after freezing, but it should not be permitted to thaw and refreeze. It is best to pull it up after the first night of frost. Leave at least some root and don't remove the outer leaves. "Replant" in soil in a root cellar, packing the soil around the root and watering it lightly. If the cabbage has no root, it can be placed in bins or boxes between layers of sand or soil.

For pit or similar storage, place upside down with at least part of the root still attached, or hang from root or stem. Cabbage can also be hung in this fashion in a root cellar, but store away from other foods, as the odor is very penetrating.

— CARROTS —

Carrots should be stored like beets.

— CAULIFLOWER —

Harvest this vegetable as late as possible, but soon after the first frost. Cut off part of the root but none of the outer leaves. Place in boxes or crates between layers of sand, sawdust, or other similar insulating material, which should be slightly moist when you pack.

— Celery —

When harvesting celery, leave its root ball and tops. Replant in soil with bunches fairly close together, compressing the soil all around. Water the soil when replanting, but be careful that the leaves don't get wet. If stored in a root cellar, light watering may be helpful every few weeks, but test soil moisture before watering. The leaves will wilt or become dry after a while; just leave them on until you use the bunch, then discard them. Darkness will turn the celery pale, but will not affect its quality.

— Chinese Cabbage —

Store like celery.

— Endive —

Store like celery, but pull leaves together with soft string or a twisted strip of soft paper, taking care not to injure them. Treat delicately as endive bruises easily.

— Ginger Root —

Ginger root can be preserved in damp sand for a very long time. When you need to use some, dig it up, rinse, grate the amount needed, and bury again.

— Horseradish —

Horseradish can withstand remaining in the soil all winter, provided it is mulched until the temperature drops below freezing. Then uncover and pull up as needed, until the weather turns warm. If you still have some in the soil by then, mulch again but use soon. You can also pull horseradishes up at the beginning of winter and store like beets and carrots.

— Jerusalem Artichokes —

These are not artichokes at all, nor do they resemble them. They are the tubers of the sunflower and grow in North America; "Jerusalem" is a corruption of the Italian word for sunflower, *girasole*. Why it is called an artichoke instead of a potato, which it resembles much more, is odd, although it does taste like one when eaten hot. Because it is so similar to a potato, store in the same way.

— KALE —

Store like celery.

— LEEKS —

Leeks should also be stored like celery.

— ONIONS —

Pull onions up very late, after the tops have turned yellow. Store with roots up in dry, airy baskets in which you have placed a layer of sand or sawdust or other insulating material. If you have a dry place that is no warmer than seventy degrees Fahrenheit, you can just hang onions from hooks on the wall or from strings secured across two walls.

Only large, round varieties of onions store well.

— PARSLEY ROOTS —

Store like beets.

— PARSNIPS —

Leave in the ground as you do your horseradishes.

— PEPPERS, SWEET —

Sweet peppers can be tricky. Some people do very well with them even up to three months; others have to eat them fast after about three weeks. It is a good idea to keep an eye on them and to check them often for dark or soft spots that signal the beginning of decay.

Pick before frost and store only hard, flawless peppers. Use shallow containers lined with plastic, but first punch several holes in the plastic. Spread your peppers out in one layer, without letting them touch. They will do better if the temperature is forty-five degrees Fahrenheit or a little higher and if the air is not too humid. A high shelf in your root cellar would be their best storage place.

31

— Potato Flour —

If you have a surplus of mealy potatoes, prepare potato flour; it will prove to be a most useful economy. It binds a sauce more effectively than regular flour—it does not lump as easily in contact with a hot liquid—and if you use potato flour instead of regular flour or mixed with it, you'll prolong the storage life of cookies, biscuits, and similar baked goods.

Peel and grate the mealy potatoes and put them in a large wire strainer half submerged in water in a large bowl. Work them well with your hands as you mix them with water, lifting the strainer several times to allow the minute particles that adhere to it to drop into the water. When all the paste has seeped through, remove the strainer and let the liquid in the bowl rest undisturbed until all the potatoes have reached the bottom. Now very gently pour out the water (don't discard it, as you can use it for soups, etc.), remove the last part of the liquid by straining carefully, then spread the potato paste thinly on a shallow baking dish. Score with a knife in several directions to speed up the drying process. Dry the paste in a very slow oven, moving it around with a spatula every few minutes. When it has thoroughly dried, grind it twice through a fine grinder or pound it in a mortar, then strain through a fine-mesh sieve.

Stored in a tightly covered jar in a cool place, potato flour will keep practically forever.

— Potatoes —

These store very well but, curiously enough, they must go through a period of conditioning before they are put up; it helps heal any bruised or skinned areas. The treatment should last about two weeks at a temperature of around fifty-five degrees Fahrenheit or slightly higher, but the relative humidity should be as high as about eighty-five to ninety per cent. This can be accomplished by placing a few trays or pans of water near the potatoes. At the end of this period, store your potatoes at a temperature of no less than forty degrees. If the temperature falls below that, the potatoes may turn sweet. In this case, a reconditioning at about

32

seventy degrees for about one week might be necessary to restore their natural taste.

Early potatoes can be stored for only about six weeks. They should be conditioned for one week to ten days at sixty to seventy degrees, and their final storage temperature kept around sixty degrees.

Warning: Do not leave potatoes in the sun for many hours after harvesting, as direct contact with sunlight makes them turn green. This oxidation, in considerable quantity, is not beneficial to your health. The removal of the discolored areas of potatoes that have turned partly green will prevent any injurious effects.

— POTATOES, SWEET —

Handle sweet potatoes with care, as they bruise easily. Condition them as potatoes, and store in a dark place. Do not allow temperatures to fall below fifty degrees as the potatoes can be damaged; or above sixty degrees or they'll turn too sweet.

— PUMPKINS —

Prepare pumpkins according to the directions we will soon give for squashes.

— RADISHES —

Handle radishes as you do horseradishes, but take care to pull them up before the frost.

— RUTABAGAS —

These, too, should be left in the ground, like horseradishes.

— SALSIFY —

Treat as you do your beets, but harvest before the frost.

— SQUASHES —

Leave a few inches of stem on all squashes except acorn and zucchini and condition for a week to ten days in a dry place at a temperature of about seventy degrees Fahrenheit. Then spread out in a single layer without allowing them to touch, in a temperature of forty-five to fifty degrees.

Butternut squashes can be harvested before fully ripe and will continue ripening while in storage.

— TOMATOES —

Harvest tomatoes a few days before frost; they should be green or at least partly green and still hard. Handle them carefully while harvesting as their skin is delicate even when they are green.

There are different ways of working with tomatoes. You can pull up the entire plant, roots and all, and hang it with the roots up. Or, you can cut off the tomatoes, leaving a few inches of stem, and place them on flat racks in a single layer. You can also wrap them individually in plastic bags with holes. Some people wash and dry them before storing, but adding moisture at this point is not advisable, unless the tomatoes have been sprayed with pesticides.

Whichever method you use, separate the tomatoes that are completely green from those that are partially green; the latter will ripen first and should be used earlier.

You can up to a point regulate the rate of ripening by means of the temperature at which you store them. At sixty-five to seventy degrees Fahrenheit they ripen in about two weeks, at fifty-five degrees they can take between three and four weeks to ripen. Do not store at temperatures lower than that, or your tomatoes may suffer a chill. Check them often for ripeness.

— TURNIPS —

Treat turnips like horseradishes, parsnips, and rutabagas. They have a very strong odor, so store separately if you place them in a root cellar.

• MEAT, POULTRY, AND GAME •

Store only freshly butchered meat, poultry, or game.

When working with meat, select a clean, tightly woven cloth for wrapping the meat and sew or tape the edges together. Now set the package in a wooden box or any other container large enough and surround meat with pieces of charcoal pressed tightly together. Try not to leave any open spaces. Then cover with thick layers of charcoal. You can use the same charcoal several times for the same purpose, but avoid using it for storage of other types of food.

Poultry should be plucked, its entrails removed, and the insides filled with charcoal before wrapping and storing it as meat.

If you don't have on hand a sufficient quantity of charcoal, simply stuff your poultry or game with charcoal, rub charcoal on the outside, sew in the cloth, then wet the cloth and hang the package in a very cool, airy place. (Unplucked or unskinned game does not need to be wrapped in cloth.)

Meat, poultry, or game stored in this way is delicious grilled or barbecued. When you are ready to use it, remove the charcoal and wipe with a dry cloth before cooking, but leave some of the charcoal powder on the meat.

This method of storage can preserve your product for at least one month. Any fresh meat or poultry you wish to preserve for about ten days or more (depending on temperature and ventilation) must first be wiped with a slightly damp cloth, then rubbed with charcoal all around. Poultry should be rubbed with charcoal inside as well as outside. Small lumps of charcoal should be packed all around the meat before it is wrapped in thick wax or freezer paper; or, better still, in a very sturdy plastic bag without holes. (If you use paper, make sure that the charcoal has not torn through. If it has, use an outer wrapping or put some tape on the hole.) Most of the air will leave the plastic bag if you squeeze it gently before tying with a metal twist, with the end of the bag over once first. Now put your package in a cloth bag and hang it in a cool, airy place.

• HARE OR RABBIT •

The following is an ancient French method of storing freshly killed hare or rabbit: Do not skin. Cut belly open and remove all entrails. Dry the inner cavity carefully, then rinse it thoroughly with a solution of equal parts of water and strong vinegar. Wipe dry and wrap the entire body in thick cloth that has been previously dipped or brushed generously with dense oil. Sew the ends of your package together with strong thread. Now store, preferably hanging, in a cool, airy place.

It will keep several weeks.

• TO STORE SMOKED MEATS FOR YEARS •

This suggestion is adapted from an American cookbook of the nineteenth century.

After curing, smoking (see special chapter on smoking), and sewing your hams or other smoked meats in bags, pack them in pulverized charcoal. The writer assures that "the preservative quality of charcoal will keep the meats till charcoal decays; or sufficiently long to have accompanied Captain Cook three times around the world."

However, keep in mind the following guidelines: Bacon should be used sooner than any other type of meat because fat meat becomes rancid more quickly than lean. With pork products, shoulders should be used before hams, not because they may not be edible later, but because hams improve with age. Pork keeps better than beef or mutton.

• STORING FISH IN COAL •

Do not clean the outside of the fish and leave the head, tail, and fins. Simply remove the entrails completely and wipe the inside cavity with a dry cloth. Stuff the fish with chopped charcoal, then put it in a box or other container between two thick layers of charcoal. Press coals around the sides of the fish also. Store in a cool, airy place.

This fish can be preserved six or seven days and even a little longer if the temperature in your storage room is lower than fifty degrees Fahrenheit.

The same charcoal can be reused, but only for fish, as it may have picked up some of the odor.

• DAIRY PRODUCTS •

Milk and cheese, in these days of refrigeration, are probably considered the foods most likely to spoil without either an icy climate or elaborate preserving methods. Yet, it is possible to keep both products sweet and pure by other means.

— MILK —

Before you store milk—in or out of a refrigerator—you should be sure that it is pasteurized. This is easily accomplished at home.

You can either heat the raw milk to 145 degrees Fahrenheit and keep it at this temperature for thirty minutes; or heat the milk to 170 degrees for exactly half a minute. Whichever method you choose, cool it as quickly as possible by placing the pot of milk immediately after heating into a larger container half filled with ice water.

You can then store the milk for at least fifty hours without refrigeration, even in a temperature as high as seventy degrees, if you add one gram of boric acid to each quart of milk. Boric acid, in very small quantities, is an excellent preserver, and you may also try it in other foods you wish to keep. It is completely harmless, provided it is added in very small amounts, such as that we have suggested.

Bicarbonate of soda (baking soda), you will recall, is also a good preservative, for milk as well as for other foods. A small pinch stirred into each quart of milk prolongs its life even on warm summer days (but try to keep the milk in a cool spot). If your milk should start to go sour, you can use it to make cheese (see Index).

— CHEESE —

A hard cheese can be preserved very well in a cool and fairly humid place. The old-fashioned springhouse or root cellar, you will remember, is a more ideal place for cheese than the refrigerator. Since it tends to harden, wrap it in a clean cloth previously soaked in white wine (or water), but squeeze the cloth first before wrapping. Later you can sprinkle the cloth from the outside with a little more liquid if the cloth becomes too dry, but the additional sprinklings should be very light and not wet the cheese too much. An outer wrapper of plastic with many holes is suggested but optional.

Strong-smelling cheeses should, however, be wrapped in plastic film or plastic bags. All cheese should be put in large crocks or tubs after wrapping, to keep rodents away.

If you are working with a hard cheese that has dried considerably, grate and store it in sealed jars in a cool place.

If a few spots of mold appear on stored cheese, remove those areas; the rest of the cheese is edible and in no way affected by the mold.

· BAKED GOODS ·

— BAKED BREAD —

If you have an excess of bread, either because you baked too much or because your family or guests have not consumed as much as you had expected, there are several ways you can keep it without freezing. In Greece, where a certain type of dark bread (often saltless) is specifically rebaked and sold, this method is a classic. Cut your loaves in very thick slices and allow to dry completely for several hours in a very slow oven. The bread is very hard but delicious. Greek peasants always keep a few bags of this dried bread at home and, even when fresh bread is available, eat it with their food, or dunk it for a few minutes in water or wine, or sprinkle olive oil on it.

— BREAD DOUGH —

If you want to have fresh-made bread every day without mixing all that dough, allowing it to rise, punching it down, and waiting for it to rise again, make a very large batch of dough (containing milk) once a week. Let it rise once, knead it a little, then cover with a damp cloth and store in a cool place, well above freezing. Then each day you can scoop out a little dough, let it rise, and bake while you cook your main meal.

— BREADCRUMBS —

Here is another delicious economy, a nutritious use for that stale bread you no doubt have been throwing away. Use crusty bread, preferably homemade, of any kind (except that rubbery white substance that, unfortunately, is the most common staple nowadays); you can save leftover bread from the table or those larger pieces from unused loaves gone stale and put them aside. Don't wait too long to dry the bread completely or it may become moldy. When you have enough to warrant making a batch of breadcrumbs, put your scraps of bread in a very slow oven until dehydrated, moving or turning them upside down several times. When they become brittle, lay one large sheet of heavy, clean paper on a surface, spread the pieces of bread on it, cover with another sheet of the same paper, and roll a rolling pin or empty bottle over this top sheet until you have fairly uniform crumbs. If you are working with chunks of bread, shatter them first into smaller pieces with a hammer, passing a clean cloth between hammer and bread.

You may wish to separate the sizes of your stale bread and save the larger ones for bread pudding.

Place the breadcrumbs in self-sealing jars that are perfectly dry and store anywhere, making sure first that the jars are tightly sealed.

You can make stuffing by this method if you dry in the oven fairly small pieces of bread. It, too, should be stored in sealed jars. Add spices and herbs when ready to stuff the bird.

— RICH CAKES —

Plum cake, spice cake, or pound cake will keep a long time.

Sprinkle with one or two teaspoonfuls of good brandy, let it soak in, then wrap in clean cloth, and sprinkle with more brandy. Store in a crock with half a fresh apple on top before you cover tightly. Once a week for six weeks warm the cake in the oven, removing the apple first. Renew the brandy and apple every two weeks.

Plum cake will keep for a year; the other cakes, for six months.

Most breads and cakes won't keep too long outside a refrigerator, especially in the summer or in hot or humid climates; but you can prevent home-baked goods from developing mildew or becoming stale quickly if you put a sliced apple in a sealed container with the bread.

If you have slightly stale bread you wish to freshen up, an old trick is to sprinkle water or milk on all sides of your bread to rehydrate it and put it in a hot oven for a few minutes. Eat it while it is still warm.

DRYING

Drying is the most natural way of preserving food. Nature makes available the seeds for next year's crop by drying the outer layers of many fruits and vegetables left exposed to the sun and air; man simulates her effects by means of solar heat or exposure to warm air and ventilation, a method that extracts all the water and liquid that would otherwise lead to fermentation and rotting.

Modern industrial science has perfected the techniques of drying and succeeded in applying them to the mass production of a great variety of foods. Powdered eggs and powdered milk, instant coffee and soups are but a few examples. The modern American housewife, relying as she does on convenience foods, has a goodly supply of commercially dried foods. One of the advantages of dried foods is that they occupy very little space. Furthermore, drying (with the exception of simple storing) is the most economical and easiest method of preserving food available to us. Since its source is the sun, solar drying is obviously the cheapest, but oven drying is not much more costly—the quantity of gas or electricity it uses up is minimal.

Sun drying is good for most fruits and vegetables, and for many other foods as well. It is recommended especially for fruits, as it retains most of their natural flavor. You must, however, be sure of the weather. Attempt it only on hot summer days, because the quicker the drying process, the better. The first time you try it, experiment with some of the most commonly dried fruits—apples, apricots, prunes, and figs.

Of course, if in the area where you live you cannot rely on hot sun, you can use your oven with equal success. If you plan to dry huge quantities of produce, you can purchase a home dryer, but you will find the oven perfectly suitable for all average drying needs. To make the most use of yours, add as many racks as possible. Buy extra racks of the same dimensions as those in your oven, or make them yourself. With a pair of pliers, you can open up several strong metal coat hangers and shape them into a grill or a frame, then cover with sturdy, rustproof, ungalvanized wire mesh, reserving some for covering the oven racks you already have, which will prevent the food you are drying from falling through. Later, when you have finished, the wire rack can be folded in front and back, slipped out of the oven, and stored for another time. Foods dried in tiny units—berries, for example—can be dried in trays or pie plates, but must then be shaken fairly often.

The same oven racks covered with mesh can be used for drying in the sun, in which case you will not be restricted by a specific size (as in the case of an oven). You can use any number of things for drying racks: trellises, slats, window frames or screens, and so on.

If you do not have constant sun and do not wish to keep your oven on for the length of time required during the August "dog days," for example, a good attic or top-floor room is a suitable place to do certain drying. We have always dried our herbs in the attic, in paper bags or spread out on wide swathes of wrapping paper. Unless very well ventilated, however, the attic is not suitable for other drying.

Remember, dry in the sun only during the summer months, and when the weather promises to be fair. Expose your food to the sun in the morning and leave it outdoors all day, but *bring it indoors at night* and store in a dry place until the next morning. This is very important, for if you leave your food outdoors all night it will reabsorb most of the humidity you need to extract;

besides, the tissues will be altered and therefore the taste. If it threatens to rain, bring in your racks as well. If you use oven racks for your sun drying, you can easily place them in the oven at night or on rainy days. And, of course, you can then alternate the two methods of drying.

Many factors determine the length of time it would take for each product to dry. Aside from the heat of the sun, the amount of ventilation and relative humidity can shorten or prolong the process considerably. The size and texture of each food is also significant. If we omit to mention even an approximate time for sun drying a specific food, this does not mean you should not attempt it, but that the length of time is flexible.

When drying in the open air, in sun or in shade, be sure to place a double layer of cheesecloth over your foods to protect them from flies and other insects. Secure the cloth to the sides of the dryer so that it will not be blown away by the wind together with some of the food. Similar cheesecloth or thin muslin under the product you are drying will prevent it from sticking to the wire mesh or racks.

When drying in the oven, the most important thing to remember is to check your food often, especially during your first experiments or when drying something you haven't tried before. There is no sure way to determine in advance the exact temperature or time necessary. Your oven may not be perfectly gauged, your kitchen may be especially humid, and the food can vary in type or size. If the season during which a fruit or vegetable has ripened was very wet, its produce will contain more moisture and therefore take longer to dry.

Set the oven temperature no higher than 150 degrees Fahrenheit (unless otherwise specified) and shift trays or racks into different positions at least once an hour. Remove the bottom and top racks and switch (switch also the middle racks); then place them on top and bottom, and so on. As the temperature of your oven is higher near the metal walls, switch also the pieces of food from the center toward the walls of the oven, and vice versa. This will promote as uniform a drying as possible.

Since the drying process is a mixture of heat and ventilation, leave the oven door either completely or partially open. If the door is a spring type that closes automatically, prop it open with a metal wedge. You can run a small electric fan, at low speed, about two feet from one side of the oven door to create better ventilation and to quicken the drying. Make sure, however, to cover any thin or flaky substances with cheesecloth so that they won't be scattered.

If your oven is electric, you will have three additional things to tend to: (1) Use only the heat coil on the bottom of the oven; if the top coil is not independently operated, remove it; (2) use a slightly higher temperature than that indicated in the directions; and (3) be sure to keep the oven door closed while preheating.

The few general rules for both gas- and electric-oven drying can be summed up just as briefly:

Don't situate the top and bottom racks closer than three inches from the top and bottom of the oven.

Don't overburden your trays. This will delay the process, result in uneven drying, and require you to stir the food more often.

Remove and alternate racks at least once an hour; top and bottom racks dry faster. Stir the pieces of food if they are small, or turn them if they are larger every time you check and move the trays. If the pieces at the outer edges seem to dry faster, push them toward the middle, or remove them if they appear to be done earlier than the rest.

While drying food, avoid leaving the house for a prolonged period of time. You may forget to check your racks and move them; or occasionally a piece of food may catch fire. The chances of this are slight but if it should happen turn the heat off immediately, close the oven door, and open the windows.

Dried fruits should be leathery, and when cut in half with a knife, should not exude even one drop of moisture. Berries, beans, peas, corn, and other small items of dried food will rattle in the tray, or be very hard to the touch. Leafy vegetables, thinly sliced vegetables, and herbs turn brittle when they are dry. Other vegetables become leathery and hard.

When your food has dried, remove it from the heat and let it cool naturally in a dry place. If it is a food that has curled up some in drying, press it gently without crushing it. Then put it in an airtight container—a jar, wooden box, or plastic bag—and cover or seal it without crushing the food, which should fill the space well.

Label all your products with the date they are stored. Plastic bags can be labeled by putting the label inside, facing outwards. Then put them in a cool, dry place. Darkness is also desirable, particularly for green vegetables and herbs.

Before storing any dried food for any length of time, leave it in an accessible place and check it during the first two weeks. If you notice any moisture or mold, reheat the food for at least a half-hour and repackage. Most dried foods will retain their color, flavor, and the better part of their nutritive content for about a year. The only exception is dried greens, which lose their nutritional value after four or five months.

To reconstitute dried foods you simply have to rehydrate them, or restore the moisture that the drying removed. This is accomplished by immersion in lukewarm water for a few hours or overnight. Beans, soybeans, and any other foods that have dried with a hard outer layer can be rehydrated by pouring boiling water over them and letting them stand in this water for an hour or two.

Don't throw out the water in which you have rehydrated foods. It can be used for cooking them or other foods, or as the base for gravies or sauces.

Water, of course, is not the only liquid in which to freshen

dried foods; any other thin liquid with a flavor that will combine well with the food you are freshening will do just as well. Mushrooms, for instance, gain appreciable taste dimensions if freshened in a dry white wine as do cherries freshened in ginger ale and onions in consommé.

• FRUITS •

— APPLES —

The color of the flesh of apples can be preserved by a brief soaking—no more than ten minutes—in an anti-oxidant solution of one teaspoonful of ascorbic acid to one quart of cold water. Unless the apples are very small, cut them in half, in quarters, or in thick slices before soaking and drying. Never peel them, even if your apples are of a sour type; drying is quicker and the yield higher if they remain unpeeled. Place the apples on racks in single layers. Let them dry in the sun for three to four days; or dry them in the oven for three to six hours, with temperatures between 120 and 140 degrees Fahrenheit.

Note: Although perfect, barely ripe, unfallen fruit dries best, you can use unripe apples or groundlings. In this case, peeling is recommended, to be followed by a soaking in a *hot* anti-oxidant solution before drying.

— APRICOTS —

Choose apricots that are *not* completely ripe. Halve and pit them and leave them for ten or fifteen minutes in a solution of bicarbonate of soda and water (one tablespoon to a quart). Then place them on racks with their cut sides up. In the oven, they will dry in six to twelve hours at 140 degrees Fahrenheit; and in the sun, in three to four days. When they are completely dry, press them and spread them gently with your fingers, as they will be curled.

Apricots, perhaps more than most other fruits, lose a certain amount of color during drying. Although the soda treatment will cut down the loss somewhat, don't expect them to be as bright an orange as before. Commercially dried apricots retain their vivid hue because they have been treated with sulphur, and we don't recommend sulphuring to the home drier.

— BERRIES —

The firmer varieties of berries—blueberries, currants, cranberries—can be dried successfully, although their best use is in canning and pickling, and in jellies and jams. Dry firm berries immediately after picking. Break their skins first, either by pricking with a sterilized needle or by dipping them half a minute in boiling water, then dropping them into cold water for a few seconds. Drain and expose them to hot sunlight. If they aren't quite dry when the sun goes down, finish them in the oven, with the temperature between 120 and 140 degrees Fahrenheit.

The softer varieties of berries—strawberries, blackberries, thimbleberries, and such—should be similarly treated.

— CHERRIES —

You don't have to remove the pits when drying cherries; they impart a slightly nutty taste you may like as much as we do. Wash the cherries and spread in the sun in one layer, and be sure to shake them several times a day. Sun-drying should take approximately three days; they are dry when they are as wrinkled as dried prunes.

If you use the oven, keep your temperature between 120 and 140 degrees, as for berries. Pitted cherries will dry in from four to six hours; unpitted will take longer.

Many varieties of cherries are grown in America as well as in Europe, some sweet and some sour. The latter, when dried and stored, make an excellent base for sweet-and-sour sauces, especially good with pork, wild boar, tongue, and other fatty meats. You can also use them for pies or to make a concentrated syrup (see Index).

— COCONUTS —

Puncture each nut in the "eye" with an icepick or sharp-pointed knife and drain off the milk, which is good to drink. Leave in the hot sun for three or four days, or in the oven at 350 degrees Fahrenheit for an hour or so. When the shell begins to crack, tap it sharply with a hammer and it will spring apart into pieces of manageable size. Now you can cut or break the coconut meat

46

into smaller pieces or shred it on a shredder. Finish drying the smaller bits in the oven at a much lower heat, no higher than 150 degrees.

— FIGS —

The figs used in drying must be very ripe, with their very soft skin slightly torn. If it isn't torn, you can break it here and there by dropping the figs into boiling water (or boiling bicarbonate and water) for approximately one minute. Then cool immediately in cold water. You can dry them either whole or halved. If you wish to halve them, hold them upside down while applying a slight pressure at the bottom. Do not separate the two halves but lay them flat in the sun, with the internal side exposed first. After they have dried for one day, turn them and dry the other side. Repeat until they have the appearance of dried figs. Halved figs should dry in about six days in a very hot, dry climate; whole figs will take one or two days longer.

You can, of course, dry them in the oven, with a temperature of 120 to 145 degrees Fahrenheit. Whole figs will dry in eight hours or more; halved figs in about six hours.

— GRAPES (RAISINS) —

Select well-ripened, or even slightly over-ripe, sweet grapes; muscat or white grapes, seeded or seedless, are good. If you are lucky enough to have your own vineyard, pick the grapes yourself, choosing fruits that are most exposed to the sun. Remove all the fruits that are imperfect or unripe, but you can use those that have begun to shrivel in the sun as long as they are not rotting. Bring to a boil a solution of one tablespoon bicarbonate of soda to a quart of water, and plunge the grapes into it for half a minute. Rinse in cold water and dry in a well-ventilated, shaded spot. When they are dry, place them on racks in the sun, making sure the grapes don't touch. Turn them often and leave them in the sun for a few days. The grapes become raisins when they have lost almost all of their moisture.

You can dry them in the oven, with the temperature ranging from 120 to 140 degrees Fahrenheit, as for berries; they will probably dry in six to ten hours.

— ORANGE AND LEMON RINDS —

Peel your fruit and remove the white parts. Then dry the rinds in the sun or in a slow oven, turning from time to time. Store in an airtight container.

You can make a nice hot drink by pouring boiling water over the dried rinds and adding a little honey. Or, you can burn a few dried rinds, like incense, to give a pleasant scent to a room.

— PAPAYAS —

Prepare as per the following directions for peaches.

— PEACHES —

You can dry peaches halved and pitted, with their skins left on, but the home preserver will probably have better results if she peels and slices the fruit first. Soak the slices for ten minutes in an anti-oxidant solution, then steam for three minutes. Dry in the hot sun for two to three days; or in the oven for four to six hours at no more than 140 degrees Fahrenheit.

— PEARS —

You don't have to peel pears either. Halve and core the fruit, then quarter or cut in half-inch slices. Drop them into an anti-oxidant solution for ten minutes and place them on your racks in single layers. The timing in either sun or oven is the same as for apples, three to four days, or three to six hours respectively.

— PLUMS OR PRUNES —

You may dry plums whole, with their pits inside, or halve and store them. Whole (unpitted) plums can be boiled for three to five minutes, and halves steamed for ten minutes. Now they are ready to go into the sun, where they should remain for four to six days. Turn them at least twice a day.

In the oven, the temperature should start at 120 degrees Fahrenheit (for whole plums) or 130 degrees (for halves), be increased to 150 degrees after the first hour, then reduced to 140 degrees when the plums are nearly dried.

• NUTS •

Instead of being dried in a slow oven, nuts should be roasted, but briefly. Whether you roast them with or without their shells depends on how you want to store them, as well as on the porousness of the shell. Peanuts and almonds, for instance, can be roasted in their shells perfectly well, but a Brazil nut's covering is too efficient an insulation to allow the heat into the nut.

Place your freshly harvested nuts no more than two deep in a shallow baking pan in the oven, then roast at 350 degrees Fahrenheit for about half an hour, stirring occasionally. During the last few minutes, shell and sample one nut to see if they are done. If you prefer to roast nuts out of the shell, first blanch them by plunging them into boiling water for about two minutes, then drain and skin. Spread on cloth to dry, then place the nuts in a single layer in a shallow baking pan and roast at 350 degrees for fifteen to twenty minutes, stirring occasionally.

Store in jars as they are, with a little salt if desired.

In a dry place, they will keep for many months.

Plunge dried, shelled chickpeas (actually a vegetable, with a taste reminiscent of nuts) into boiling water for a few seconds, then drain and roast in a 400-degree oven for about twenty minutes. They will become very hard, and, like roasted peanuts, are an excellent accompaniment to drinks.

• SEEDS •

Most seeds are dried when you gather them; or if not, they are easily dried in the sun or a low oven. They are storable for long periods, and offer an excellent source of protein.

• VEGETABLES •

Many vegetables can be dried successfully, but some kinds should be blanched before drying to reduce the enzymatic action. Boiling them for a few minutes or, better still, steaming them is recommended, as the water would otherwise rob them of a good amount of their healthful minerals and vitamins.

Generally speaking, vegetables dry better in the oven, often at slightly lower temperatures than fruits, and proper ventilation is even more important. Because most vegetables don't contain the added safeguard of natural sugars, they tend to decompose more rapidly than fruits, so they should be dried immediately after harvesting. If the sun is not sufficiently hot or the air dry, select the oven. This is especially recommended for green vegetables, as they may lose some of their color and taste if dried in the sun.

— ARTICHOKES —

Choose small, tender artichokes. Remove the stems and outer leaves and, with a sharp knife, chop off the tips of the remaining leaves. Cut them in four parts lengthwise, and pry loose the choke (if any) and discard it. As you cut, put the artichoke sections into a bowl of cold water containing the juice of one lemon for just a minute or two. Strain and steam for about five minutes. Now they can be sun-dried, or oven-dried, in the same manner as green beans (instructions to follow).

You can string artichokes up with needle and thread, still in quarters, making sure that they hang separate from each other and do not touch. Choose a well-ventilated place. You can, if you wish, alternate your methods of drying until they are quite sere.

Artichoke hearts or bottoms from which all sign of choke has been removed can be given the lemon-water treatment and then dried in the oven on very low heat.

— ASPARAGUS —

Dry only the tips. Soak them in an anti-oxidant solution for a few minutes, then spread to dry, without permitting them to touch, in the hot sun for one day; or in an oven with a temperature up to 150 degrees Fahrenheit for four to six hours.

Asparagus can be rehydrated in wine, in melted butter, or directly in a cream soup.

— BEANS —

Leave lima beans, peas, or any kind of bean whose pod you don't eat on the vines, past the time you would normally pick them for eating until the pods are just beginning to dry. Shell and steam (in small amounts at a time) for about ten minutes. Oven-drying is preferable for beans, but you can spread them thinly on trays or racks and dry in the hot sun for a day or two. Oven heat should be kept between 140 and 160 degrees Fahrenheit. Drying will probably take six to eight hours.

Pick your wax, string, and other beans of which you eat the pod fully grown or slightly smaller. String and steam the whole bean for ten minutes, a few at a time, then dry in the oven, using the same temperature range as for shell beans; drying will take four to six hours.

A more colorful method of drying snap (or green) beans is to string and hang them. Thread a needle with a long piece of stout thread or string. Leave your beans whole and pierce them through about a third of the way from one end. Now steam them (or plunge them for a few minutes into boiling salted water), string and all. Hang them to drip in a warm, shaded, well-ventilated place, making sure the beans don't touch. You can finish drying them in the sun, in your oven, or use the space over your stove, if it is used often enough to provide the necessary warmth.

— BEETS —

Select young, tender beets for drying. Cut off all but one-third to one-half inch of the greens and stems and steam for twenty minutes or so. Then trim, peel, and slice. Dry in your oven at a heat of 130 to 150 degrees Fahrenheit for six to eight hours or until the slices are very leathery.

— BROCCOLI —

Use only the flowerets, not the woody stalks. Proceed as with asparagus, but steam for about five minutes after immersing in the anti-oxidant solution.

— CABBAGE —

Choose large, firm heads. Remove the outer leaves and slice the ball into one-inch sections. Steam for about five minutes, then drain, and pat dry with a towel or cloth. Place on trays or racks in the sun, or in the oven, with the heat no higher than 130 degrees Fahrenheit. Be even more vigilant than with other more solid types of vegetables. Turn and separate the cabbage constantly, to prevent its leaves from sticking together while drying. The thinner parts will dry quickly, the thicker in three to four hours.

— CAULIFLOWER —

Pick (or buy) fresh, compact heads with outer leaves that are a rich green color. Remove the leaves and separate the flowerets at their base, discarding the core. Then proceed as with cabbage, though you will probably have to allow for more drying time, possibly as much as six hours in the oven.

— CORN —

Some varieties of corn can be dried on the cob, and indeed are often left on their stalks past harvest time to start drying in fields where the climate is dry and the sun hot and reliable. When the weather cools somewhat, this corn can be further dried in the air by gathering it, stripping back the husks, and using them to hang up the corn. It makes a charming autumnal decoration, and if left long enough in a sunny place, needs no other treatment. This can be done only with the kinds of corn that make popcorn and corn meal, not those that are eaten fresh.

Sweet corn, which grows in this country in several varieties, can be dried off the cob, and if handled properly keeps its flavor well. Don't leave it on the stalk until full maturity, but pick it young and tender and try to process it immediately. To loosen the corn from the cobs, husk and then drop the ears into boiling water, which you should immediately reduce to simmering. Don't leave the corn in the boiling water more than three minutes. Now cut the kernels from the cob about two-thirds of the way down; do not include the small root on each kernel. Then spread on trays and dry in the sun.

If you prefer to oven-dry, stir often, with the heat no higher than 140 degrees Fahrenheit. It should take four to five hours for the corn to dry, at which time the kernels should be very hard.

— EGGPLANTS —

Choose smallish eggplants, no larger than a large pear. Wash them and wipe dry. Hang them from their stems in the sun for a few days, just as they are. You'll know when they are ready by shaking them: If you hear the seeds rattling inside, they are dry. Store in plastic bags or jars.

— MUSHROOMS —

Choose only young, perfect, and absolutely fresh mushrooms. Wash them if they seem to need it, then separate the caps from the stems. You can slice them or not, depending on their size and your preference. If whole, steam them for six to seven minutes; or plunge them into boiling water for three minutes (less time if sliced). You can sun-dry mushrooms; you can oven-dry them (use the same temperature range as for beans); or you can string them with needle and thread, making sure that when you hang them up they don't touch. Tie knots in the string so that they don't slide down and pile up at the bottom, and suspend strings of different lengths from the ceiling of a well-ventilated room or tie the string across, like a clothesline.

— ONIONS —

Onions lend themselves well to drying as slender rings or as flakes or chips. Peel and slice or chip into pieces of uniform thickness. Don't steam or use anti-oxidant, but spread out on pans and dry in the oven for four or five hours at 130 to 140 degrees Fahrenheit. Watch them closely for burning, especially during the last hour of drying.

— PEAS

Green peas for drying should be gathered young and tender. Shell them and proceed as specified for shell beans, allowing a shorter drying time.

— PEPPERS —
SWEET OR HOT, RED OR GREEN

Peppers should be allowed to mature on the vine. Hot peppers should be strung whole and hung in the sun to dry. In Hungary and in other middle European countries, the fronts of village houses are colorfully festooned with long looping strings of peppers drying in the sun.

Sweet peppers are more frequently oven-dried. First stem and halve them and scrape out the seeds and white membrane. Cut in fairly large chunks and steam three to five minutes, then dry in the oven at 120 to 140 degrees Fahrenheit, stirring often.

— PUMPKINS —

Cut the pumpkin up into several large pieces. Peel and scoop out the seeds. Now bake until it is soft and dry and then pound and push it through a colander. Spread a thin layer of pumpkin meat—about one-quarter inch thick—on lightly greased round pie pans. Now dry the circular forms in the sun, or in the oven at no more than 140 degrees. When they are dry, which will be in an hour or so, you will be able to roll up each piece into a tube or cylinder for easy storing in a tight box or bag. Each package will be enough for a pumpkin pie.

Instead of baking, you can shred the raw pumpkin coarsely and steam the shreds, a few at a time, for six or seven minutes. Then spread loosely in the sun to dry, or dry in the oven at 140 degrees Fahrenheit. They should dry completely in the oven in from three to five hours.

— ROOT VEGETABLES —

Root vegetables—carrots, beets, turnips, parsnips, rutabagas, Jerusalem artichokes, and such—store so well in a root cellar that drying them is really not necessary. But they can be dried in the sun if you want to try it. First wash them thoroughly, then slice, and steam for six to ten minutes. They will need about a month in the sun.

To oven-dry, follow the instructions for shredded pumpkins.

— TOMATOES —

Most home preservers don't dry tomatoes, as there are so many other wonderful ways of preserving them. But they can be dried. Choose ripe, but not over-ripe, tomatoes. Cut in quarters and squeeze out as much of the liquid as you can without crushing them too much. Remove most or all of the seeds. Sprinkle the pieces with salt and spread them on drying racks in the sun for two to four days, or in the oven at 140 degrees Fahrenheit for a few hours. Tomatoes dried this way are good to have on hand for soups, stews, sauces, and other cooking.

You can leave cherry or egg tomatoes on their branches whole, and let them dry in the sun for a few days, filling in with oven-drying, and then finishing the drying process by hanging them in the kitchen or attic. But keep a careful watch that they don't attract pests.

In both cases, your finished product should be fairly leathery but not completely hard.

You can then put inside each tomato a small piece of fresh garlic, a fresh basil leaf, and either a little ground pepper or a small piece of hot pepper, if you like the taste. Close the two halves and put the tomatoes, pressing them slightly, in jars. Fill with good oil and seal. Leave the jars in a visible place and check them after a couple of days, as they may need a little more oil. Seal again and store in a cool place.

Do not use this produce for at least three months. With a slice of cheese or cold meat, it will make a very tasty sandwich or can be used to make pizza. It will be useful also in preparing tomato sauce, or in stews, casseroles, and such.

— Yams —

Bake whole yams until soft and then dry as you do pumpkins.

• HERBS AND GREENS •

The following method can be applied to the drying of parsley, tarragon, basil, thyme, sage, rosemary, mint, dill, oregano, bay and celery leaves, fennel, anise, savory, and many other herbs or greens.

Herbs should be gathered just before the plant begins to flower and while the leaves are still green and tender. Their drying is a gentle and tentative process because they are so delicate; their flavor resides in the oils, which will dry out if too hot, or be destroyed by the sun. Some of the more thickly leaved herbs, such as sage and thyme, can be dried partially in the sun (in temperate climates) and then in a slow oven. But never let your oven temperature rise any higher than 100 degrees Fahrenheit for drying any herb. And watch your timing carefully; the whole process should not take more than a couple of hours.

The more delicately leaved herbs should be kept out of the sunlight entirely and dried in the dark. You may want to wash them—ever so carefully—in cool water before you start to dry them (curly parsley can be dipped first in boiling water for about ten seconds). But washing is usually not necessary, and should be avoided if possible because it reduces the aroma.

Some herbs can be left on their stems, gathered in clusters, and put head first into a paper bag. Then hang the bag with a bit of string tied loosely around its neck from a rafter in your attic or a warm upstairs room.

Our own method of drying herbs is simplicity itself: We usually spread them on a large piece of wrapping paper in the attic, cover them with another piece of paper to keep out the light, and leave them four or five days.

Parsley roots, shredded and dried in the same way as herbs (perhaps a little longer), are just as tasty as parsley leaves. Soak them in a small amount of cold water before using. If you are adding them to liquid dishes such as soups or stews, there is then no need to soak; you can chop them instead, if desired.

• MEATS •

Beef can be dried if it has first been cured. Most of us can recall the dried chipped beef on toast we were served in our childhoods. Before being chipped, or sliced exceedingly thin in small pieces, the beef was dried. If you want to try the following Pennsylvania Dutch method, prepare yourself as follows:

10 lbs. fresh-killed beef
(round steak is good, but other cuts may be used)
1 cup salt
4 tbs. brown sugar
½ tsp. saltpeter

Mix the salt, sugar, and saltpeter well, making sure you have not left any lumps. Divide this mixture into three equal portions. Place your meat in a large bowl, rub thoroughly with a third of the mixture, and let stand one day. Repeat with the remaining parts of the mixture on the second and third days. Turn the meat several times a day, and let stand for seven more days.

On the eighth day, hang the meat in a cool shed to dry thoroughly. If the threat of bugs is a problem, you can rub the meat with some charcoal powder to discourage them. When the meat is thoroughly dry, wrap it in muslin or a double layer of cheesecloth and keep in a cool place. It will store safely for several months. But if, after six months or so the meat becomes too hard for you to piece, soak it in cold water for twenty-four hours and gently wipe dry. Then rewrap and hang again in a cool place.

You can apply this same method to veal, lamb or mutton, and venison. Fatty or organ meats, however, do not lend themselves to the drying process.

• FISH AND SHELLFISH •

Almost any fish can be dried, provided it is very fresh and has been well salted first. Fish containing a high percentage of fat, however, can be preserved for a shorter period of time than leaner fish.

Open the throat of the fish, remove the gills, and allow the fish to bleed. When the bleeding has stopped, wash the fish thoroughly in cold water and cut off the head, making sure you leave the plate below the gills. With a very sharp knife, cut down the left side of the backbone (or the right side, if you are lefthanded); with the knife slanted against the bone, try to remove the upper section in one piece. Then push the knife point against the backbone and slide it toward the tail. Repeat until all the backbone has been removed. Open the belly with scissors and remove all the organs and blood. Do this under running water and make sure you remove everything from the belly. Then remove the scales with a knife: Hold the fish by the tail and rub the blade several times toward the head, all around the body. If the fish is not too scaly, you can use a stiff brush instead of a knife.

Prepare a brine of one cup salt to one gallon of cold water and soak the fish in it for half an hour. Drain well. Then roll the fish in a shallow dish full of pickling salt. Use about a pound of salt for each four pounds of fish, and get as much of the salt as you can onto the fish, inside and out. Place the fish on boards or racks in a shady, well-ventilated place. Let them dry for at least two days or longer, depending on the size of the fish and the amount of humidity in the air. If you have trouble with flies or other insects outdoors, you can build a fire of green wood under or close to the drying spot to keep them away. Bring the fish indoors every night and weigh them down evenly with boards and weights to help squeeze out the moisture.

The process may take as long as six or seven days and nights, depending on conditions. Don't cut it short but make sure the fish is very dry before you store it by pressing the flesh between your fingers; if it leaves no impression, the fish is dry. Wrap in wax paper and pack it in wooden boxes.

To prepare shrimps, add one cup of salt to every two quarts of water and bring to a boil. Drop in the shrimps still in their shells and simmer for about ten minutes. Then remove the shells completely, the tails if they are still attached, and devein. Spread the shrimps in a single layer in the sun, and turn often during the first day. If the sun is hot, the shrimps should dry in about three days. At night, however, they must be brought inside and left in a dry, airy place. When the shrimps have dried completely, store them in jars or paper bags in a cool, dry place.

They will keep many months. When you are ready to cook the shrimps, simply soak them for two or three hours.

4

SMOKING

Now that so many industrial methods of preserving meat are being openly questioned and challenged, you may want to consider curing and smoking your meat at home. At this writing, the commercial use of sodium nitrite for bacon is receiving considerable attention, although there is no conclusive evidence yet that eating a modest amount of hickory-smoked ham or cheese is dangerous.

The flesh of the pig, so long a world favorite, lends itself best of all to smoking, though this age-old process effectively preserves other meats, fish, game, poultry, and even some fruits and vegetables.

Smoking is, of course, a drying process carried to an interesting new extreme. The removal of moisture makes an uncongenial atmosphere for the growth of the micro-organisms that lead to spoilage; but smoking is more than "super-drying." It also adds color and flavor to food, depending of course on the kind of smoke you use and what you burn to produce it.

Hickory-smoked, for example, the label that we sometimes see on hams, bacon, and other American products, means just that. The flesh has been permeated with smoke produced by the burning of logs or branches or chips from the hickory, an indigenous

North American tree that gives off a special smell (and hence flavor) when burned. But a number of other woods will do as good or as beneficial a job. Most hardwood trees will give you good fodder for smoking: maple, apple, beech, cherry, pear, alder, oak, buttonwood, or pecan (which is a kind of hickory). Hickory and other kinds of chips can be bought in hardware stores, as can sawdust. In some parts of the country you have a ready supply of sweet bay that you can use, or the roots of palmetto or manzanita. And, if you have trouble getting hold of enough wood from trees, you can do a fair job of meat-smoking with dried corn cobs.

Avoid conifers or soft woods; because of resins, these woods lend a bad taste. And, if in doubt about your smoking fuel, just burn a small piece of it and smell the smoke it gives off. Trust your olfactory nerves, and their close connection with your sense of taste, to tell you if you will like your large catch of perch smoked with the emanations of that cord of fireplace wood on your back porch.

You may use regular kindling, charcoal, or a combination of both, to get the fire started. But before hanging anything to smoke, be sure the fire has burned down to embers. Then lay on your hardwood in small pieces, chips, or sawdust, to get the smoke started. You can moisten sawdust before putting it on the fire, or you can sprinkle it with water after it has started to burn, to produce a good smoke. Juniper berries, added to wood chips, produce an interesting smoked flavor for meats.

Smoking, of course, is not usually sufficient to protect your food from deterioration. First it must be treated with salt, sugar, or some other spice or spoilage-retarder for a while as is, for example, "smoked, sugar-cured ham." The details of the pre-smoking process for each product are given individually.

Certain products, such as fish (if not too large), ham, cheese, and foods that are small in size don't have to be cooked after they are treated and smoked. But of course you will have to cook game and poultry.

• THE SMOKEHOUSE OR SMOKER •

The first thing you will need is a smokehouse of some kind, since smoking in your oven is definitely not recommended. If you live on a farm where there is such a structure, you are fortunate indeed. Otherwise, look around: That little square brick house just beyond the rim of the hill that is too small for a garage and too elaborate for chicks may be the place. A smokehouse can even be a smallish wooden box that you keep in the cellar, on the porch, or in the provisions closet, and take out and put to work in the fireplace from time to time.

If you are not a make-it-yourself type, you can purchase an electric aluminum meat and fish smoker for about thirty-five dollars that will smoke up to twenty-five pounds of meat at a time. Its dimensions are 11½" x 12" x 24". The only provision, aside from space, you will have to make for it is regular house electric current and a means of allowing some of the smoke to escape. A smaller variety, called the Scandinavian food smoker, is sometimes available at about eighteen dollars.

You can convert an old icebox or refrigerator into a smoker. First place an electric hot plate on the floor of the appliance, running the cord out the open space in the back or through a hole you make in the bottom of the side; or place on the floor a small tub or large pot in which you can kindle a fire. Now make a hole in the floor of the refrigerating space (unless there's already a drain there, in which case you already have a place through which the smoke can come. Then drill some holes in the very top of the appliance, to allow the smoke to escape. To regulate the heat inside, you will need simple dampers for these holes, which you can make from metal (the tops or bottoms of large juice or fruit cans, for instance) and attach with screws—one screw to each damper, so that they can slide back and forth over the holes. If your old icebox still has its shelves, fine. If not, find some discarded shelves in the dump, or make some out of coat hangers, window-screening, or ungalvanized, rust-proof chicken wire. Or, rig up some hooks suspended from the top of the appliance to hang large things on.

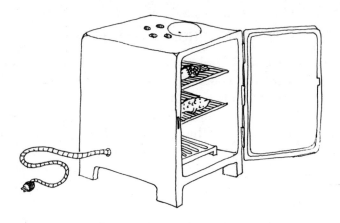

You can instead cut the top out of an oil drum. Burn out the insides to remove any oil odors, and put a window screen over the top of the drum. Then place an old washtub, upside down, over the screen. The tub may already have holes in its bottom; if not, drill or punch some in with large nails. Now you can make a fire in the bottom of the drum and lay your food on the screen for smoking.

OIL DRUM
SMOKER

If you prefer to make a smokehouse of wood, the size of the trays or racks you are using for your shelves should determine the size of wood you cut, and the hardness of the wood determine the tree from which it comes. Cut four slabs for the sides and hinge a fifth for a door. Attach shelf holders—stout nails only partially pounded in will do—and fit on a top with holes in it. Put a metal pot or pan in the bottom, and you are prepared for your smoking venture.

If you have a little outdoor space you can give over to smoking, you might want to try building a trench-and-pit smokehouse, shown in the accompanying illustration. Try to find a spot that includes an incline, since smoke and heat rise. At the lower level dig a good-sized pit in which to build your fire and cover it with a metal top. Carry a trench, from high up on one side of the pit, up the incline at an angle; it should connect at its other end with the bottom of an airtight wooden barrel. Line the trench or flue with stovepiping, or with round plumbing tiles. You can hang your meat on round wooden dowels stretched across the top of the barrel, and put a wooden barrel cover on top of the dowels. That will hold most of the smoke in and allow some to escape under the edges of the cover.

BARREL
TRENCH + PIT
SMOKEHOUSE

We even know of a farm couple in the Adirondacks who every autumn temporarily convert their garage into a smokehouse, in which they smoke their bacon and ham. They found lying around the farm a large square metal cube missing one side. They hoist it to the garage ceiling with the meat suspended inside on hooks. Then they simply build a fire (of maple chips) on the cement floor underneath. Your garage, of course, must be free of oil or gasoline or their lingering odor.

If you live in a city apartment, you will have to rely on your fireplace or terrace, after first checking the local ordinances. Or, you might consider a hibachi—a small, modest grate normally used for grilling meats—and adapt it to your smoking needs.

Whatever means you choose, a well-calibrated oven thermometer, one that will register changes in temperature by the tens and twenties, is recommended. And experiment with the regulation of smoke and heat before you entrust a costly big ham or side of beef to the smoker. Controlling the heat of a smoker is a knack that is developed with experience, especially if you start your fire from scratch. An electric unit that can be regulated to various heats is an ideal generator, but in any event, whether you use one or make your own fire, remember that wetting your wood chips before burning them will produce instant smoke. The more chips, the hotter the smoke, generally speaking. And, of course, the size of your smoker will be a factor, too; the smaller box will get hotter with less burning. Also, the more nearly closed your dampers, the hotter the inside of the box will become.

We are all familiar with kippered herring, the fish that is dried, salted, and smoked. Kippering requires smoking at a very high heat, over 180 degrees Fahrenheit, a kind of smoking that is hard for the home smoker to attain and regulate. So we are limited to what is known as "cold smoking," at 120 to 140 degrees. If you are using a handmade wooden smoker, you'd best have smoked salmon for your Sunday breakfast rather than kippered herring.

Above all, don't try to smoke with anything other than a hard wood, and don't smoke by burning cardboard or wet newspapers.

The use of a little oil will keep food from sticking.

· MEATS ·

— PORK —

Fresh pork, sometimes called fresh ham, is a highly perishable meat that must be dry-cured before it is smoked. Unless you do your own slaughtering, the only parts of the pig available to you will be shoulders, hams (hind legs), or bacon. If you plan to smoke fifty pounds of fresh pork, you will need:

4 lbs. salt
1 lb. sugar (white or brown)
1 oz. saltpeter

Mix these ingredients together and divide them in half. Rub all surfaces of the meat well with the curing mixture; if working with a ham, pack the shank end well. Put the meat into a clean crock or glass dish and leave it in a cold place (above freezing, 36 to 40 degrees) for six to eight days. Then rub the pieces of meat with the other half of the curing mix and put them back into the cold place for the rest of the time needed for cure: For hams and shoulders, you can figure about two days per pound; for bacon, one and a half days per pound.

At the end of this period, brush smaller pieces of meat to remove the excess curing mixture; larger cuts, however, should be soaked in cold water for about a half-hour. Hang the meat to dry somewhere away from insects overnight. If you are smoking bacon, you can begin in the morning. Larger cuts will need a week or so.

Get your smokehouse up to about 120 degrees Fahrenheit and smoke the meat for a day with the dampers open. Close the dampers the second day and smoke for another day or two, testing the meat for color. When the color looks right to you, take it out; it probably is smoked enough. Don't let the heat rise above 120 degrees or you may scorch the meat. If you can maintain a lower heat, 90 degrees or so, even better; but of course you will have to smoke it for a longer period.

You can substitute honey (approximately three cups) for the sugar, though it is rather difficult to work with.

— HAM —

The following method of smoking ham does not actually require a smokehouse. If you live in a house with a fireplace, you can preserve a twelve- to fifteen-pound ham for as long as six months.

In mid-September, sift some good wood ashes out of the fireplace. Blend with about one-quarter pound of ashes, one pound of salt, and one-quarter pound of black pepper. Rub it over the entire surface of the ham, then put ham into a basket in a cool place. Every three days wipe off the ash mixture, then re-coat with the same blend. Continue to do this for two weeks.

Prepare a piece of burlap by boiling it for ten minutes in three gallons of water, to which you have added a pound of salt. Remove from heat and allow bag and water to cool. Squeeze bag as dry as possible and hang it in the sun to dry completely. Tie the ham in it and hang it for two weeks more in the cool place.

In mid-October, climb up on your roof and, using a sturdy chain, lower the ham down the chimney until it is suspended about four feet above fire level. In the winter months that follow, however, use only hard wood in your fireplace.

Take the ham down about mid-March, remove the blackened burlap, and rinse the meat with warm water and a bit of baking soda. The ham is ready to eat, hot or cold (thin-sliced), whichever way you prefer.

Ham will also keep for several weeks in a cool place without spoiling, if you protect it from insects by packing it in pulverized charcoal.

Pork and smoking seem to go together, but you can use your smoker to preserve nearly any other meat that you want to keep for a while. The rules for smoking pork can be applied to beef, veal (though it's not commonly smoked), lamb, the larger fish, venison, and other game.

— Venison —

Bring to boil enough water to cover your game. Dissolve in it:

> *2 cups salt*
> *1 cup sugar*
> *1 cup cider (any kind)*
> *1 tsp. ground cloves*
> *1 bay leaf*

Now put in your meat and cook it about five minutes to the pound at a low boil. Drain and let dry for about an hour, then smoke for about seven or eight hours, at 120 to 140 degrees Fahrenheit, the length of time depending on the weight of the meat; allow one and a half hours to the pound. Bear, rabbit, and opossum can be similarly smoked.

— JERKY —

Those thin strips (¼- to ½-inch thick) of smoked venison, elk, deer, or beef should be cut and rubbed with salt, then smoked on racks in your smokehouse with heat as low as you can get it. Smoke for five to eight hours; test for dryness from time to time and turn the strips over midway through the process.

When the strips are completely dry, wrap them in cheesecloth and hang them in the air, either outside or inside your house in a cool place. They will keep for months.

— BEEF TONGUE AND HEART —

Put a tongue and heart in water, to which you have added:

¾ cup salt
⅓ cup sugar
1 to 1½ tsps. crushed black pepper
1 garlic clove

Cover and simmer for forty-five minutes to an hour (about forty-five minutes per pound of meat). Drain until quite dry, then rub both parts all over with a garlic clove that you have cut across its fattest part and then crosscut. Smoke for no less than sixteen hours at 120 to 130 degrees Fahrenheit.

This is an effective method for smoking duck and pheasant as well, but you may not want to smoke fowl as long; probably one hour to the pound will suffice.

— PASTRAMI —

Pastrami can be made simply by marinating. For one and a half pounds of pastrami, combine the following ingredients:

1½ lbs. beef shoulder
1 qt. water
12 tbs. salt
3 tbs. brown sugar
2 tbs. parsley, chopped fine
2 medium onions, chopped fine

2 garlic cloves, minced or pressed
1 tsp. saltpeter
dash cayenne pepper
dash black pepper
3 or 4 cloves
2 tsp. mixed pickling spices (see Index)

Make sure that the meat is entirely covered by the solution, and put in the refrigerator. Refrigerate for six or seven days, but turn the meat frequently. Then remove the meat, wipe dry, and hang it in a cool, airy place until its surface is completely dry.

Smoke pastrami at about 100 degrees Fahrenheit for four hours. Then raise the temperature to as close to 180 degrees as you can get it and smoke for another two or three hours. If you can get your heat only halfway there, just increase the length of smoking time at the higher heat.

If you don't eat all the meat when it is hot from the smoker, cool and wrap it. It will keep a week or so in a cool place, or even longer in the refrigerator.

Care must be taken not to dry out poultry, the smaller fish, and seafood too much. The following instructions will guide you in the preparation of these foods.

— CHICKEN —

2 lbs. salt
1 lb. sugar
1½ ozs. saltpeter
6 qts. water
3 fryers, about 2 lbs. each

Dissolve the first three ingredients in the water and bring to a boil. Soak the chickens, completely submerged, for thirty-six to forty-eight hours. Remove the birds and place in clean, cold water for an hour. Hang them up to dry (or drain on a rack). Then truss and tie in stockinettes.

Hang them in your smokehouse by the legs and smoke for about an hour, with the dampers closed, at 140 degrees Fahrenheit if you can get the heat up that high for so brief a period. Then lower the heat, open dampers, and smoke at between 120 and 130 degrees for five to six hours more. Check for color and remove when they turn golden brown.

Chicken cured and smoked this way can be stored in a cool place for a week or two, in the refrigerator for a month, and frozen for about three months.

— Turkey —

Domesticated or wild turkey can be similarly smoked, but may require moisturizing during smoking. For this you will need:

> *3 gallons water*
> *4 lbs. salt*
> *1½ lbs. sugar*
> *1½ ozs. saltpeter*

Bring to a boil the water in which you have dissolved the other ingredients. Pack the turkey into a crock and pour the brine, slightly cooled, over it. If you wish, and if it is a fairly large-sized bird, you may inject the turkey with the brine mixture, concentrating on the joints around wings and legs, before soaking it. Weight the bird to keep it submerged and leave it in a cool place from four to five days, or even longer for a large turkey that you have not thus injected.

Then soak the bird in fresh, cool water for four to six hours to remove excess salt. Drain and truss and wrap in a stockinette. Hang by tail or wings in smokehouse and smoke at 140 degrees Fahrenheit for eight to ten hours; or, at 120 degrees for twelve to fourteen hours.

After the first two hours, you may want to place a pan of water over the fire to restore some of the moisture to the bird. Smoke it until you like the color of the skin.

The turkey will keep in a cool place for about a week or in the refrigerator for a month. If you wrap it in plastic or moisture-proof paper and freeze it, you can keep it for three to four months.

• FISH AND SEAFOOD •

A large fish that you can't eat up all at once may be smoked for keeping.

The flavor of a large fish will be improved by curing and spicing. The following method will work with nearly any medium- to large-sized fish from stream, lake, or sea with fairly firm flesh, or with steaks of salmon, halibut, and other larger fish. The following ingredients will accommodate up to ten pounds of fish; if you are working with more, just increase the proportions accordingly.

2 qts. ice water	*1 oz. saltpeter*
3 lbs. salt	*1 oz. each: black pepper,*
1 lb. sugar	*mace, powdered clove,*
(white or brown)	*allspice, minced bay leaf*

Don't skin the fish, but scale and bone it as much as possible; gut it and leave the head on or not, as you prefer. Soak it for an hour or two in the ice water in which you have dissolved one pound of salt. Drain for a half-hour while you prepare a mixture of the remaining two pounds of salt and the rest of the ingredients. Rub the fish carefully with this spice mix, inside and out, and leave it on for about twelve hours. Scrub it off (to get rid of all the salt), then dry the fish in the air for six to eight hours.

Smoke at 90 to 100 degrees Fahrenheit for six to eight hours, then lower your heat and continue smoking at 70 degrees for two days or more. The longer you smoke the fish, the longer you will be able to store it.

The smaller the fish, the more likely you are to leave the heads on; some tiny fish, such as sardines, need not be gutted or boned.

Soak them in the same kind of brine, rub with a similar spice mixture, dry in the air, and smoke on racks.

Omit the higher initial temperature and start "cold-smoking," keeping the temperature between 70 and 90 degrees for the whole time.

Smoked for twenty-four hours, small fish will keep in a cool place for about two weeks. If you want to store them longer, smoke for five days or more, night and day.

— Oysters and Clams —

If you have a ready source of these delightful mollusks, you can enjoy a rare smoked delicacy that is both a tasty tidbit and a source of health-giving vitamin D and minerals.

Steam oysters for fifteen minutes in the shell, then shuck and soak for another fifteen minutes in a brine of a half cup of salt to a quart of water. Rinse and drain. Slice ¼ to ½ inch thick. Smoke for an hour at low heat, about 100 degrees Fahrenheit, with dampers wide open. Then close dampers and increase heat to 140 degrees and smoke for another hour or slightly less. Check often and remove when color becomes pleasing.

For clams steam the shells open and shuck them. Soak in the same brine for ten minutes. Rinse and drain, then steam again, for about ten more minutes. Smoke at a low temperature, 80 to 90 degrees, for a preliminary hour, then proceed as with oysters.

If covered with a bit of olive oil, oysters and clams smoked in this manner will keep about a month in a cool place.

— Salmon —

Smoked salmon—sometimes called "lox"—is often a brilliant orange in color. Some very delicious salmon, however, has silvery or white flesh instead—for example, the King Salmon of the American West Coast—with a nutritional value equal to that of its more brightly colored cousin and a flavor that is often superior.

To smoke either kind of salmon, first make a brine of one cup salt to two quarts water, bring to a boil, then chill. Bone and filet or cut the fish into chunks. Submerge in brine and soak for one to three hours, depending on the size of the pieces. Then rinse and soak fish in fresh cold water for a day, changing the water three or four times. Drain and dry fish in a ventilated or breezy place where the temperature doesn't go above 70 degrees Fahrenheit.

Then smoke at no more than 80 degrees for eight to twelve hours, until a membrane has formed on the surface of the fish. Now raise the temperature as hot as you can get it, close to 180 degrees if possible, and smoke for another two hours. If you can't get it up that high, smoke for a longer period at a lower heat.

The salmon will keep in a cool place for a week, and in the refrigerator somewhat longer.

— Smoked Fish Indian-Style —

To preserve a good catch of small fish, gut the fish and discard the heads and the backbone down to the tail. Open the flesh to a flat piece and cut incisions in the flesh lengthwise. Wash and wipe dry. Prepare a mixture of two tablespoons pepper to a pound of salt, and rub both skin and flesh with it. Store in a cool, dry place for ten to twelve hours, then rinse off the seasonings.

Now cut some wands of green wood, whittle them to points, and spear the fish on the sticks, with the other ends stuck into the ground. Leave the fish waving in the breeze for four or five hours.

Dig a pit, and using any of the hardwoods good for smoking, kindle a fire and let it reach the red-coal stage. Then arrange your fish on sticks so that the filets are hanging over the smoking fire. Now make a tepee of poles around the pit and higher than the fish. Cover the framework of poles with boughs, leaves, grasses, whatever you can find to make a fairly solid layer of green material that won't curl up in the heat and fly away. You will have in effect a natural, if temporary, smokehouse.

Smoke the fish no less than six and no more than twenty-four hours. At the end of the smoking period, cool the fish, wrap, and store in a cool, dry place. Depending on how long you've smoked them, they will keep without refrigeration from several days to several weeks.

This method smokes small fresh-water fish such as trout, pickerel, and the like to mouth-watering goodness.

• CHEESE •

Once you have made your cheese (see Index), you may want to smoke it, to change its flavor and to render it storable outside a refrigerator for a longer time. Its consistency can be hardened somewhat, too, by the smoking process.

Hickory is a good wood for smoking cheese, but any available hardwood of your choice will do. However, avoid the soft woods: pine, cedar, and the other evergreens, which will give your cheese a creosotic taste.

The heat should never be allowed to get high or your cheese will melt. Long, low-heat smoking at 70 to 90 degrees Fahrenheit for ten to twelve hours is best.

SIMPLE AND ASSORTED PROCESSING

There are several extremely simple ways of preserving various kinds of food, some of which are not widely known. For many foods, for example, salt and/or oil are good preserving agents. The salt should be natural salt that has not been iodized or treated to flow more freely. The oil should be preferably olive oil. In many instances you can reuse the same oil (either to make a fresh batch of the same preserve or in salads) after you have eaten the preserved product. The flavor of the oil is usually enhanced by the foods that were submerged in it and this can only improve the taste of your salads, unless you have stored the jars in a warm place and the oil has turned rancid. Oils other than olive can be used, but they should be of high quality and rather dense. Oils generally used for frying are too thin and watery and don't keep the product as well as do the thicker oils. Olive oil imparts to preserved foods its delicate, distinctive taste, while other oils can make the product less interesting by absorbing some of the taste of the preserved food while not giving any enhancement in return. For all these reasons, olive oil is by far the best, and since the biggest portion of the jar is taken up by whatever food you are preserving, only a very small amount of oil is used and the expense is not very high.

Some other preserving agents are lemon, vinegar and salt-peter, boric acid, salicylic acid, and bicarbonate of soda. Boric acid and salicylic acid used sparingly, in the exact amounts indicated, are completely harmless.

The following is an all-purpose brine for any type of meat, fish, or vegetable. If bottled and corked properly, it can keep for a very long time for ready use whenever it is needed.

> 2 lbs. coarse salt   ½ tsp. mace
> 10 bay leaves   ½ tsp. ground juniper
> 2 tbs. dry basil leaves or   berries
> 5 tbs. fresh leaves   ½ tsp. ground pepper
> 2 tsp. coriander seeds

Boil all ingredients in three gallons of water for fifteen minutes. Allow to cool, then strain through fine sieve, and bottle.

Every few weeks, if not used, boil mixture again and replace water that has evaporated.

Meats should be punctured deeply in several places with a sharp, long needle, then rubbed vigorously with saltpeter on all sides, and submerged in the liquid brine. Then put a wooden plank on top and weigh it down with a large stone, so that the meat is completely immersed in the liquid.

• VEGETABLES •

— ARTICHOKES IN OIL, HOME-STYLE —

The following is a very old Florentine method of preserving artichokes: Choose very small, tender artichokes, possibly the size of a walnut, or slightly larger, before they have formed a choke. If they are bigger, halve and remove chokes. Blanch for five minutes in a solution of half water and half vinegar to which you have added a generous amount of salt. The liquid should be just enough to cover them. Remove from fire, drain, and spread out on a dishtowel, upside down if whole, or with the inside half down if halved, to cool and dry. Then spread them on a cloth in trays, in single layers, in a well-ventilated, shady place until completely dry, or about one hour. Put in jars, stuffing them gently, and cover with olive oil or a good-quality salad oil and pepper-

corns. They should be sufficiently stuffed so that they don't
float. Seal tightly and store in a cool, dark place.

If you have salicylic acid on hand, omit the salt and use one
small pinch for every two cups of oil. This prolongs their preservation.

Two or three days after putting the artichokes in jars, check
to see if they are still submerged in oil, as they may have absorbed
some of it. If they are not submerged, open the jars and add more
oil, then seal and store.

— ARTICHOKES IN OIL, GOURMET-STYLE —

Also from Italy but a more refined method is to rinse the same
tiny artichokes, removing the outer leaves if necessary, and in
lemon juice instead. Blanch in dry white wine together with a
little aromatic vinegar (one or two tablespoonfuls per cup of
wine), bay leaf, cloves, peppercorns, and a few lemon slices for
five minutes. Drain and dry thoroughly by placing them upside
down on a nonmetallic strainer, or a layer of cheesecloth
stretched and taped on top of trays. Cover with dishtowels so that
the artichokes don't get discolored.

Do not discard the liquid in which you blanched the artichokes.
It can be used as a salad dressing, as a marinade for fish or meat,
or for boiling fish. The bay leaves and peppercorns should be removed and drained and, when completely dry, can be added to
the jars in which you store the artichokes. Stuff artichokes gently
in jars, and cover with olive oil or a good-quality salad oil. Seal
the jars and check after a few days to make sure the artichokes
are still submerged. If they have absorbed some of the oil, add
some more, seal tightly, and store in a cool, dark place.

— ASPARAGUS TIPS —

Select stalks that are very fresh and green, possibly rather thin,
and cut out the hard white part of the stems completely. Bring to
a boil water, salt (to taste), a few cloves, and a thinly sliced
lemon, preferably unripe. When the liquid boils, add the asparagus and boil for about ten minutes, or until tender.

Remove to warm jars, handling the asparagus very delicately
so as not to break the stems, and insert with tips up. Cover with

the liquid in which they have boiled, and fill jars completely. Seal and store in a cool place.

— BEANS, GREEN —

The following method is derived from a cookbook from Pennsylvania that bears the date 1883.

Pick green string beans while still young and tender. Sprinkle the bottom of a wooden keg or half barrel with pickling salt, add a layer about three inches deep of string beans, then another layer of salt, and continue alternating until you finish with salt. Cover with a piece of board that fits inside the container and place a heavy weight on it. A brine will form.

When ready to use, soak them overnight in plenty of water after rinsing under running water. Then cook in the same manner as fresh.

— BEANS, SHELL —

The New England state of Maine is the source of this recipe for baking and keeping beans. The high protein and iron content of beans makes them a good substitute for meat. Unlike meat, beans have always been plentiful and cheap.

Other parts of the country may depend on pea beans. Kidney and other kinds of beans lend themselves equally well to the process.

Beans are baked in the traditional way in a special iron kettle with legs, a handle like that of a pail, and a cover that fits around the top, but any covered iron kettle with a secure overhanging cover and a handle will do. If you have the classic round bean crock for baking beans, reserve that for cooking them in your oven. If your iron kettle does not have legs, it should be supported by a rack or grill to keep its bottom off the coals.

Dig a hole in the ground about three feet deep and two feet wide. Place a flat rock on the bottom of the hole, then add some pieces of scrap iron or more rocks. Fill the hole with hardwood, then light it and burn out the hole for half a day. You will need good hot coals to cook the beans.

Soak the beans overnight or pour boiling water over them about

76

two hours before you start cooking them. Then drain and put beans in the kettle with a chunk of salt pork or bacon and a tablespoon or so of salt, depending on your taste and the quantity of beans. If you are a vegetarian, add some oil of a dense quality or vegetable shortening instead. Dilute in a little warm water enough molasses to sweeten the beans, again varying the amount to suit your taste.

The kettle should be about three-quarters full of beans. Cover with boiling water with a few inches to spare; leave some empty space at the top as the beans will absorb the liquid and swell.

You are now ready to cover and lower the kettle. It is a good idea to hook to the handle a few feet of sturdy wire, which you can use not only for lowering and later lifting the kettle, but also to mark where you have buried the beans. Surround the kettle with the hot coals and iron scraps or rocks, still leaving the bottom rock on which you place the kettle on its own feet or on the grill. Now fill the hole up with earth, packing it tightly and stamping it down. Make a firm seal, as any opening will allow air to get in and ruin your beans.

Leave the pot buried for a day or so, then dig the earth off and pull the kettle out by the wire. The beans are ready to eat.

Beans prepared in this fashion will keep in a cool place for several weeks.

— Beets and Cauliflower —

Boiled beets, sliced or diced coarsely, and boiled chunks of cauliflower can be preserved either separately or together for a few weeks in jars in the refrigerator. Pour into the jars about two-thirds of the liquid in which they have boiled and one-third strong vinegar (preferably aromatic vinegar). You can add ground pepper, tarragon, basil, garlic, etc., to suit your taste. Coriander seeds are especially recommended for cauliflower. Make sure to cover completely with liquid. Close jar, shake well, and store.

To serve in salads, just drain and add salad oil. The liquid in the jar can be reused three or four times. If it has become too vinegary, add a little water, boil the mixture for a few minutes, and use again.

77

— CUCUMBERS IN BRINE —

Since you cannot freeze or dry cucumbers, if you don't want to serve them pickled all the time, you may try preparing them Swiss-style.

Peel young, smallish cucumbers and slice very thinly. Sprinkle in a container with a flat bottom some pickling salt and fill with alternating layers of sliced cucumbers and salt. Cover with salt. The amount of salt must be sufficient to assure that the cucumbers will be covered with their own liquid after about an hour. If they are not, add some more salt at the top and wait another hour before covering the jar. When ready, add about half an inch of good oil and seal tightly.

When ready to serve, rinse in running water, then put in a bowl and cover with water for a few hours. Drain and add to mixed salads or serve alone with a dressing of oil, vinegar, and pepper (omitting salt).

— EGGPLANT IN OIL —

Peel a medium-size eggplant, slice about half an inch thick, then spread it out on clean cloth and salt the slices on both sides. Allow to stand twenty-four hours, moving them to another dry cloth when the first becomes soaked. Then squeeze gently between two pieces of absorbent paper or cloth and blanch in small quantity of two-thirds water and one-third vinegar for two minutes. Drain and dry on cloth. When dry, put in wide jars horizontally (you may have to halve the wider slices). Add a little oil, chopped fresh garlic or chives, and two or three peppercorns in between each layer. If you prefer not to eat garlic, add only a halved clove every two layers and remove before serving the eggplant. Adding oregano or basil to each layer enhances the final taste. Seal tightly and store in a cool, dark place.

— GRAPE LEAVES IN OIL —

For this Greek delicacy choose medium-size leaves and cut the stems, leaving about one-quarter inch attached to the leaf. Then boil in a little salted water for four minutes (or only three, if the leaves are thin and tender). Pat thoroughly dry with a cloth, and put a few leaves at the bottom of each jar, pressing gently so that you do not break them; then add a little oil and fill up each jar with alternate layers of leaves and oil, always pushing them down carefully as you stuff the jar. Cover with more oil, to the top of the jar, then seal and store the leaves in a cool, dark place.

These leaves are often preferred to those preserved in brine. They keep almost as long, and after you have fished out all the leaves, you can use the oil for any purpose.

— WILD GRAPE LEAVES IN BRINE —

Use leaves that are fresh and light green, and after pickling, pull out ten or twelve at a time when you want to stuff them. You will need the following for your brine:

1 cup salt

1 gallon water

cloves, mace, cinnamon, and peppercorns to taste

Actually, use whatever spices suit your fancy, since the spices aren't really necessary to preserve for several months the fine nutty taste of the leaves. Their color changes to a darker green, but they don't otherwise alter. Just be sure the leaves stay submerged in the brine when you place them in wide-mouthed jars, spreading them so that they lay flat. Cover the jars and store in a cool, dark place.

If you have cultivated grapes, pick the leaves of those vines and proceed as directed.

— PEAPODS —

The idea of preserving peapods may be new to some of you, but actually it is an old European culinary trick for adding taste to soups, stews, and many other dishes.

The next time you use peas, wash the pods before you shell them and drain; the pods will be dry by the time you have finished shelling the peas. Place them on oven trays in a single layer and bake them in a high oven until they have become quite brown. Do not allow the pods to become too dark, or they will taste burned. Pack tightly in jars, seal, and store in a dark, cool place. When ready to use, add in a small quantity to your dish. If you prefer, discard them after cooking your soup, stew, or whatever before serving.

— Soup Greens —

2 lbs. carrots   1 lb. tomatoes
1 lb. turnips   2 lbs. onions or leeks, or
1 lb. cauliflower   1 of each
1 lb. celery   2 lbs. salt
½ lb. parsley

Wash and scrape the carrots and turnips, wash the cauliflower, celery, parsley, and tomatoes, clean the onions and leeks. Now mash everything through a food mill or chop finely, and put the mixture into a large bowl or crock and mix with the salt. Remove to jars and cover, sealing tightly.

When ready to prepare your soup, add a few potatoes (to absorb the salt), water, and whatever other ingredients your recipe calls for, but omit salt.

— Sweet Red Peppers in Oil —

This recipe comes from Italy, where red and yellow peppers are combined to make a very colorful dish. If you are growing yellow peppers, by all means mix them with the red.

Roast your peppers whole directly atop the flame, if you have a gas stove or fireplace, or place them in a hot oven, until you can remove the skin easily. Don't allow them to cook too long if you use the oven, as they should not become too soft. When cool enough to handle, remove the stems and crowns, then cut peppers in half and remove seeds. Now cut into pieces or strips (or leave halves intact), sprinkle some pickling salt on a tray, and spread the peppers on the tray in a single layer. Sprinkle with salt again. Let stand a few hours, then drain and wipe dry. Now heat one cup of good oil mixed with one-half teaspoonful of salicylic acid and warm up the jars in which you plan to store the peppers. When the oil is very warm, pour it into the jars and add the peppers, stuffing them a little and alternating layers of peppers with oil until the jar is completely full but the peppers are covered with oil. As you fill the jars, add any fresh herbs you might have. Seal tightly and store in a dark, cool place.

You can, of course, use the oil as a salad dressing after you've eaten these delicious peppers.

— Whole Tomatoes, Uncooked —

Boil two cups of water and drop into a large jar four tablespoonfuls of salt and four of strong wine vinegar. Pour the water into the jar, stir, and let cool. Then wash fairly small, ripe tomatoes and put, unpeeled, into another jar. Cover with the prepared liquid and fill the jar to overflowing. Seal and store in a cool, dark place.

— Naturally Preserved Tomatoes —

Peel ripe tomatoes by plunging them in boiling water for about thirty seconds, and quarter or cut them into pieces, then put in a large bowl and cover with a folded cloth. Leave overnight, or up to fourteen hours, to ferment. For each two pounds of tomatoes, measure one-half teaspoonful of salicylic acid, and after you have removed some of the juice given out by the tomatoes, add the salicylic acid to it, then mix in a bowl with the tomatoes. Now place the tomatoes in medium-size jars, packing them to about one-half inch from the top. Fill the remaining space with good, dense oil, after pressing the tomatoes down a little.

Stored in a cool, dark place, tomatoes preserved this way will keep for months.

— Tomato Concentrate, Uncooked —

Cut and squeeze washed and dried tomatoes into a wide crock or bowl. Cover with cloth and allow to ferment twenty-four hours, then pass them through a sieve to remove skin and seeds. Now put the pulp in a very clean, thickly woven cloth or jelly bag, and hang container to get rid of most of the liquid. After three or four days squeeze the bag to let out the remaining liquid, and spread tomatoes out in the sun or in a very slow oven until fairly thick. Mix into the paste one-half teaspoon of salicylic acid for each two pounds of purée and put in jars, filling them to the top. Store in a cool, dark place.

This paste will last about one year.

— Tomato Purée, Uncooked —

Purée very ripe tomatoes by passing them through a strainer or food mill. Add one-quarter teaspoon of salicylic acid for each two pounds of purée, mix well, and pour into bottles. Cork tightly and store in a cool, dark place. If, however, you use dark green bottles you can store them in a place that has light.

This purée can keep several months and maintains the taste of fresh tomatoes.

• HERBS •

— Basil in Oil —

Wash and dry thoroughly medium-size basil leaves, and place them in layers in a jar, alternating with olive oil or good-quality salad oil.

Use as you would fresh basil, which in fact this is.

You can reuse the same oil for more basil in oil, or as a salad dressing.

— Basil in Salt —

Pick medium-size basil leaves, rinse in cold water, and allow to dry and wilt a little in a shaded, well-ventilated place for a few hours. Then sprinkle some salt in a jar and fill it with alternate layers of basil leaves and salt, ending with a final layer of salt. Close tightly.

Basil preserved this way retains its aroma and tastes almost like fresh basil. Use as is but cut down the amount of salt specified in your recipe.

— Parsley in Salt —

Rinse very green parsley leaves and let dry in a shaded, airy place. Then chop and mix with two tablespoons of salt for each cup of chopped parsley. Put in a jar and seal. Reduce the amount of salt when using this parsley in recipes.

• PEANUTS •

To preserve peanuts in the shell for a short time, you will need:

3 lbs. ripe peanuts, freshly harvested, in shells
10 ozs. salt
1 gallon water

Clean the peanuts, in their shells, in warm water and mild soap. Rinse in clear water, then place in a large saucepan, and cover with the brine. Cover the pan and boil for forty-five minutes or until the kernels are tender; toward the end of your cooking open one of the peanut shells and sample. Cool and let peanuts remain in the brine for fifteen to twenty minutes, then drain and dry them. When dry, they will keep in a cool place for five days (a bit longer in the refrigerator) without going sour.

• MEATS •

Although there is some general disagreement as to whether the term curing is subsumed by smoking or vice versa, for the purpose of this book we shall define curing as salting—either with plain salt or with a brine or similar solution. The solution may be a combination of salt and water; water to which salt, sugar or another sweetening agent, and saltpeter have been added; or the result of salt drawing liquid out of the food it is rubbed on or into.

The curing of meat is frequently, but not always, followed by smoking. The home smoker has been advised in Chapter 4 to thus prepare the various foods before smoking them, and the following is a standard curing procedure that can be applied to most kinds of freshly slaughtered meat, whether subsequent smoking is intended or not.

You will first have to cut your fresh meat into pieces of even size, weigh it, and chill it in the refrigerator. It should then be packed into a crock, wood, or glass container (just so long as it is watertight and not made of metal) with the top layer of meat skinside up.

Now make a brine with the following:

4½ gallons water
8 lbs. salt
2 lbs. sugar
2 ozs. saltpeter

Boil the water for at least five minutes first, and filter out any sediment as you pour it into a sterilized container. Now heat the water again, adding the other ingredients, and stir until it comes to a boil. Skim the surface and cool the brine to 40 degrees Fahrenheit before pouring it over the meat. Be sure that when the brine has settled down around the meat it not only covers the food but rises an extra inch or so above the top layer. Some of this liquid will evaporate during the curing process.

Now leave it in a cool place for a length of time determined by the weight of the meat, three and a half days per pound of meat.

— CORNED MEATS —

Use 1½ tablespoons of saltpeter for each pound of coarse salt. With a large needle, puncture the meat deeply in several spots and rub with the salt. Place in a crock, together with a couple of bay leaves and a sprig of thyme. Weight the meat with a plank on which you have placed a heavy stone, but turn it after a few days. Leave in corning process eight to ten days if in a very cool place, less if the temperature is warmer.

— CORNED VENISON —

For this recipe that dates back to the early 1800s, you will need the following:

1 gallon water
approx. 4 lbs. venison
¾ cup brown sugar
4 cups salt
2 tbs. baking soda

2 tbs. cream of tartar
(or baking powder)
1 tsp. each allspice and
caraway seed

Remove the fat from the meat, but do not truss or tie it. Put it into a crock, then boil a gallon of water to which you have added the rest of the ingredients. Let cool and pour over the meat. Immerse the meat in the liquid and keep it down with a board and stone. Cover the crock with muslin and leave it for two weeks; if hung in a dry, airy place, the meat will keep for several weeks.

— MEAT IN CURDLED MILK OR YOGURT —

This flavor-enhancing method comes from Switzerland, where it was used effectively prior to refrigeration.

By thoroughly submerging any piece of meat in milk (which will curdle if it has not already curdled) or yogurt, you can preserve it perfectly for at least eight days. The covered container should be placed in your cellar or in a very cool place, and the piece of meat should of course be kept weighted down and submerged by a clean heavy stone or by a plate covered with a stone or other weight. Add more milk, if needed, and turn the meat every couple of days.

Before using the meat, drain it. You don't have to wipe it dry if you plan to use it in a stew or for Swiss steak or a similar dish.

— Meat in Lemon and Vinegar —

Preserving beef, veal, lamb, game, or poultry for several days is easy by means of this one-hundred-year-old Italian custom.

If you are working with poultry or game, remove entrails and cut off the neck. Dry any bloody portion with a clean cloth. Rub inside and out with lemon and strong vinegar mixed with salt and ground pepper, then fill the insides with paper towels or clean rags.

If you are preparing meat, rub the whole chunk thoroughly with the marinade.

Wrap with a clean cloth you have sprinkled almost to soaking with lemon and vinegar and hang in a cool, well-ventilated place.

— Meat in Salt —

All types of meat can be preserved for a few days by rubbing it all over with salt. (If poultry, remove the bones first.) Use one cup of salt for each two pounds of meat. Place meat in a wooden bowl or crock and weight it down so that it will be submerged in its own liquid when the salt draws it out.

When ready to use, wash salt away in cold water, dry, and cook as desired, without salting.

Should you wish to preserve it longer, add to the salt one tablespoon saltpeter, twelve juniper berries, two bay leaves, six cloves, and six ground peppercorns for each two pounds of meat. Keep the meat weighted down and turn it once in a while. An Italian version of corned beef, it will keep for about two weeks.

— MEAT IN VINEGAR —

Select tender cuts of meat. Sprinkle with flour and fry in oil or butter or fat until cooked. Place in a crock, cover with vinegar, keeping it submerged with a weight, then cover container and store in a cool place. It will keep at least one month.

• FISH •

While this process is most commonly used to make corned beef, it can be used for a variety of meats and is an excellent way to preserve fish, particularly the smaller, firm varieties.

Scale and clean the fish immediately upon catching, and remove all blood and guts. Wash the fish well, inside and out. Then prepare a mixture of coarse salt and pepper using about one tablespoon of peppercorns to one cup of salt; a little more than one tablespoon of the mix will accommodate up to a pound of fish. Rub the cavity well with the corns, then sprinkle a little on the outside as well. Put the fish in a basket, box, or crock and cover the container with a wet cloth, suspended ½ inch above and not resting on the fish. Keep in a cool place and remoisten the cloth from time to time. The fish will keep two or three days without refrigeration. Rinse well in fresh water before smoking, freezing, or cooking.

— MARINATED FISH —

Here is another effective preserving method used in Switzerland before (and since) refrigeration.

Clean the fish thoroughly inside and out, but keep the head and tail. Rinse well. Now chop a large quantity of soup greens (except turnip), salt, pepper, and bay leaf, and simmer fish and greens in good-quality dry white wine for about fifteen minutes (depending on the size of the fish). Be generous with your greens. The amount of wine should assure that the fish is still covered after it has cooked. Remove from fire and allow to cool. Strain the vegetables and again bring to a slow boil, simmering for a few more minutes. If the fish has been cooked in an enamel or stainless-steel pot, you can store it in the same pot; if not, place it in a deep platter with the marinade. Weight the fish down with a stone, then cover the pot or container tightly, weighting down the lid if necessary. Store in a cool place. Every few days, remove the broth, simmer a few minutes, and when it has cooled, pour it once again over the fish.

This marinated fish can be stored for ten to twelve days.

When ready to use, either drain and cook as desired but shorten the time of cooking considerably or just warm up the fish in its marinade and serve hot. It can also be served cold, as is, with horseradish sauce, pickles, green sauce, or relish (see Index for recipes).

— HERRING IN OIL —

Larger herring or similar fish with a thicker skin can be "pickled" in oil.

Cut off the head and peel off the skin. Using a very sharp knife, cut along the back of the fish carefully, then open it in half and remove the spine and back fins. If you find eggs and milk, don't discard. Put them aside for the moment, but remove and discard the tail. Cut the two filets in half lengthwise. Place them in a crock or fruit jar, then cover them with their eggs and milk (if any). Saturate with olive oil, letting it sink in well and adding more if necessary to completely cover the fish. Seal and store. These filets will keep for several months in a cool place.

• DAIRY PRODUCTS •

Butter and eggs, like milk and cheese, can be kept quite safely without refrigeration, just as they were always kept before the advent of modern appliances. The procedures involved are only slightly more complicated than those for simple storing, and the results are well worth the slight trouble.

— BUTTER —

From Cow's Milk

If the cream you intend to use is fresh and unpasteurized, pasteurize it as follows: In a double-boiler, heat one quart of heavy cream to about 160 degrees Fahrenheit or slightly higher, then cool it as quickly as possible to 50 degrees. To do so, pour the warm cream into a cold pot and place in the freezer for about fifteen minutes, stirring every few minutes.

Now pour the cool pasteurized cream into an electric blender or mixer. If you use a mixer, cover the top of the bowl with aluminum foil pierced through the center with the small ends of the beaters, so that you will not spatter the cream all around. Beat at a high speed for about ten or fifteen seconds, or until the cream is whipped and the portion near the beaters thickens and starts to become butter. Lower the speed to lowest and continue beating until the buttermilk separates. Then pour off the butter-milk, measure it, and save it for drinking, soups, or baking. Replace the buttermilk with the same amount of cold water, cover the butter with it, and beat again at the lowest speed until more liquid is formed, which should be removed but not added to the first batch of buttermilk unless you wish to dilute it. Meanwhile, add two or three cubes of cracked ice to some cold water that you will again add to the butter, extracting it and replacing it with colder water until the water you remove comes out clear. It is important to remove all the buttermilk, so continue until you have succeeded in separating all the liquid from the butter. Press out the remainder of the liquid by kneading the butter with a wooden spoon. At this point you can salt the butter, if you wish, by using one-half teaspoonful of salt to each pound of butter. Mold into any shape you wish, then cover or wrap in plastic.

From Goat's Milk

If you have your own goat, you can prepare butter in the following way:

Goat's milk does not separate as easily as cow's milk. Place it therefore in shallow pans, covered, instead of using bottles, because you will need a wider surface. Let the pans of milk stand in a cool place for eighteen hours or so, depending on the temperature in the room. Use containers that can be heated, because after this first setting period you'll have to heat the milk very slowly until the cream just begins to wrinkle on top. As you move the containers to and from the stove, transport them very gently. Put them back in the same cool place, covered, and allow to rest another eighteen hours. You can then skim off the cream.

If using an electric mixer, proceed as in the preceding recipe; it will, however, take longer for the butter to form.

You may wish to add some artificial food colorings as well as salt during the last step, since goat's butter is completely white. You will like its texture, which is softer and creamier than that of cow's butter, and if you have removed all the buttermilk, this butter will keep much longer than cow's butter, even if you don't refrigerate it.

Preserving, Clarifying, and Restoring Butter

There are a number of ways to preserve butter for quite a while without refrigeration. Sweet butter, incidentally, can last much longer than salted butter.

To preserve in salt water, make a brine with water and salt strong enough to float an egg (the egg must be fresh; eggs that are not fresh float even in saltless water) and boil for about five minutes. Allow to stand overnight, then gently strain the liquid through a muslin or several layers of cheesecloth without pouring off any sediment that might have settled at the bottom of the pot. Place the butter directly in a large crock, without outer wrappers. You can store it either as a solid piece or in pieces you precut according to your needs and wrap individually in cheesecloth so that you can later pull them out one at a time. Pour the brine over the butter, covering it with a few inches to spare. As you remove part of the butter and the level of the liquid has lowered, always make sure the remaining butter is totally submerged. You can either make more brine or remove the butter to a smaller jar. If you add new butter to the same jar, wrap it in cheesecloth and tie a string to a corner tagged with the date on which you immersed it. The string can be left hanging outside. The crock should be kept covered tightly. If the butter tends to float, keep it submerged by placing a clean stone or other object inside the jar.

Stored in a cool place, this butter will keep fresh up to six months.

The Scots make a sweet brine with two and a half quarts of water, one pound of fine salt, one ounce of saltpeter, and two ounces of sugar or honey. Boil all ingredients for a few minutes, allow to cool, then strain and pour on sweet butter, completely submerging it. Store as in the previous method.

A very old American system is to make the same brine described in the first method and pour it into a tub. A smaller tub that fits into the large one is then placed inside with sweet butter in it. Place a cloth bag filled with salt in the inner tub and cover. The liquid brine in the outer tub should be about one inch below the top of the smaller tub. Cover both tubs tightly.

Butter stored in this fashion has been reported to keep for one year in a cool place.

You can also make a solution with one and a half teaspoons of baking soda and half a teaspoon of tartaric acid for each quart of water. Stir well and submerge the butter completely. If you have a large quantity of butter, however, separate it into different containers. The containers should be sealed perfectly, because the preserving agent is the carbonic gas formed by the mixture of the acid and the bicarbonate in an airless atmosphere.

Butter preserved in baking soda can keep up to six months.

Or, if you like, make a paste using one tablespoon of honey for each half-pound of butter. Butter preserved in honey can last up to six months in a cool place. This method is especially popular in Switzerland, where this butter is often served with a Continental breakfast.

For cooking purposes, clarified butter is by far better than whole butter. Clarifying butter simply means to remove the particles of whey and casein. The process removes some of the butterfat, cuts down the cholesterol, and of course makes the butter less fattening. Clarified butter is also far preferable to whole butter for pan-frying any food, and is recommended by the best cooks for its superior taste. Furthermore, you can bring whatever you are sautéing to a high temperature more quickly and the butter won't darken or burn.

To clarify butter, melt it over low heat in a double boiler. With a slotted spoon, skim the foam from the surface, if any. When the whey has separated from the fat, carefully pour it into another container and discard the whey at the bottom. Placing melted butter in the refrigerator for a while may simplify the separating process.

Butter that has gone rancid can be restored by clarifying it before adding a piece of very dark toast. Remove the toast after about half an hour, or when the butter has lost its rancid taste, and store the butter in a cool place.

Or, you can soak it in a solution of one tablespoon of baking soda for each quart of water. After two hours, wash and drain, then spread on slanted surface to allow the whey to run out. Add half a tablespoon of salt for each pound of butter, work well, reshape, and store in a cool place.

— BUTTERMILK —

The liquid you have left over after making butter is buttermilk. The buttermilk is pure if no water has been added during the butter-making process, and if the butter was made out of cream and not from a mixture of milk and cream. Although it is also called buttermilk, the latter is actually a diluted version of the real thing.

Squeeze out all the buttermilk from the butter. If this refreshing drink is kept for a day or two, it acquires an acidity that some people prefer.

Keep your buttermilk in glass jars or bottles or crocks, never in metal containers.

— YOGURT —

Yogurt actually did not appear in the United States until 1940. Middle Easterners have relied on it for thousands of years as a most delicious food, low in calories and cholesterol, that aids digestion and slows down aging of the internal organs.

Making yogurt out of the milk you have on hand is also a good way to preserve it, especially when you find yourself with an excess of milk that would turn sour. All you need is some yogurt culture, which you can purchase in specialized food markets or dairy markets. Try to obtain Bulgarian culture, which is the best.

Scald a quart of milk, taking care not to allow it to reach the boiling stage as this may affect the taste of the yogurt, and then cool it to lukewarm. Now stir a few tablespoons of the culture into your milk and pour into a glass jar or bottle (do not use metal containers), and place the jar or bottle inside a larger kettle half-filled with lukewarm water. If you wish to have a creamier yogurt, you can add some powdered milk to the mixture, or even evaporated milk, in the proportion of one ounce per quart of milk.

Store in a warm place for several hours. The temperature should be around 120 degrees Fahrenheit, and no higher or the yogurt bacilli will perish. You can use the lowest temperature in your oven, the bottom of "warm," but some people get good results by leaving their developing yogurt on top of the turned-on television set, or in a pre-warmed thermos bottle, or wrapped in warm sweaters or blankets. Still others rely on the warmest room of the house. The yogurt will be ready after seven to ten hours. When you have stored the culture and milk in a warm place for about six hours, test its consistency and taste it every half-hour or so, and immediately chill it in the refrigerator or in a cool place.

If you buy commercial yogurt from the market, you don't need to buy the culture for your first home-made batch. Just add four tablespoons of yogurt to your quart of milk, stir it in after you have scalded and cooled the milk to lukewarm, and proceed as for yogurt made from culture.

If you have goat's milk or sheep's milk available you'll be able to make authentic Middle Eastern yogurt. The milk of goats or sheep is the milk used in the Middle Eastern countries, as well as Eastern European countries, where yogurt originated. Just follow the same procedure, although you may have to wait a little longer for the yogurt to form. This yogurt is smoother and stiffer than that made out of cow's milk. It is also considerably tastier.

Add yogurt to your cooked dishes at the very last moment, so that its temperature won't rise above 120 degrees Fahrenheit and remove its health-giving properties.

Refrigerate yogurt if you can, but it will keep several days without refrigeration.

— Eggs —

Before attempting to preserve eggs, you must make sure they are absolutely fresh. There are two basic ways to determine their degree of freshness.

Dissolve one and a half tablespoons of salt in one quart of

cold water and gently slide your eggs into this solution. An egg laid the same day sinks to the bottom; if it drops only midway, it is three days old; if it floats, it is older than three days.

Or, you can examine your eggs one by one by placing them in front of a bright bare bulb (remember when they put the egg in front of a lighted candle?), with the pointed side up. Study it without any other light in the room, and if you can't see through, create some shade around the egg. If the light shows through the top of the egg only about ¼ of an inch, the egg is fresh. If more light than that shows, the egg is not fresh.

The best time of year to store eggs is in the spring, when they are usually fresher and cheaper, but any time you find fresh, inexpensive eggs buy them in quantity and store them. Of course, if you have your own chickens and a surplus of eggs, these are perhaps the best circumstances, because you'll be sure to store eggs that have been laid the same day.

To preserve eggs properly, you must protect the shell to avoid (or substantially curtail) the penetration of air and to prevent the moisture and nutritional value of the egg from exuding through the pores of the shell. A protective coating, and storing the egg pointed side down, packing eggs closely together, will maintain the egg's freshness. Positioning the egg upside down actually prolongs the life of the egg because the egg deteriorates when the bottom of the yolk touches the shell.

Before you preserve eggs in any of the ways we shall describe, examine them under strong light to make sure that none of your eggs is cracked. A cracked egg will certainly rot, and thus endanger the freshness of the whole batch. And, to avoid cracking, bring your eggs to the container, after placing them in a cool room for storage rather than working, let us say, in the kitchen and then carrying the container down to the cellar. And do not move the container during storage, so that the eggs will remain intact.

It is advisable, whichever method you choose, to use several containers. This way, if one egg breaks, the damage will be minimal.

Eggs in Lime

First pour two quarts of boiling water on four pounds of powdered lime and stir mixture with a stick. Then add another five

93

quarts of boiling water and two cups of salt, mixing again until solution has the consistency of thin cream. Allow to cool. You can then either add the eggs to the liquid or the reverse, any way you think there would be less chance of breakage. We prefer putting the eggs into the containers first, delicately lowering them one by one. In this way, should one crack, we can remove it more easily; it also makes it easier to judge how much liquid to pour into each jar. If you have more than one container, mix the solution well before pouring it, so that the proportions will not be altered. The eggs must be totally submerged in the liquid at all times; if when you remove some the rest of the eggs begin to show through the surface, add a little water. The containers should be covered and labeled, especially if you plan to store more than one batch of eggs at different times.

Sometimes the white of the eggs stored in lime might become more liquid than that of fresh eggs. You may not be able to make dishes that call for fluffy egg whites, but the quality of the eggs remains good nevertheless.

Eggs in lime can be preserved as long as two years.

Eggs in Paraffin

Melt paraffin in a double boiler. When it has melted and cooled somewhat, roll the eggs in it, one by one, removing them as soon as they are coated. Let the paraffin solidify around the eggs. If the spot where the drying eggs touch the table is not coated, dip those areas into paraffin again. Place the dry eggs in boxes or jars between layers of charcoal or sawdust. You can accommodate the eggs with pointed side down, in layers if the container is deep. Pack charcoal dust or sawdust in between the eggs. Cover container and store in a cool place.

Eggs can be preserved in paraffin for about six months, and you can use the same coal dust or sawdust several times.

Eggs in Oil

Wash and carefully dry the eggs, or allow to dry in a ventilated place. Very gently place them in a large, wide-mouthed jar half full with oil. If an egg breaks as you put it in the jar, just remove all the eggs, boil the oil, allow it to cool, and start again. The eggs should always be covered with oil and the jar kept closed.

These eggs will keep at least four or five months. You can reuse the oil for the same purpose, but not for eating as it will absorb some of the eggshell taste.

Eggs in Vaseline or Melted Suet

Coat each egg carefully with Vaseline or suet, then place them, small end down, in a container packed with charcoal, although you can use bran. They can be positioned close together, but be careful not to break them. Cover with charcoal or bran and close the container.

They can be stored for about three months.

Eggs in Charcoal Dust or Wood Ashes

Spread about two inches of charcoal dust or wood ashes in the bottom of a container, then add the eggs, pointed ends down and not touching. Pack and cover with an abundance of dust or ashes and close the container well.

They will keep for two or three months. You can prolong their storage life by parboiling them for two minutes and drying them well before storing them, but then you can only use the eggs you have parboiled for boiling purposes.

Eggs in Sawdust, Flour, or Bran

Follow the same procedure as for eggs packed in charcoal dust or wood ashes. Flour is preferable to sawdust because it allows less air to penetrate. You may especially want to try this method if you have flour that has gone stale or has developed bugs, but strain it first.

Soft-Boiled Eggs

Use eggs that have been standing at room temperature and boil for exactly two and a half minutes, then immediately submerge them in cold water. They do not require individual wrapping, but need only be placed among rags or tissue paper. As always, store them with bottoms up and cover container well.

They will keep several months. When ready to use, for soft-boiled eggs heat them in hot water until just before boiling. For hard-boiled eggs, boil four or five minutes.

Eggs in Waterglass

This is an old American method of preserving eggs. Waterglass is easily purchased, perhaps under the more scientific name of sodium silicate or potassium silicate, or sometimes as a mixture of both. If you have a choice, use sodium silicate and try to buy the powder rather than the waterglassed solution, so that you will be able to gauge the proportions better. Use about one and a half cups of powdered waterglass for each two quarts of water, less if the waterglass is already mixed with water. Boil and partially cool your water before mixing. Store in a cool place, and check to make sure that the eggs are always completely submerged in the liquid.

They will keep for up to six months. They may not produce good poached or boiled eggs, and sometimes the white may become more liquid, so avoid using the white for dishes that require stiffly beaten whites. This change, however, will not affect the quality of the eggs.

Eggs in Salt

Bury your eggs in a layer of salt, pointed ends down, and cover with another layer of salt. According to some sources, you can thus preserve them for a few days, and to others, for up to two months.

Thousand-Year Eggs

The Chinese thousand-year egg, sometimes called the hundred-year egg, is more likely a hundred-day egg. The ancient practice of coating eggs (in shells) with a thick paste made of equal parts of lime, salt, and ashes held together with a little water, and drying and burying the eggs in a box in the ground for about a hundred days, produces a gray color on the eggs' surface. Hence their aged look. The paste makes the egg white firm and gelatinous and changes its color to dark green. The yolk becomes amber-colored and chewy. The taste of this "ancient" egg will be practically unrecognizable—a true delicacy!

A slight variation, also Chinese, is to make the coating paste with one part mud to three parts powdered lime and immediately roll the eggs into rice husks or the chaff of any cereal.

When you disinter the eggs, be very careful as you shell them lest they break. Rinse the shelled eggs in cold water, drain, and cut in quarters, lengthwise. Serve uncooked with soy sauce, grated ginger root, and a dash of vinegar. It's a delicious hors d'oeuvre.

Duck Eggs

Make a brine of one cup of salt to one gallon of water and soak duck eggs (or eggs of similar aquatic fowl) in it. The whites will become salty and the yolks a bright orange. They can be stored for about one month and should be used only for cooking.

— CHEESE —

Cheese in Oil

In America cheeses are not customarily pickled, but this is not the case in Europe. In Italy, for instance, some small fresh cheeses are preserved in oil and herbs in the following manner:

small, fresh cheese	bay leaf
thyme	fennel sprigs (or anise seeds)
rosemary	olive oil

Place your cheeses in layers in a wide-necked jar, alternating with layers of herbs. Fill the jar with oil until cheeses are completely submerged. Seal tightly and let stand at least four weeks before using. The oil will make a delicious salad dressing.

Small goat cheeses are among the cheeses that can be preserved this way.

Brandied Cheese

The following method transforms moldy semi-hard or hard cheeses of any type into a delicacy.

Cut off the affected portion only (the rest of the cheese is still perfectly edible) and, if hard enough, grate. If not, chop it fine

97

or pound it in a mortar. Add two teaspoons of good brandy for each pound of cheese and mix well. Put in a jar, pressing tightly as you fill it, then press again when the jar is full, so as not to leave any air bubbles. Cut a disk of strong absorbent paper the exact size of the inside of the jar. Sprinkle the paper with more brandy and seal tightly. Store in a cool dry place and do not use for at least six months.

Brandied cheese is a real gourmet treat that keeps many years.

PICKLING

The easily grown cucumber lends itself so well to pickling that its name is practically synonymous with this process. The cucumber pickle is a standard staple item in many cultures. In the old country stores of New England, for example, large wooden pickle barrels stand by the door, giving off a pungent odor that lets us know we're in the right place. But there are many other ways to pickle a cucumber. And there are many other foods that you can preserve by pickling and eat months, even years, later.

Meat, fish, poultry, fruits, vegetables, nuts, and cheeses can be variously pickled. One of the simplest and safest methods of preserving food, pickling eliminates the need for steam pressure, very high heat, or subzero temperatures, and the finished product takes up little more storage space than the food would have in its natural form. Pickling interestingly changes the taste, the consistency, and sometimes the color of most foods; and also safeguards against the ever-present threat of mold and bacteria.

The rules are few. To begin with, as for all methods, use firm, whole, unblemished fruits or vegetables and try to get them into the pickling fluid as soon as possible after harvesting. And be especially fastidious; unsterilized jars or scruffy foods are an overwhelming challenge to the best pickling ingredients.

Use soft water for pickling or to make a brine. To soften hard water, add one teaspoon of baking soda to one gallon of water, boil fifteen minutes, and let stand twenty-four hours. Then ladle it carefully, without disturbing the sediment at the bottom.

Use pickling salt (not iodized table salt), and be sure that your spices are fresh. Dried herbs may be used in lesser than specified amounts; herbs lose some of their volume in the drying.

Above all, do not use metal containers or spoons in pickling. And never keep pickles, or anything preserved in vinegar, in ceramic or pottery ware. Arsenic and other poisons are sometimes used in glazing, and seldom do you know what was used to finish the earthenware. The vinegar can break it down and make it accessible when you eat the pickle.

In the instructions that follow, the ingredient that will be mentioned most frequently is vinegar. Unless advised otherwise, use apple cider vinegar, the "common" vinegar found on the shelves of most American markets. But you are not limited to plain vinegar; if you have only red-wine vinegar or prefer its taste, use that instead. If the food you are preserving is light in color and you don't wish to darken it, use white vinegar in some recipes even though it is not specified.

A word needs to be said about pickling spices as a product or as a term. In reading recipes you sometimes come upon an item in the list of ingredients that suggests: 4 tbs. mixed pickling spices. Confusing, true, but think of curry powder, which is a combination of several spices ground together. Pickling spices, labeled as such, are often sold in specialty shops or markets or health-food stores; and the combination can include anywhere from four to sixteen different spices. Red pepper, coriander, dill seed, and chopped bay leaf are usually the basics, but a number of others may be added.

If you have these four basics already in your preparation, you can just ignore the ingredient that reads "pickling spices." On the other hand, if you have a ready supply of this product already mixed, there are a number of foods that you can preserve nicely with just pickling spices and vinegar, wine, or water simply by combining them.

Don't confuse pickling spices with allspice, which gets its

name not from an assortment of spices but from its flavor, although in fragrance and taste it seems like a blend of cinnamon, nutmeg, and clove. It's not a mixture at all but rather the whole or ground-up berry of an evergreen tree that grows in the Caribbean.

Before you start pickling in earnest, make up a number of spice or herb bags, tiny drawstring bags that you can suspend in liquid and then retrieve later. We made a supply from very old and loosely woven muslin.

• VINEGAR •

Wine that has been opened and left standing for a while tends to turn sour, unless it is a "pasteurized" wine like so many wines produced commercially in the United States. Untreated wine is usually of a better quality and just as safe to drink. The process is used by the manufacturers so that their wines will travel better (many wines can be thoroughly spoiled by transportation); it also means that they can be shelved for a longer time at any temperature and under any conditions without deteriorating. These are not vintage wines, of course, but the more common varieties whose aroma is so negligible to begin with that it cannot be much affected by pasteurization.

Vinegar, like bread or yogurt, needs a starter, which can be used over and over again. This starter can be vinegar itself, cider, or wine that has begun to turn. The procedure is quite simple, and the implements you need few.

The proper container is made of wood and has a bung hole on top and a spigot on the side a few inches from the bottom. It is still fairly easy to find a wooden tub, small barrel, or keg, with or without the spigot, which you can purchase separately. If the container you have is not equipped with a spigot, pierce a hole the size of the spigot at the desired height and insert the spigot. If you plan to make both wine and cider vinegar, set out two separate kegs and use the same container for the same type of vinegar again and again. You can simplify your equipment by using a large plastic bottle, but a spigot is always necessary since when making vinegar it is very important to extract the liquid from the lower portion of the container. You can siphon it off,

101

but you must take great care to remove only the lower part of the liquid. And the use of plastic presents another difficulty in that it is inert and will not turn the liquid to vinegar as readily as wood, so that with plastic the process requires even more care and patience.

— WINE VINEGAR —

To properly prepare a wooden keg, scrub it clean and allow it to dry completely. Then warm enough good-quality wine vinegar (to about 130 degrees Fahrenheit) to fill your container. Leave the vinegar in the keg for about twenty-four hours, then siphon off about two-thirds of the vinegar and bottle it (you can start using it immediately). Now funnel in through the bung hole unpasteurized wine of any type in the same amount as the vinegar you have removed. Allow to rest at a temperature of about 70 degrees for eight days, with the bung hole closed. You will now have vinegar, though this first batch may be fairly weak. Pour off as much as you wish through the spigot (leaving at least one-third in the container) and bottle it. Before pouring in more wine, insert a tube in your bung hole funnel as the vinegar in the container will have formed a "mother" (a rather thick film) on top, which must be broken so that the wine you add gets under the film.

If you use the same container, you can go on making vinegar indefinitely, provided you always leave some vinegar in it as a starter.

If you make your own wine, a good time to make wine vinegar is just after you finish making the wine, as you will then utilize the fermented solids from the grapes. After you have siphoned off the wine you plan to drink, leave the must in the bottom of your vinegar-making keg in the open air for two or three days, uncovered. When the smell of vinegar rises, pour into the container about one-tenth its capacity of lukewarm water. Repeat this operation with the same amount of water for eight to ten days until the container is full. Now open the spigot (or siphon off from the bottom) and extract the liquid a little at a time, pouring it back on top through a funnel and tube, so that it will penetrate under the mother, which should have started to form.

102

Pierce one hole only and insert the tube without disturbing the mother. Repeat this operation once a day, and in about one month you will have a very strong, excellent vinegar. When the vinegar is ready, strain the liquid through a cloth, pressing it to squeeze out all the juice, and bottle it. Store in a warm place for at least a month.

If you have a cellar in which you keep wine, don't use the same room to make vinegar or your wine may turn.

— Cider Vinegar —

If you have made your own wine, you probably have also made cider and will appreciate a good cider vinegar.

We offer two foolproof recipes, one using sweet cider as a starter and another made with hard.

For sweet cider vinegar, take all the peel and cores from a few tart apples (the green variety that you would normally use for apple pie is best, but other kinds will do almost as well), cover. them with lukewarm water, and let stand for twenty-four hours in a warm place. The foam that you will find at the end of this period is the beginning of the mother. Scoop off this film or foam, pour it gently into a jug of sweet cider, and allow it to float. In five to eight days you will have vinegar. Strain the water in which the apple cores and peels were soaked and you will find that this has become a much stronger vinegar. You can either mix the two or keep them separately and use them for different purposes.

To make hard cider vinegar, to each quart of hard cider add four tablespoons of whiskey and two of rye meal. Mix well and leave in a warm place, covered, for three to four weeks for a fairly strong vinegar with an excellent taste.

Whether you use the vinegar you make yourself or the commercially manufactured brands, you can enhance the flavor by adding a variety of herbs or spices. Choose from chopped onions, chives, garlic, grated ginger root; or any herbs, especially tarragon, thyme, sage, or basil. The herbs should be fresh, and in sprigs that you can insert in the bottle and just leave there. Even some flowers added to regular vinegar give good results—dandelions or nasturtiums, for instance.

When you add herbs or spices to vinegar, it is a good idea to use a bottle that has an inside cap with holes, so that the pieces won't fall out. When the bottle is finished these can be added to a marinade, or they can be reused once or twice by adding new vinegar to the same bottle.

— AROMATIC VINEGAR —

Boil one quart of good wine vinegar. While you are waiting for it to have boiled down to half its original quantity, put in a bowl:

2 chopped chives   *a sprig or ½ tsp. thyme*
1 clove of garlic (pressed)   *½ tsp. freshly ground pepper*
1 bay leaf   *½ tsp. salt*

When the vinegar is ready, pour it in the bowl with the spices and let stand for two hours. Then strain through a fine sieve or cloth and pour it into the bottle in which you plan to preserve it. Cover tightly when completely cool.

This is a very strong vinegar. Use it sparingly, or add a minute quantity to your usual wine vinegar to enhance its aroma.

— RASPBERRY VINEGAR —

1 lb. raspberries
2 cups white vinegar*
2 tsp. sugar or 1 tsp. honey

Mash the berries, add the vinegar, and let stand four days. Then add the sweetener, bring everything to a boil, and simmer for fifteen minutes. Strain and bottle.

Should you want to use this vinegar as a base for practically any sweet-and-sour dish, increase sugar to one cup. This vinegar is also very good for fruit salads.

• SIMPLE PICKLES •

In this year's Famous-Name seed catalog, nineteen different breeds of cucumbers were listed, among them pickling cucumbers, bred for smaller size so that they can be pickled whole. Actually you can pickle any cucumber, regardless of its size or kind.

---

* If you prefer, you can substitute cider vinegar and only half the amount of sweetener.

— Bread and Butter Pickles —

½ peck cucumbers — 1 qt. vinegar
8 medium-size onions — 2 tbs. mustard seed
½ cup salt — 1 tsp. turmeric
2 qts. cracked or shaved ice — 1 tsp. celery seed
5 cups sugar

Slice cucumbers and onions into rather thin rounds. Mix them with the salt and shaved ice, weigh them down, and leave for three to four hours. Drain. Now add the rest of the ingredients and heat not quite to a boil, stirring carefully. Then pack pickles and liquid into sterilized jars, seal, and store.

— Dill Cucumber Pickles —

½ peck cucumbers — hot red peppers
1 gallon cold water — 1 qt. vinegar
fresh dill sprigs — 3 qts. water
garlic cloves — 1 cup salt

Clean and soak cucumbers in the cold water for a day and a night. Put into each sterilized jar a couple of sprigs of dill, a peeled garlic clove, and a pepper. Then pack the cucumbers, whole, into the jars. If your cucumbers are large, you can slice them first. Now make a brine of the vinegar, water, and salt, boil it a minute or two, and add it to the jars. Seal tightly and store.

— Sour Cucumber Pickles —

½ peck cucumbers — 1 cup sugar
1 cup salt — 2 tsp. each: cloves, peppercorns, mustard seed, celery seed
1 gallon cold water
6 cups vinegar

Clean and scrub the cucumbers. Put them into a brine of the salt and water and leave them for a day and a night, then drain. Cut them up into strips. Make a pickling liquid of the remaining ingredients, boil for five or six minutes, then pour over the cucumbers. Let them stand for another day and night. Then drain and reserve the fluid. Pack pickles into sterilized fruit jars. Reheat the liquid just to a boil and pour into the jars. Seal tightly and store.

105

— SWEET CUCUMBER PICKLES —

½ peck cucumbers	1 tbs. cinnamon
4 cups sugar	2 tbs. cloves
2 cups vinegar	2 tbs. peppercorns
2 cloves garlic, peeled and chopped	

Slice the cucumbers, after washing, into either rounds or strips. Make a syrup of one cup of sugar and the vinegar and boil for five minutes. Pour over cucumbers and leave for a day and night. Every day, for three days, drain off the syrup, add another cup of sugar, reboil, and pour over the cucumbers. Then drain the syrup off once more, and pack the cucumber slices into sterilized jars, meanwhile sprinkling the flavorings between layers. Bring the syrup to a boil once again, omitting the sugar this time, and pour it into the jars. Seal and store.

• FRUITS AND VEGETABLES •

Many other fruits and vegetables from garden and field can be pickled as successfully as cucumbers, perhaps more so because of their unusual shapes and flavors.

— APPLES —

This pickling recipe for apples will do just as well for pears and most melons of firm texture.

½ peck apples (or mixture of fruits)	2 or 3 sticks fresh cinnamon
4 qts. cold water	2 or 3 tbs. allspice
1 qt. white vinegar	2 qts. sugar

Skin or peel the fruit, core it, and cut it up into pieces of similar size. Let it stand for about half an hour in the cold water to which you have added a couple of tablespoons of vinegar. Rinse and steam for ten minutes. Tie the cinnamon and allspice into a spice bag. Combine the remaining vinegar and sugar, dilute with a little water, add the spice bag, and bring to a boil. Simmer a few minutes, then pour over the fruit and let stand for about twelve hours. Drain off the syrup and cook it over medium heat until it thickens. Add the fruit and cook until its tenderness pleases you. Pack the fruit and liquid into sterilized fruit jars, adjust the lids, and process in a water bath for ten minutes (see Index). Seal, cool, and store.

— ARTICHOKES —

Use small, young artichokes, plants too tender to have yet formed a choke. Leaving part of the stem on, steam the small artichokes until almost tender. Now measure equal parts of white vinegar and white wine (or red vinegar and red wine, if you prefer the stronger flavor and color) to cover the vegetables. Bring to a boil and let boil until tender. Drain and place the artichokes in sterilized jars. Cover the vegetables with olive oil (or other good vegetable oil) and place one clove and a few peppercorns in each jar.

— ASPARAGUS —

Don't try to pickle asparagus that are too thick or over-ripe; select rather the thinner, more pliant stalks, or use only the tips of the sturdier stalks.

Cook asparagus for five minutes in lightly salted water; or steam for ten minutes. Drain and soak in a solution of white vinegar and salt, a half-cup to the quart. Leave in this marinade for ten days, making sure the vegetable is always submerged. Then drain and cut off any white, wooden part that still remains. Place in a wide-mouthed jar with tops up. Pour on a new solution of vinegar and salt (in the same proportions). Cover tightly and store in cool place.

— BEANS, GREEN —

1 qt. any green beans	2 cups water
1 sprig fresh dill	2 cups vinegar
2 cloves garlic	½ cup salt
½ tsp. crushed red pepper	
(or ¼ tsp. powdered red pepper)	

Clean and trim vegetables but leave them whole. Sterilize a quart jar and put the first three ingredients into it. Now combine the remaining ingredients and bring to a boil. Pack the vegetables standing up into the jar and pour in the boiling solution. Seal and store. Don't use until two weeks have passed.

That's all you have to do to produce those crisp, crunchy, slightly pickled beans that you often find as snacks on a buffet table.

— Beets —

beets, with greens removed	*peppercorns*
horseradish	*vinegar*
mace or bay leaf	*lemon juice (optional)*

Boil the beets in water for one to two hours, until they are tender, testing them with a toothpick to be sure. Drain, cool, peel, and slice them. Shred the horseradish. Layer the beet slices in a crock, with a sprinkling of horseradish, small bits of mace or bay, and a few peppercorns between layers. Heat enough vinegar to cover the beets completely, adding a small amount of lemon juice if you wish. When it is boiling, pour it over the beets. Cover securely and leave in a cool place. You can preserve a good supply of beets this way.

You may want to remove a few small ones as soon as they are cooked tender and treat them this way:

6 small whole cooked beets	*6 tbs. oil*
1 small bunch parsley	*6 tbs. red-wine vinegar*
3 garlic cloves	*salt and pepper, to taste*
½ tsp. tarragon leaves	*(or 2 or 3 anchovies, chopped)*

Peel and slice beets. Chop parsley and herbs fine. Add oil, vinegar, and spices (or anchovies) and mix together vigorously. Pour some of this mixture into the bottom of your jar, then add layers of beets and the marinade alternately, ending with the beets completely covered. Cover tightly and store.

If you don't want to cook the beets first, here's a simple way to preserve them raw. Use only small, young beets.

Cut scrubbed or peeled beets into cubes about one-half-inch square. Place in jars and cover with red-wine vinegar and salt to taste. Seal tightly and store in a cool place.

All three methods will keep your beets nicely for a month or two; in fact, you should not leave them stored for any less than a month.

— BLUEBERRIES* —

For mildly spiced relish that is excellent with poultry or game dishes or as a spread, prepare:

1 qt. blueberries

2 cups sugar

¼ cup cider vinegar

¼ tsp. each: ground cinnamon and allspice

⅛ tsp. ground clove

Stem and wash the berries. Combine with the rest of the ingredients, bring to a boil, then turn down heat and simmer until the desired thickness is achieved. Pour into warm jars, seal tightly, and store in a cool place.

— CABBAGE, GREEN (SAUERKRAUT) —

3 cabbages, 1 large and 2 smaller, separated into leaves

juniper berries

peppercorns

caraway seeds

salt

1 cup water

Rinse and trim the large cabbage, then quarter it and remove its core. Shred very fine. Rinse the leaves of a smaller cabbage and line the bottom of a large crock or barrel with them. Pack the shredded cabbage in tightly, and sprinkle it with a few juniper berries, peppercorns, caraway seeds, and salt. Pour over this a cup of water and cover with several leaves from the third cabbage. Top this with a sterilized piece of muslin, then a wooden board. Place a heavy weight on top of the board and move container into the sun, and when little white bubbles appear on top of the cabbage, move it to a cool, dry place. In two weeks, remove cloth and top layer of leaves, replace with fresh leaves and a fresh cloth, and cover with the weights again. Repeat this last procedure three more times, a week apart each time. At the end of five weeks you can eat the sauerkraut; or you can store it for up to a year, in the brine, in a cool place, where the temperature doesn't rise above 40 degrees Fahrenheit.

* This relish can be made as well from mulberries or Juneberries (the ubiquitous wild berries also called shadberries, serviceberries, or Indian pears).

109

— CABBAGE, RED —

Cut cabbage across in very thin slices and lay it out on a large dish. Sprinkle liberally, layer by layer, with salt. Cover with another dish and let stand twenty-four hours. Drain off the liquid, and put the cabbage into a jar. Add to vinegar a little mace, cloves, crushed black peppercorns, and a little cochineal, bruised fine. Boil mixture briefly, then cool and cover the cabbage completely with this liquid. A nineteenth-century source recommends tying the jar down with leather or skin, and storing it in a cool, dry place. It will keep for months.

— HYDEN SALAD —

You may want to pickle your cabbage in the manner of this excellent nineteenth-century recipe from Virginia.

4 qts. finely chopped cabbage
4 qts. green tomatoes (whole if small, chopped if large)
2 cups chopped green peppers
4 cups chopped onions
salt

2 qts. strong vinegar
1 lb. sugar
2 tbs. each:
turmeric, cloves, celery seed, salt, cinnamon, ground or powdered mustard, fresh ginger (less if powdered)

Sprinkle the four vegetables with salt, mix well, and let stand overnight. The next day, pour boiling water over the mixture, drain, and squeeze dry. Then mix the vinegar with all the remaining ingredients, bring to a boil, and boil ten minutes. Put vegetables into sterilized jars, pour in the pickling liquid, filling the jars up to the top. Cover tightly and store.

— CHERRIES, SOUR —

Choose good-quality cherries. Wash, drain, dry, and stem them as desired. Pack into sterilized jars, cover with wine vinegar, and seal jars tightly. Store for a month before using.

— CHERRIES, SWEET —

Choose cherries that are firm and fleshy. Wash, drain thoroughly, and cut off part of the stems (or all, if you prefer). Put cherries into a crock or glass dish, together with a piece of cinnamon stick, two or three cloves, and a sprig of thyme. Now boil some red-wine vinegar and pour it over the cherries, covering them completely. Cover and let stand for four or five days. Drain off the vinegar and boil it for five minutes. Put the cherries into hot, sterilized jars, fill jars with the hot syrup, seal tightly, and store.

After a month of storing, serve these pickled sweet cherries with roasts or boiled meats or use them as stuffing for game.

— CRAB APPLES —

5 lbs. crab apples   7 cups sugar
1 qt. vinegar   1 tbs. whole cloves
2″ cinnamon stick

Wash crab apples, leaving skin (and stem, if desired), and prick several holes in each. Bring to a boil remaining ingredients, and crab apples, and cook slowly until tender. Pack apples in sterilized jars and fill jars with the hot syrup. Seal securely and store.

— EGGPLANT —

3 lbs. eggplant   olive oil
salt   mint leaves
white vinegar   tarragon leaves
garlic, minced

Try to match your pickling jar to the girth of the eggplant so that you will be able to put up whole rounds, rather than half-slices.

Peel eggplant and slice very, very thin. Sprinkle rounds lightly with salt on both sides, and place them on a clean cloth over a grate to drain for a day and a night.

Place slices in layers in a crock or glass dish. Pour white vinegar over them, almost to cover. Put a plate or wooden board directly on the eggplant, then heavy weights atop the board. Leave them another day and night.

Now drain the slices and spread them on another clean cloth on a grate, cover with boards and weights, and leave for about six hours.

Pour a little olive oil in the bottom of your jar, then insert flat layers of the eggplant slices. Sprinkle herbs, garlic, and a few drops of oil between the layers, and press gently every few lay-

111

ers as you fill the jars. Cover with oil, let it sink in, and add more oil. Be sure that the eggplant is completely covered with oil and seal tightly.

You can pickle summer squash and zucchini by the same method.

If your eggplants are young and slender, you may want to pickle them in this slightly different way, using the following ingredients:

eggplant	*marjoram*
white vinegar	*basil*
salt and pepper	*hot red peppers, sliced*
garlic, minced	*olive oil**

Slice eggplants lengthwise, in sections (like you would an orange), and spread them out on a board, none touching, in the sun for a few hours. Then boil them for eight to ten minutes in enough vinegar to cover and a little salt. Drain the eggplant sections on a clean dry towel.

After twenty-four hours, pack the eggplant (upright if possible, like pickle slices) in sterilized jars, adding to each jar a little pepper, a little minced garlic, a few leaves of the herbs, and a few slices of hot pepper. Cover the vegetables with olive oil, let it sink in and be absorbed, then add more oil. Be sure the eggplant is completely submerged in oil before you seal the jars.

Do not unpack and eat for at least two months. They should keep well for about six months.

— GRAPE TENDRILS —
(*Viticci Sott'Aceto*)

In Italian, the word *viticci* means only the tendrils of the grape, which are used as extra flavoring in some liqueurs as well as in pickling. If you can obtain some *viticci*, try the following recipe from Italy.

Choose only tendrils that are young and tender, and while you wash them, bring a pot of water to a rapid boil. Drop the tendrils into the boiling water and remove them when it comes to a

---

* You may substitute some other vegetable oil for the olive oil if you wish, but there is something just right about the combined taste of eggplant and olive oil.

second boil. Immediately submerge them in cold water, drain, and dry them with a dishcloth. Put the tendrils in a sterilized jar and add a clove or two of garlic, a few stems of parsley, and if you wish, a whole hot red pepper. Separately, bring some vinegar to a boil and pour it over the tendrils. Let cool, then remove garlic, parsley, and pepper. Cover the tendrils with more of the same vinegar. Seal the jar tightly, and do not use for at least two months.

Pickled tendrils can be used as a garnish for antipasto or as an accompaniment to any meat dish, especially roast or boiled beef.

— HEARTS OF PALM MUSTARD PICKLE —

2 qts. diced hearts of palm (use only upper portion)	1 tbs. turmeric
	½ tsp. cayenne pepper
2 tbs. salt	1½ cups white sugar
1 qt. water	½ cup cornstarch or arrowroot
1 qt. white vinegar	1½ tbs. each: celery seed,
2 tbs. lemon juice	mustard seed, dry mustard

Soak palm sections in the salt and water for two days. Drain and then rinse in several rinses of fresh, cold water. Make a pickling fluid of all the remaining ingredients. Bring it to a boil, then lower heat and cook, stirring constantly, until it thickens slightly. Add the hearts of palm, bring just to a boil again, then pour into sterilized fruit jars. Seal and store. It will keep for months.

— LEMONS —

Choose small lemons, wash, and dry thoroughly. Stick into each lemon at least four cloves. Place lemons in a sterilized jar and fill it with olive oil, making sure that the lemons are completely submerged. Seal tightly and store without opening at least two months. The fruit will keep very well for six months or more.

Lemons treated in this manner can be used for several dishes, including boiled or broiled fish. The oil from the jar can be used in salads or as dressing for any boiled fish served cold, or with raw fish.

There is no reason to believe that any other citrus fruit would not keep in the same manner, though the very high acidity of the lemon probably preserves it the longest.

113

— Mushrooms —

fresh mushrooms	*½ cinnamon stick*
white vinegar	*2 garlic cloves*
1 tsp. salt	*2 bay leaves*
peppercorns	*4 or 5 cloves*

Clean mushrooms (cutting off stem tips) and wipe them with a clean cloth. Cut into large chunks or quarters, depending on their size. Put into a saucepan, add enough vinegar to cover the mushrooms, and the salt; but do not add mushrooms until the vinegar has come to a boil. Boil them for five minutes. Then turn off the heat and add to the pot a few peppercorns, half a cinnamon stick, the garlic, bay leaves, and cloves. Cover the pot and let stand for half an hour. Then drain the mushrooms, setting aside the vinegar. Place mushrooms in a sterilized jar, removing the garlic and bay but leaving the peppercorns and cloves. Cover with fresh, cold vinegar and seal. Store for a month before eating.

These mushrooms may be eaten without cooking.

— Onions —

2 lbs. small white onions of uniform size	*bay leaves*
salt	*1 sprig thyme (or ½ tsp. leaves)*
white vinegar	*peppercorns*
1 clove garlic	*1 clove*
1 cinnamon stick	*olive oil*

Peel onions and plunge them for one minute into boiling, lightly salted water. To one pint of vinegar, add garlic, half the cinnamon stick, one bay leaf, the thyme, a few peppercorns, the clove, and a pinch of salt. Add onions and boil for ten minutes. Drain and place onions in sterilized jars. Bring another pint or more of vinegar to a boil and let cool. Pour it on onions, and add (to each jar) a bay leaf, a piece of cinnamon stick, and at the top, a little olive oil, which will float and help preserve the onions. Make sure the onions are totally submerged. Cover tightly.

— PEACHES —

Choose large, hard peaches. Wash and drain thoroughly. Cut in half and remove pits, then peel and plunge into a bowl of lemon juice. Roll peaches in the juice as you put them into the bowl. Leave them in the lemon juice for five or ten minutes, then put them into sterilized jars. Cover with a good-quality white vinegar. Seal tightly and store.

— PEARS —

To preserve some of that lush crop of Bartlett or seckel pears that can't possibly be eaten up when they are all ripe, gather together:

pears, whole	*sugar*
salt	*green food coloring*
water	*sprigs of mint*

Wash the pears, leaving them whole and with the stems attached. Prepare a light brine of two teaspoons of salt to each quart of water you use. Peel pears and put them immediately into brine to cover. Make a light syrup of one cup of sugar to each three-quarters cup of water. Bring this syrup to a boil, add a few drops of green food coloring, then the pears. Let the pears heat through (if ripe) or boil a minute or two (if still hard).

Now line your sterilized fruit jars with sprigs of mint, reserving some to pack between the pears, and nearly fill the jars with pears. Then cover them with the boiling syrup.

Process in your water-bath canner (see Index), boiling for about ten minutes. You will have a minty green cold dessert to follow some of your fall or winter meals of brown and orange and yellow foods.

— PEPPERS —

1 peck small sweet peppers	*1 whole garlic clove*
2 cups salt	*2 tbs. grated horseradish*
10 cups cider vinegar	*4 tbs. sugar*

Wash the peppers well and make a few slits in them. Don't slice them open or remove the seeds or white parts. Sprinkle with salt, pour over enough cold water to cover, and let stand about eighteen hours. Drain and rinse them in several waters. Now make a pickling fluid of the vinegar and the rest of the ingredients, adding a cup or two of water if you wish, bring it to a boil, then turn heat down and simmer for twenty minutes. Remove the garlic clove and pack the peppers into sterilized jars. Then fill the jars with the pickling fluid, still very hot. Seal and store in a cool place. Use after two months.

— TOMATOES —

We don't recommend pickling ripe, red tomatoes; you can preserve them in so many other ways. Pickle only green tomatoes, using the following recipe:

½ peck green tomatoes	1 lb. sugar
12 large onions	2 tbs. basil, oregano, or dill
5 tbs. salt	2 tbs. celery seed
1 qt. strong vinegar	black pepper

If the tomatoes are very small, leave them whole; if large, chop them up. Peel and chop the onions. Sprinkle salt over the two vegetables and let them stand overnight. The next day, drain the water off, and add the vinegar, sugar, herb, and celery seed. Pepper to taste. Place everything in a large pot, bring to a boil and then simmer for half an hour. Pour into warm, sterilized jars and cover tightly.

The amount of sugar may be increased, or even doubled, if you desire a very sweet pickle.

• NASTURTIUM SEEDS •

The spicy seeds of the nasturtium are favored over capers (the bud of a Mediterranean shrub and hence always imported) by some Americans.

Gather seeds while they are green and let them stand in the sun for a few days to dry. Now steep them for a day or so in cold vinegar. Drain seeds and put them into fresh, boiling vinegar for ten minutes. Pour seeds and vinegar into clean jars, cover tightly, and store in a cool place for six months.

• NUTS •

Pickled nuts are an interesting new taste experience. This recipe is particularly good for green walnuts, but a mixture of walnuts and other very unripe nuts can be used. It will accommodate twelve pounds of nuts, picked early while they are still tender and green and their shells have not yet become woody.

> 12 lbs. nuts
> 3 cups salt
> 3 gallons water
>
> 2 tbs. each: mustard seed, allspice, peppercorns
> 2 tsp. each: mace and ground clove
> 1 gallon vinegar

Scald and defuzz the nuts (if necessary) and soak them in the salt and water for about ten days (one cup for each gallon), replacing the brine twice during that period. Be sure the nuts stay submerged. Drain and thoroughly dry nuts and prick several holes in each. Now mix the spices together. Arrange the nuts in layers in a large-necked jar, distributing the spice mixture well among them. Boil the vinegar for five minutes and pour it into the jar. Seal tightly and store in a cool, dark place for four to six weeks before eating.

· RELISHES ·

— Mixed Vegetable Relish —

This is in a sense a vegetable stew, except that it's not a stew but a condiment that will keep for months in a cool, dry place and liven up many a winter meal of a starchy or bland nature.

Slice or chop one cup each of the vegetables in the following recipe:

> cucumbers
> sweet peppers
> onions
> cabbage
> tomatoes (green or very firm)
> carrots
> string beans (or wax, or both)
> celery
>
> turnips
> ½ cup salt
> 2 qts. water
> 2 cups vinegar
> 2 cups sugar
> 2 tbs. turmeric
> 1 tbs. each: mustard and celery seed

Let vegetables soak overnight in a brine of salt and water. (You may want to soften the root vegetables first by parboiling.) Drain

117

and add the vegetables to the vinegar, sugar, and spice mixture. Bring to a boil, then lower heat and simmer for ten or twelve minutes. Pour into sterilized jars and seal.

— SWEET PEPPER RELISH —

6 lbs. sweet peppers	2 tbs. salt
3 lbs. onions	½ cup sugar
1 qt. vinegar	1 tsp. each: celery seed, mustard seed, dry mustard

Your peppers can be red, green, or a mixture of both and your onions any kind. Core, deseed, and devein the peppers and peel the onions. Grind both vegetables in a food grinder or blender. Pour boiling water, to cover, on the vegetables, let stand a few minutes, then drain. Now mix the rest of the ingredients, bring to a boil, add the peppers and onions, bring to a boil again, then simmer for ten minutes, stirring occasionally. Pour into sterilized bottles or jars, seal, and store.

You can add green tomatoes if you treat them the same way as the peppers and increase the amounts of all your other ingredients a bit.

This standard relish is a familiar embellishment.

— CORN AND PEPPER RELISH —

To preserve some of that wonderful late-summer corn, assemble:

2 qts. corn kernels	2 cups each: chopped peppers, celery, onions
½ cup water	
2 tbs. dry mustard	1 qt. vinegar
½ cup flour or cornstarch	1 cup sugar
	2 tbs. salt
	2 tbs. celery seed

Cover corn kernels with water and boil for about five minutes. Make a paste of the water, mustard, and starch and add to the drained corn. Combine the chopped vegetables with the rest of the ingredients, bring to a boil, and cook for fifteen to eighteen minutes. Combine both mixtures, again bring to a boil, then simmer and stir for five to ten minutes. Pour into sterilized jars, seal, and store.

118

— Grape Relish —

This relish wastes nothing but the seeds. You can use any sort of skinnable table grapes and, if you wish, match your vinegar to their color.

7 lbs. grapes
1 cup vinegar
6 cups sugar
1 tsp. each: ground clove, allspice, cinnamon

Wash grapes and separate skins from pulp. Cook pulp until tender and put through a sieve to remove the seeds, which you may discard. Simmer the skins in one cup of water until softened. Now combine skins and pulp and add them to the rest of the ingredients. Bring to a boil, then simmer until thickened. Pour into sterilized jars, seal, and store.

— Chow-Chow —

You will need two cups of each of the vegetables in the following recipe:

small whole green cucumbers	*beans, wax or green, cut in 1" pieces*
large ripe cucumbers, chopped	
small white onions, peeled	*½ cup salt*
sweet peppers, seeded and chopped	*1½ qts. vinegar*
	1 cup sugar
green tomatoes, chopped	*4 tbs. flour or cornstarch*
cauliflowerets	*3 tbs. dry mustard*
celery stalk and leaf, chopped	*1 tbs. water*

Mix the vegetables with the salt and just enough water to cover, and let stand overnight. Drain and rinse the vegetables well, and add them to the vinegar and bring to a boil. Lower heat to medium. Mix a paste of the remaining ingredients and stir it bit by bit into the simmering vegetables. Keep stirring for a few minutes or until thickened to your favorite consistency. Pour into sterilized fruit jars, seal, and store.

119

— PICALILLI —

Picalilli is a mixed vegetable relish from the other side of the
world. Let's add some cabbage, and some red pepper for hotness.
If you think, however, it might be a bit too zingy for your Western palate, just leave out the cayenne pepper.

*1 small head cabbage, green
or red, chopped or shredded*

1 qt. green tomatoes, chopped

*4 sweet peppers, seeded,
veined, and chopped*

*3 medium-size onions,
peeled and chopped*

½ cup salt

3 cups vinegar

2 cups brown sugar

*a spice bag containing a stick
of cinnamon and 1 tsp. each:
whole cloves, allspice, whole
mustard seed, and cayenne
pepper*

Combine all vegetables with the salt and leave overnight, then
drain. Now combine the vinegar and all the rest of the ingredients
and bring to a boil. Add the vegetables, bring to a boil again, then
lower the heat and simmer, stirring occasionally, until the mixture has thickened to your taste. Discard spice bag, pour mixture
into sterilized jars, seal tightly, and store.

— GREAT-GRANDMOTHER PARKER'S "FAVORITE" —

The following ingredients will make a big batch of "Favorite":

1 peck green tomatoes

12 medium-size onions, peeled

8 sweet peppers

1 cup salt

2 qts. vinegar

4 lbs. brown sugar

2 lbs. white sugar

*½ lb. each: mustard seed,
celery seed*

1 tbs. each: cinnamon, allspice

*1 tsp. each: dry mustard,
black pepper*

Put the vegetables through a food grinder, add the salt, and
let stand in a crock overnight. In the morning drain the vegetables and add all the rest of the ingredients. Bring to a boil, then
turn down the heat and let simmer for five or six hours, until
mixture turns a rich dark-brown color.

It keeps forever and is an excellent accompaniment to baked
beans and brown bread, or a more Spartan lunch of cottage
cheese and wheat-bread toast.

— Mostarda di Cremona —

This relish is a specialty of the province of Cremona in the Lombardy region of Italy. It is a sweet mustard and fruit combination in which the following fruits are used: cherries, slightly unripe figs, plums, pears, grapes, melon, apricots, citron or orange rind; and always pumpkin.

Cut up large pieces of fruit to get the different kinds into more or less uniform size. Cook each item separately in a little water and sugar or honey until each separate fruit is still in a whole piece and a little tenderized. Drain the syrup from all the various fruits and combine in one pot. Add more sugar (or honey), bring to a boil, and let cook until the syrup thickens a little. Separately melt some dry mustard in a little warm oil or water. Add this to the syrup while still hot and mix well. Place the fruit in sterilized jars and pour warm syrup into the jars to cover the fruit completely. Close tightly and do not use for at least five days.

This is one of the most cherished specialties in Italy. It is usually served with boiled beef or braised pork, but can of course be used as any relish.

— Fruit Relish —

6 *pears*	2 *cups vinegar*
6 *peaches*	2 *cups sugar*
6 *apples*	1 *tbs. salt*
6 *onions*	1 *tbs. mixed pickling spices*

Mix all ingredients together, bring to a boil, then lower heat and simmer until the mixture thickens to your taste. Pour into fruit jars, seal, and store.

You can vary the taste, color, and texture of this relish by peeling, chopping, and adding some ripe, red tomatoes. Use up your leftover ripe tomatoes in this way, but don't add more than the same volume of the combined fruits. Double all the other ingredients, but otherwise proceed as directed.

• CHUTNEYS •

— Nectarine Chutney —

9 or 10 nectarines	½ cup brown sugar
2 tart green apples	1 tsp. mustard seed
2 lemons, juice and rinds	½ tsp. chili peppers, crushed
3 cloves garlic	½ cup green ginger
½ cup water	½ cup pecans
½ cup vinegar	

Peel, stone, and cut up the nectarines. Peel, core, and cut up the apples. Chop the lemon rind; crush the garlic. Add to all the rest of the ingredients. Bring to a boil in a saucepan, then simmer for twenty-five to thirty minutes. Seal in sterilized bottles.

— Gooseberry Chutney —

3 lbs. gooseberries	3 cups brown sugar
4 medium onions	2 tbs. salt
1 cup raisins (golden or brown)	½ tsp. each: mustard seed, cayenne pepper, turmeric
3 cups vinegar	

Chop the onions and add them to the gooseberries and the rest of the ingredients. Bring to a boil in a saucepan, then lower heat and simmer for one-and-a-half to two hours. Seal in sterilized bottles.

— Tomato Chutney —

4 to 5 lbs. ripe red tomatoes	1 or 2 cloves garlic
1 qt. vinegar	3 lbs. sugar
2 lbs. raisins	2 lbs. salt
	4 tbs. cayenne pepper

Dip and peel the tomatoes, then cut them up and boil in the vinegar for fifteen to twenty minutes. Now mash the raisins and garlic in mortar and pestle or blender, adding just enough of the vinegar to moisten. Combine the vegetables and vinegar, add the sugar, salt, and cayenne, and bring everything to a boil. Then turn down to a simmer and cook for two hours. Seal in sterilized bottles.

— Mango-Papaya*-Pineapple Chutney —

This is a really superb chutney that will not only grace your meals of curried fish, poultry, or meat, but will also preserve a healthy quantity of those fruits that glut the market at certain times of the year in certain sub-tropical parts of the United States.

2 fresh pineapples	1 tbs. ginger syrup
1 tsp. salt	1 cup seedless raisins
2 lbs. green mangoes	½ cup pitted dates
2 sweet peppers	1 tbs. cinnamon
1 small hot red pepper	1 tsp. each: allspice, ground clove
2 medium onions	
2 cloves garlic	1 cup brown sugar
2 ozs. preserved ginger	1 cup vinegar
1 cup chopped ripe papaya meat	1 cup boiling water

Peel, core, and shred the pineapples, then salt them and let stand for about ten hours. Peel and slice the mangoes. Chop the sweet peppers and mince the hot pepper. Chop the onions and mince the garlic and preserved ginger. Combine all ingredients and bring to a boil. Then simmer for about an hour, stirring from time to time. Seal in sterilized bottles.

* Known as papaws, paw-paws, or custard apples in some regions of the United States.

— MANGO CHUTNEY —

In India there are many ways to make chutney, but the following recipe is one of the most popular. Assemble the following ingredients:

2 lbs. green mangoes, peeled and chopped

1 lb. sugar

1½ cups honey

1 lb. raisins, halved

2 tbs. freshly grated ginger (or 2 tsps. powdered ginger)

6 tbs. salt

6 cloves of garlic, crushed

1 cup chopped almonds (optional)

¼ tsp. powdered mace

3 tbs. lime juice

2 tbs. tamarind extract (if unavailable, use lemon juice)

1¾ cups cider vinegar

dash Tabasco sauce or cayenne pepper

Mix all ingredients well in a wide bowl, cover with clean cloth, tape or tie cloth around the bowl, and put in the strong sun (moving it indoors at night) for at least two weeks. In India the mixture is kept in the sun up to six weeks, as the longer exposure improves its taste, but leaving it in the sun three or four weeks makes a very good chutney. Should the sun fail you during this period, on cloudy or rainy days you can place the bowl, uncovered, in a very slow oven. You can accelerate the process by using the oven for a few hours after sundown every day.

When the sauce is ready, remove to jars, close tightly, and store in cool place. It lasts indefinitely. Use as you would a relish.

— GREEN MANGO CHUTNEY —

Here is a simpler chutney that you can make by just letting it sit in the sun for a while.

2 lbs. green mangoes

1 lb. raisins

½ lb. chili peppers

5 cloves garlic

½ lb. sugar

½ lb. crystalized ginger

½ cup mustard seed

1 lb. sweet or bitter almonds

1 tbs. salt

1 qt. vinegar

Peel and slice the mangoes. Then put all ingredients except salt and vinegar into your food chopper or blender. Grind or blend for a few seconds until you get the consistency you like. Add the

124

salt and vinegar, then seal tightly into sterilized bottles. Put the bottles in a sunny place and let stand, revolving them so that every side will get the same amount of sunlight. Don't put the bottles away on your pantry shelf until they have been exposed to six or seven weeks of sunlight.

— TANGERINE CHUTNEY —

4 tangerines	½ tsp. ginger
1 apple	½ tsp. cinnamon
½ cup vinegar	1 tbs. curry powder
1½ cups water	½ cup orange marmalade
1¼ cups sugar	1 tsp. ground cloves or
2 cups fresh cranberries	coriander
½ cup white raisins	

Peel tangerines, remove membranes and strings, cut sections in half, remove seeds. Peel and chop the apple. Combine all ingredients in a saucepan and bring to a boil on medium heat. Cool, then pack into sterilized jars and store in refrigerator, where it will keep for many months. Tangerine chutney is delicious served with pork or turkey.

— WATERMELON CHUTNEY —

The great thing about this chutney is that you can eat the soft flesh of the watermelon first, fresh and sweet and pink and moist, because all you will need for the chutney is the rind, the white part, from which you will remove the green outer casing.

rind of 1 watermelon	3 cloves garlic
1 tsp. powdered alum	1 lb. raisins
6 tbs. salt	1 cup preserved ginger
1 lb. apples (or pears)	2 cups sugar
3 medium-size onions	1 sliced lemon
vinegar	juice of 2 more lemons
1 tbs. celery seed	2 tsp. each: cinnamon, allspice,
2 tbs. mustard seed	ground pepper, ground clove

Cut the white rind into rather small pieces. Add the alum and four tablespoons of salt to enough water to cover the rind; boil it for fifteen minutes and drain. Peel, core, and cut up the apples (or pears); peel and chop the onions. Cover the apples and onions with vinegar, then add two tablespoons salt and the softened rind. Let stand three hours, then drain, reserving the vinegar.

Mash the celery seed, mustard seed, and garlic. Add this mash to the reserved vinegar, along with the remaining ingredients, and bring to a boil. Stir well and add the watermelon mixture. Turn heat down and simmer until watermelon rind is transparent and texture becomes syrupy. Cool and let stand eight to ten hours. Bring to a boil again, then seal in sterilized bottles.

• MEAT, POULTRY, AND FISH •

— BEEF —

The combination of beef and vinegar is not too pleasing to the Western palate, but fortunately there are a number of other ways to pickle beef. For the first, you will need:

10 lbs. beef	*1 oz. saltpeter*
2 tbs. each: ginger, allspice, black pepper	*½ cup brown sugar*
	6 tbs. salt
2 tsp. ground clove	
1 tsp. mace	

Bone the beef, remove the fat, and cut into steaks or chunks. Mix together all the ingredients up to saltpeter and rub the meat well with the mixture, covering all the surfaces well. Then mix together the sugar and salt and sprinkle it over and between the pieces of meat as you pack them into a stone crock or agateware kettle. Leave meat there for two weeks, turning it over every day. At the end of that time, it will keep in a cool place for an additional couple of weeks.

You will perhaps prefer the following method and ingredients:

10 lbs. beef	*1 oz. cayenne pepper*
8 lbs. salt	*1 qt. molasses*
1 oz. saltpeter	*8 gallons soft water*

Bone and defat the beef and cut it into manageable pieces. Rub a pound of the salt into meat thoroughly and let it stand for twenty-four hours (to draw off the blood). Permit it to drain and then pack it in a crock. Combine seven pounds of salt and the rest of the ingredients, boil and skim well and, when cool, pour over the beef.

— Beef Tongue —

1 tongue of beef	3 bay leaves
4 tbs. salt	3 or 4 cloves
2 tbs. salnatron (crude sodium carbonate)	½ tsp. each: pepper, coriander
½ cup dry red wine	

Wash the tongue in cold water. Without drying it, rub it thoroughly all over with two tablespoons of salt and of salnatron. Pour one tablespoon of salt in a bowl, then place tongue over it, curving it slightly to the shape of the bowl. Sprinkle the fourth tablespoon of salt on top of the tongue, then cover with a small plank of wood or a flat plate. Add a heavy weight to the top and leave in a cold place for four days.

On the fifth day, mix the rest of the ingredients in a small pot. Bring to a boil and remove immediately. Uncover the tongue, turn it upside down, and discard the pinkish liquid around it. Pour the boiled wine mixture over and cover again with wood and weight. Return it to a cool place, and in three or four days, it will be ready to cook. Don't try to store it any longer without cooking.

To cook the pickled tongue wash thoroughly in cold water, then place in pot, cover with water, add a few carrots and celery leaves, bring to a boil, and simmer for about two hours. Remove from fire and peel thoroughly. Slice and serve hot with some horseradish or piquant relish on the side. You can slice half and save the other half to be served cold on another occasion. Drain remainder, wrap in wet cloth, and leave hanging in a cool place. It can keep for four or five days.

— GAME —

Quail, partridge, woodcock, or any of the usual game birds can be preserved by this method. It can also be used for other poultry if the idea of pickled domestic fowl appeals to you. You will need the following:

4 to 6 game birds
1 slice bacon
(or equal volume salt pork)
1 cup mixed raw onion, carrot, celery, sweet pepper (chopped fine)

cider or wine vinegar (or dry white wine)
salt and pepper, to taste
dill or basil or tarragon

Clean, pluck, and singe but don't skin your birds. Remove feet and heads. Put the bacon or salt pork into the bottom of your kettle and add the chopped mixed vegetables. Spread the game on this base and cover them with vinegar or wine. Add salt and pepper to taste and the herbs of your choice, one or two or three. Cover securely and put into an oven preheated to 400 degrees Fahrenheit and leave there for thirty to forty minutes.

Pack the birds into sterilized fruit jars. Strain the liquid in which they were cooked and pour it into the jars, leaving some space at the top. Screw jar lids on loosely and process in your pressure canner for forty minutes (see Index). Cool, adjust lids, and store in a cool, dark place.

— PICKLED HERRING —
(*or Other Small Fish*)

Pickled herring is universally accepted but you can, of course, pickle any smallish firm-fleshed fish. All you need are:

a catch of small fish
vinegar and water
salt

Behead, gut, and clean your whole catch. Take off the very thin flesh of the belly, as well as the dark flesh right next to the backbone, but leave the bone attached. Wash and drain. Cover the fish well with a solution of equal parts of cold water and vinegar in which salt has been dissolved (about one-half cup to the quart). Leave the fish four to seven days, checking each day the condition of the skin; if it should change color or get wrinkled, stop brining and rinse and dry.

Now pack the fish tightly in layers, interlarded with a little salt and covered with a solution of one quart of vinegar to two quarts of water plus one-half cup of salt. Now let stand fourteen to twenty-one days. Do not store longer in the brine.

A day before eating, remove the fish and soak it overnight in cold, fresh, saltless water.

— MARINATED MACKEREL —

a few mackerel	1 bay leaf, shredded
salt	a few peppercorns
onion, thinly sliced	a few cloves
carrots, chopped	dry white wine
parsley, chopped	white-wine vinegar

Remove the tails and heads of the fish. Rinse the fish well, dry with a cloth, sprinkle with salt. Let stand an hour. Cover the bottom of a large skillet with onion, carrots, parsley, bay leaf, peppercorns, and cloves. Place fish in one layer on top of this cushion of vegetables, herbs, and spices, making sure fish does not touch bottom of skillet. Prepare enough liquid to cover the fish, half wine, half vinegar. Gently pour over fish without disturbing the bottom layer. Bring to a boil over medium heat. Then lower the flame to a bare simmer, for six or seven minutes. Remove from fire and allow to cool. Put the liquid through a coarse sieve, pressing a little with a wooden spoon so that some of the vegetables and herbs will go into the liquid.

You may serve the mackerel immediately or preserve it in sterilized jars, wide enough so that the fish can be placed horizontally. Pack fish tightly. Bring the marinade to a boil and reduce it somewhat, boiling for about ten minutes. Cover the fish with this liquid, leaving a small space at the top of the jar. Add olive oil (or other heavy oil) up to the top and seal tightly.

This fish will keep several weeks in a cool place, longer in the refrigerator.

129

— PICKLED EEL —

This is the traditional Christmas Eve dish of Italy. It's also a Scandinavian specialty, and many Americans are fond of it. This recipe calls for the skin to be left on, but you may sometimes want to cook or preserve an eel skinless.

1 2-lb. eel	2 or 3 cups vinegar
oil	2 garlic cloves
6 bay leaves	a few peppercorns
salt	sprig of rosemary
pepper	3 or 4 cloves

Scrub the eel with a brush and water without removing the skin. Cut it in five or six segments, discarding the head and tip of the tail. Remove the insides completely and wash the pieces of eel under running water, then dry. Pour very little oil in the bottom of a pan and put in the pieces of fish, packing them close together. Add three bay leaves and salt and pepper to taste. Bake in a moderate oven for one hour or until the eel looks done, turning the pieces halfway through. Remove from oven, let drain, then put into a crock or jar, again packing them close together without squeezing. Bring to a boil two or three cups of vinegar, one teaspoon of salt, three bay leaves, and the rest of the herbs and spices. Pour over the eel and cover the container. For the first few days turn the pieces twice a day. Don't eat it until at least four days have passed, but it will keep for months in a cool place.

— PICKLED SHRIMP —

The following shellfish-preserving recipe can be applied to crabmeat or crayfish or lobster as well:

2 lbs. shrimp	½ cup salt
3 qts. water	3 cups vinegar
2 tsp. each: hot red peppers, white peppercorns, whole cloves, whole allspice, mustard seed	1 tbs. sugar
	1 tsp. mixed pickling spices
	lemon slices

130

Shell, devein, and wash shrimp in cold water. Start simmering in two quarts of water the spices, salt, and 1 cup vinegar. When it has simmered thirty minutes, add the cleaned shrimp and bring to a boil again. Lower heat and simmer a scant five minutes. Drain the shrimp and pack them in sterilized fruit jars. Now make a new solution of the remaining water and vinegar; add sugar and pickling spices, and pour into the jars. Add a slice of lemon to each jar, seal tightly, and store in a cool, dark place.

7

Ꮓ· CAᒥᒥIᒥᏃ ·Ꮓ

The renewed interest in home canning is understandable because it is a natural way to keep the nutritional value and flavor of foods that you may come by in greater quantity than you can possibly eat up at once. It deals with a food surplus economically, requiring as it does so comparatively small an investment of time and so little equipment. It is good homemaking to cache a windfall of fruit or a harvest of vegetables for another season's eating.

All you really need for most home canning is a supply of jars and airtight covers, tongs for handling hot glass and metals, and a water-bath canner: any large metal container with a tight-fitting lid and an inside wire or wooden rack for the jars to rest on so that water can circulate underneath as well as around and over them. The kind of rack that has divisions to keep the glass jars from touching as they boil is best.

If you plan to can any foods low in acid such as meats and most vegetables, however, you must use a pressure canner, a device that resembles a pressure cooker except that it is larger and equipped with a steam gauge. Botulism is one of the dangers of canning fish and meat, and botulism, as you know, is often fatal. The natural acids in fruits destroy decay-producing bacteria, but the absence of such acids from meats and vegetables dictates the use of the greater heat of steam.

Nevertheless, even when you have the help of natural acids, meticulous hygiene is necessary when canning fresh fruits and tomatoes. No more than two hours should be allowed to elapse between gathering and canning. If that is impractical, be sure to wash, dry, and keep covered in a cool, dry place the produce you picked the day before canning.

There are two distinct methods of canning: the cold pack, or raw pack, and the hot pack. You either pack the food into the jars raw or cold, or heat or partially cook them first in water, in syrup, or in their own juice. The advantage of the cold pack is an aesthetic one: A more attractive package is made by packing raw, cold fruits or vegetables into a jar in their original shape and texture. The effect is lost when they have been even slightly softened by pre-heating. Some fruits, however, will either float or shrink, or both, when packed raw and leave too much liquid space in the jar. The canning table in this chapter will help you choose and pursue your method.

There is on the market a machine that the home preserver can buy and use to can produce which gives you at the end of a steamy day in the kitchen a row of metal cans with airtight seals that have to be opened with a can opener. Despite the efficiency of canning in this way, however, most home canners prefer to use glass containers, the kind called fruit jars, that permit them to see what is inside without elaborate labeling. Metal does keep out light as well as air, but jars can be stored in a dark, cool, and dry place, so that light won't change the color and flavor of the stored foods. The instructions in this book therefore will be exclusively concerned with putting up food in jars rather than in cans.

Canning in the United States has always been associated with the names Mason and Ball. Mason or Ball jars have become generic terms for canning jars. These jars are fitted out with a cover made of parts that act together to insure a tight seal. Traditionally jars were sealed by means of a rubber ring with a glass top that was set over the rubber and was then fastened down with a metal brace attached to the neck of the jar. The kind more frequently in use now is a two-piece metal top, one piece a screw band and the other a metal disk lid with a rubber sealing compound underneath. Also in current use is a porcelain-lined screw cap with a rubber ring. Neither the rubber rings nor the metal disk lid should be used more than once, since the heat of the canning process always warps them a little. The metal screw band can be used several times. The jar can be used for many seasons, as long as it is whole and has no cracks or chipped or sharp edges.

• WATER-BATH CANNING FOR FRUITS •

To prepare your equipment, wash your hands in hot, soapy water, and then wash the jars in a new batch of hot, soapy water. Rinse jars twice in hot water, then leave them in the water until you take them out to fill them. Cover lids and bands with hot water until you remove them to cover your filled jars. Sterilize similarly all knives, peelers, slicers, and corers.

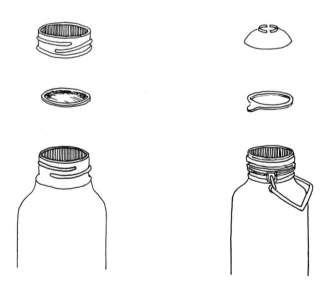

To prepare your produce, clean any soil or other foreign substances from fruit, and wash a few at a time under cold, running water, or in several changes of clean, cool water, lifting fruit out each time. Sort the fruits according to size, shape, color, and degree of ripeness, so that no one jar will contain fruits of different quality. Now peel, core, slice, or pit those fruits that require it. This, too, is a matter of aesthetics, as there is no hard-and-fast rule about which fruits to can with skins on or off. The vitamin content may be increased slightly if you leave skin on; the texture of the final product improved if you peel. For easy peeling, plunge fruit for a few seconds (you can handle it best in a wire basket or cheesecloth) into boiling water, then dip in cold water and drain.

WATER BATH
CANNER

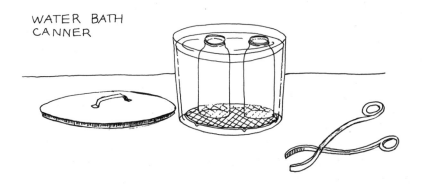

• ANTI OXIDANTS •

Some fruits, such as apples, pears, and peaches, will start to change color as soon as they are peeled; they start to oxidize immediately on contact with the air. If you want them to retain their original color, treat them with an anti-oxidant. As soon as you have peeled or cut them up, put them into one of the following three solutions:

(1) 1 tsp. ascorbic acid (vitamin C) to 1 gallon of water, or
(2) 1 tsp. citric acid to 1 gallon of water, or
(3) 2 tbs. salt and 2 tbs. distilled vinegar to 1 gallon of water.

If you use no. 3, rinse the fruit well before you add syrup to it.

Leave the fruit in the anti-oxidant solution for ten to fifteen minutes, depending on the size of the pieces.

Some canners, concerned about the loss of nutrients in soaking (or boiling), only sprinkle anti-oxidants in solution on fruit; others go so far as to rub each half or slice of pear or apple with one of the acids in crystalline form. We say that the loss of your valuable time in sprinkling or smearing each slice is probably not worth the slight saving of vitamin content.

These anti-oxidants are useful in preparing fruit for drying as well, as a preliminary step in making fruit salads and desserts, and before freezing.

· SYRUPS ·

It is not necessary to add syrup when canning most fruits, for you can rely on their own natural sweetening for flavor. The juiciest apples—the McIntosh, for instance—have their own syrup built in. However, the addition of some sort of syrup to the jar will in some cases improve the taste of the fruit and help it to retain its shape and color; and furthermore, syrup is in itself a means of preservation.

If it is your habit to substitute honey for sugar whenever you can, use honey (or corn syrup) instead of the sugar specified in the next few pages, scaling the amount down to between half and two-thirds (as you do when converting a regular cooking recipe from sugar to honey). But, remember, honey has a distinctive taste of its own that may blend very well with certain fruits, but overpower the taste of others.

In any case, to make the canning syrup, use only water or fruit juice and sweetening.

To make a heavy syrup, use four to five cups of sugar to one quart of water; for a medium syrup, three cups of sugar to one quart of water; and for a light syrup, two cups of sugar to one quart of water. A featherweight syrup can be made by combining one cup of sugar and one quart of water.

Cook the mixture over low heat until the sugar is entirely dissolved. The heavier the syrup, obviously, the sweeter the taste of the preserve. Some theorize, also, that the more sugar

136

you use, the longer your fruit will keep; this is a moot point, so let your taste be your guide.

Depending upon the fruit, you will need one to one and a half quarts of syrup for each quart of fruit. Instead of making the syrup, and then cooling and reheating it, try to make the syrup while you are preparing your fruit and keep it hot until you are ready to pour.

• COLD PACK OR RAW PACK •

Lift your sterilized jars out of the hot water and line them up. Pack your cleaned, peeled, cored, anti-oxidated fruits into the jars quite firmly, in layers, cavity side down or in (if there is a cavity), leaving about a half-inch at the top of the jar. Pour hot syrup into the jars, enough to cover fruit, and let it settle in. Run a knife or some other flat object between fruit and jar to let out any air bubbles that may have formed. Now put on jar lids, bands, and covers, and screw them tightly. Put filled jars onto rack, and rack into canning pot. Pour hot (not boiling) water into pot so that the jars are in a bath up to at least an inch over their heads. Cover canner and boil with cover on. Times for boiling can be found in the table to come.

• HOT PACK •

This method is preferred by some home canners for most fruits, presumably because they want to see what changes take place in the texture, consistency, and size of their fruits before they are boiled in a water bath.

Follow all instructions given for the cold pack. Before packing the fruits into the jars, however, heat the fruit a few minutes in hot syrup (not boiling) long enough to heat through and still have their temperatures just under boiling when you put them into the jars. You don't need to pack them quite as tightly as you do when cold packing; in fact, with most fruits you can't.

• FRUIT CANNING TABLE •
Water-Bath Method

Altitude makes a difference: When time is 20 minutes or less, add 1 minute for each 1,000 feet above sea level; if time is more than 20 minutes, add 2 minutes for each 1,000 feet.

Fruit	*Pack Recommended*	*Minutes of Boiling*	
		PINT JARS	QUART JARS
Apples	Hot	20	20
Apricots	Hot	20	20
Berries (all kinds)	Cold	15	20
Cherries	Cold	20	20
Figs	Cold	90	90
Grapes	Cold	20	25
Guavas	Cold	30	35
Mangoes	Cold	20	25
Peaches	Cold	25	30
Pears	Hot	20	25
Plums	Cold	20	20
Prunes	Cold	20	20
Rhubarb	Cold	10	10
Peppers*	Cold	20	25
Tomatoes*	Cold	35	45

* Because of their high acid content, peppers and tomatoes can be processed by this method as well.

This is, of course, an incomplete list; we have selected only the most popular canned foods. There are fruits other than those on the list that you may can with safety and profit. Just choose the fruit from the table that your preferred fruit most closely resembles in character, sweetness, and so forth, and use the same directions.

• FRUIT SAUCES •

If you want to can fruit sauces or purées, again use only sound, ripe fruit. Wash, pit, peel, and cut into pieces. Simmer until soft, using a little water if needed to keep fruit from burning. Strain through a sieve or mill, or blend in a blender. Add sugar to taste. Heat again to simmering. Pack hot to within one-half inch from top of jar. Fasten lid and process in water bath about ten minutes.

• FRUIT COMBINATIONS •

You may want to can fruits in combination. Remember that each will lend flavor to the other in the canning and storing, so choose fruits that you think will complement each other. The following pages describe some combinations that we have found interesting. You may want to make up others of your own.

— PEARS AND PEPPERS —

This may sound like an "odd couple," but actually the tastes of sweet peppers and pears combine very well, and the dish makes a fine fall or winter accompaniment to meat, fish, poultry, eggs, or farinaceous foods. The color combination, too, is handsome— especially if you use a combination of green and red peppers.

Peel, core, stem, and seed the pears; cut them in halves or quarters and drop them into a salt-vinegar bath to keep them from darkening while you remove stems, seeds, and whites from the sweet peppers. You can chop the peppers, but a more attractive preserve is made by cutting them into long, thin slices. Now drain the pears and pack them into hot, sterilized jars, round side up, sliding the pepper segments between and among them.

Prepare a medium syrup and pour it, boiling, into the jars, filling them to within an inch of the top of the jars, being sure that both fruits and vegetables are covered. Process in water-bath canner, boiling twenty minutes for pint jars, twenty-five for quarts.

— PLUMS AND CRANBERRIES —

Wash your plums and, if you wish to can them whole, prick their skins a little. (If you are working with freestone plums, then halve them and remove the stones.) Pick over and wash the cranberries, discarding any imperfect ones. Pack both fruits, distributing them equally, in hot, sterilized jars. Pour in boiling medium syrup to cover them well, leaving one-half inch at tops of jars. Process in water-bath canner, boiling twenty minutes for pint jars, twenty-five for quarts.

The prune variety can also be used, or you may can a combination of all three, prunes, plums, and cranberries.

139

— APPLES AND RHUBARB —

This is as good a coupling in canning as in a pie, especially when you use a sweet, mealy apple. But *never* cook or eat the leaves of the tart and tasty rhubarb stalk; the leaves can inflict severe gastritis, or even death, on human beings as well as animals.

Clean the rhubarb stalks, cutting off all greenery and the rather woody ends of the stalks. Cut into half-inch pieces and put into a saucepan with one-quarter cup of honey for each quart of cut rhubarb. Bring to a boil and let simmer a minute or two. Pare, core, and cut the apples into pieces, dropping them into an anti-oxidant solution to keep them from darkening. Drain and then boil the apples three to five minutes in water. (Use syrup if the apples are of a very tart variety, but you don't need it if they are sweet.)

Combine the rhubarb and apples in equal parts, put into jars up to one-half inch from the top, and add a bit of boiling water to each jar. Process in your water-bath canner, fifteen minutes for pint jars, twenty for quarts.

— MANGOES AND RASPBERRIES —

Select mangoes that are not fibrous, and not too ripe. Peel, slice, seed, and cut into broad strips, saving the inside pulp for syrup. Pack them into sterilized jars, mingling with them an equal volume (or perhaps a bit less) of washed, picked-over raspberries, leaving nearly an inch of space at the top of the jars. Prepare a light syrup of the pulp, sugar, and water, and bring it to a boil; pour into the jars to within a half-inch of the top. Boil in your water-bath canner, fifteen minutes for pint jars, twenty for quarts.

— GUAVAS AND BLUEBERRIES —

This may take a bit of doing, as the crops tend to ripen with time and geography between them; but if you can manage it, you will have a truly Pan-American preserve, and one that affords a unique and delightful melding of tastes, textures, and hues.

140

Wash, peel, and cut off the ends of a mixture of sweet and sour ripe guavas. Slice and pack into sterilized jars, mingling among them an equal volume of washed, picked-over blueberries. Now bring to a boil a very light syrup, add a bit of lime juice to it, and pour the boiling syrup into the jars, covering the fruit but leaving a half-inch of space at the top of the jars. Process in your canner, boiling pint jars twenty-five minutes, quarts thirty.

— PEACHES AND BLACKBERRIES —

Probably the slight woodiness of the blackberries will satisfy your desire for texture sufficiently that you will want to skin the peaches first. So peel, stem, and stone the peaches and cut them in halves. Pick over the blackberries, removing all sticks, stems, leaves, bugs, and imperfect or unripe berries. Drop the peaches as you peel them into an anti-oxidant solution. Drain and pack them into hot, sterilized jars. Remember to pack them convex side out, with blackberries arranged between the peach halves, leaving at least a half-inch at the top of the jars. Prepare a light or medium syrup, bring it to a boil, then pour it into jars, filling them up to a half-inch from the top. Now process in your water-bath canner, twenty-five minutes for pints, thirty for quarts.

— TOMATOES AND FIGS —

Use only firm, ripe tomatoes. A combination of small yellow ones with larger red ones would look pretty on the shelves (and on your plate later). Dip them quickly into boiling water, then into cold for easy peeling. Peel and stem. Leave them whole, or cut into halves or quarters. Now wash the figs and stem them. Sprinkle them with baking soda and pour boiling water over them, and let stand for five minutes. Again, you may leave them whole or cut in half, depending on their size and your preference (remember that to open them up is to lose their seeds during processing). Pack both tomatoes and figs, in equal amounts or perhaps lighter on the figs, into sterilized fruit jars. Add no water or syrup, but put a bit of salt in each jar, one teaspoon to quart jars, one-half teaspoon to pints. Process in water-bath canner, boiling pints thirty-five minutes, quarts forty-five.

141

· THE PRESSURE CANNER ·

The pressure canner differs from the ordinary pressure cooker only in size; it has to be large enough to accommodate the pint-size fruit jars you wish to pack your food in. But if you want to use jars smaller than pint size and put things up in rather small amounts, your regular pressure cooker with (or without) a handle will do fine. Just be sure that there is a rack that allows for circulation underneath the jars, as well as sufficient space around, between, and above the jars.

Like any equipment used in connection with canning foods, the pressure canner must be kept scrupulously clean. Also, the steam gauge is a rather sensitive, tricky instrument that can easily, and for no good reason, go out of kilter. It's a good idea to have its accuracy checked several times a year, or just before canning season.

As with water-bath canning, the altitude at which you live makes a difference. If you live 2,000 feet or more above sea level, add one pound of pressure for each 2,000 feet. From sea level to 2,000 feet above, vegetables should be processed at ten pounds of steam pressure, which produces a heat of 240 degrees Fahrenheit. Always start timing when the steam gauge shows this temperature has been reached.

When the specified time under pressure is up, remove the pressure canner from the heat and let it stand, unopened, until the pressure has registered zero *for about twenty minutes.* Then open the petcock, unfasten the cover, and open the canner far side first, tilted away from you. Remove the jars with tongs and complete the seals at once (unless self-sealing type). Then cool by either method.

Now is the time to test your jars for accurate seal; in two or three months your peaches may have had time to mold, or your canned fish to develop a little botulism! As soon as you take the jars out of the water-bath or pressure canner, turn them over on their sides briefly to see if any liquid leaks out. If it does, either eat the food inside on that very day, or reprocess immediately, boiling fifteen minutes for water-bath, or maintaining the pressure for the originally specified time for pressure canning.

If your jar tops are the flat metal-disk kind, tap the metal in its middle: If it is slightly concave and doesn't move when you touch it, it is sealed. Sometimes these metal caps make a pleasant "ploink" sound as you take them out of the canner. That's a good signal; they have completed their own airtight sealing.

— Pressure-Canning Vegetables —

As with fruits (and tomatoes and peppers), it's best to use only very fresh, perfect specimens, separated according to size and shape or cut to uniform pieces. And again, hygiene is a must: Wash your vegetables in several waters, not allowing them to soak but lifting them out of each bath, or scrubbing them under cold, running water.

You need not add anything other than boiling water to the vegetables, no spices or herbs or vinegars or sugar. The high heat destroys any bacteria that may be present and removes the oxygen as well, thus rendering your vegetables fit to keep for a long time in a cool place. Very often salt is used as well as hot water, but in pressure canning salt is used more for flavoring than for preserving. Use one-half teaspoon to the pint jar, one teaspoon to the quart; and be sure it is raw salt, sometimes called curing salt; not iodized, free-flowing table salt.

Vegetables can be cold-packed, and the jars then filled with boiling water. But since some pre-heating before going into the canner is almost always desirable, we prefer hot-packing vegetables; the table that follows is set up that way. If you wish to substitute a few minutes of steaming, particularly with small vegetables such as beans, you may. The point is to introduce heat into the vegetables in advance of the steam-heating it will get in the pressure canner, but not to cook it completely.

— Vegetable Canning Table —
Pressure-Canner Method

The following directions are for the vegetables most commonly canned at home in this country (tomatoes and peppers appear on the previous table).

PRE-CANNING

Vegetable	Preparation Recommended	Minutes of Pressure PINT JARS	QUART JARS
Asparagus	Heat to a boil; or steam	25	30
Beans—lima, butter, etc.	Heat to a boil	40	50
Beans—wax, green, etc.	Boil 5 minutes	20	25
Beets	Boil till tender, remove skin	30	35
Carrots and similar roots	Heat to a boil	25	30
Corn—raw kernels,	Heat to a boil	55	85
hominy	Pack while still hot	60	70
Eggplant	Heat to a boil	30	40
Greens, all kinds	Heat to a boil	70	90
Okra	Boil 1 minute	25	50
Onions	Heat to a boil	25	30
Peas	Heat to a boil	35	40
Mushrooms	Heat without water, covered, 15 minutes	30	40
Potatoes, sweet	Boil until skin slips, peel	55	90
Potatoes, white	Heat to a boil	35	40
Summer squash and zucchini	Heat to a boil	30	40
Winter squash and pumpkin	Heat to a boil	55	90
Yams	Heat to a boil	40	60

As with fruits, you may combine vegetables when canning, again remembering to consider the result of the melding of flavors that will take place in the canning and storing process. Be sure that you observe the greater length of time if your teamed vegetables require different steam-pressure times. Succotash is a combination of lima beans and corn kernels and is often canned in that form.

— GREEN BEANS AND PEAS —

Throw into boiling water small, tender peas (shelled) and green beans (with their tips removed). Leave three minutes in boiling water.

In a large kettle add celery (stalks and leaves), carrots, parsley, onion, one or two cloves of garlic, and salt in the proportion of one-and-a-half tablespoons to each quart of water. Bring to a boil and let boil for ten minutes. Strain water into bowl, using thick woven cloth, and let cool.

Put peas and beans in jars, packing them together quite tightly, and leaving about three inches of space on top of the jars. Pour the cold brine into the jars to overflowing and cover tightly. Place in cauldron or canner, making sure you have enough water to reach the tops of the jars. Bring to a boil and boil for twenty minutes. Let cool until the following day. Store.

• MEAT, POULTRY, AND FISH •

If you don't start canning meat, fowl, or fish practically the moment they are slaughtered or caught (actually as soon as the body heat has gone), you must be sure to keep them under refrigeration until you do. Don't let them wait more than a day or two.

You must not can any of these foods by the water-bath method. Use *only* the pressure canner when putting them up.

The hot-pack preparation is recommended for canning any such product. Careful cleaning, drawing, boning, and removing of all the less savory parts are necessary before cutting meat, fowl, or fish into pieces of manageable size. The skin can be left on in cases where you would normally eat the skin if you were cooking the fresh meat instead of canning it.

Salting before canning is optional and a question of taste; you don't need salt to act as a preservative when pressure-canning but you may want it for flavoring. Add salt after you have packed the food into your jars, by combining it with the juice that you pour into the jars. Do not rub the flesh with the salt before packing it.

Remove as much fat as possible from meat before canning it.

Some small creatures, such as game birds and the smaller breeds of fish, may be canned without chopping them up into small pieces. If you elect to can them whole, be sure they are thoroughly cleaned first, and that your jars are large enough to accommodate them so that no part is sticking up out of the canning liquid at the top of the jar.

— MEAT —

Your utensils and cutting board (especially any wooden surfaces) must be scraped, scrubbed, and disinfected. Keep the meat cold until you actually begin your canning preparations; it will be easier to handle. Cut or saw it into manageable pieces.

Now put the pieces of meat into a saucepan and cover with cold water. Bring the water to a boil, then lower heat and simmer until meat is just tenderized. Pour off the broth, reserve it, and pack the meat loosely into your hot sterilized jars. Then pop the jars into a hot oven to keep everything heated while the reserved broth is cooling enough for you to skim off the fat.

Next, bring the broth to a boil and pour it, still boiling, into the jars of meat, leaving about an inch of space at the top of the jars. With a very clean cloth, wipe the tops and edges of jars free of any fat, and put on the tops, wiping again when the tops are sealed.

Put the clean, hot jars full of meat into your pressure canner with the proper amount of water in the bottom. Seal it and bring the pressure up to ten pounds (240 degrees Fahrenheit). Don't start your timing until the pressure has reached this level. Then maintain that temperature for seventy-five minutes if you have used pint jars, and for ninety minutes if you have used quart jars.

Remember to let the canner cool entirely before you open it and unpack it, and remember to check your seals.

— Poultry —

For chicken, duck, goose, squab, turkey, game bird, guinea hen, as well as small furry game such as rabbit and squirrel, try to work with poultry that, if not freshly killed, has been kept under refrigeration for not more than a day after killing. Cut up and separate into pieces with a bone and those without. Do as you like about the skin. Wash well.

Put the bony pieces into a saucepan and cover with water. Bring to a boil, then reduce heat to a simmer, cover pan, and cook until half-done or until pieces when cut at center show almost no pink color. Then add the boneless pieces long enough to just heat through.

Pack into hot, sterilized jars with leg pieces skin side out next to glass, breasts and smaller pieces in center. Pour hot broth into jars to cover meat, but leave an inch of space at the top. (Salt, as with meat, is optional; but if you are using it, add it to the packed jars.)

Seal jars and wipe their rims clean. Then proceed the same as when canning meat, using the same time scale.

You can also put up poultry gizzards and heart (together) and livers (alone) in the same manner.

— Fish —

Most of the rules for meat and poultry apply equally to the canning of fish and seafood: absolute freshness or no more than a day under refrigeration between catching and canning; the strictest hygiene; and scaling and getting rid of all inelegant portions. Whether to skin or not depends on the nature of the creature and its flesh; as does whether to can whole or in sections. Follow the directions for poultry.

Gefüllte Fish

One of the most popular types of canned fish is this old favorite:

1 whole whitefish	2 or 3 medium onions
1 whole carp	1 to 3 eggs
1 whole pike	salt and pepper, to taste
3 or 4 carrots	pinch of sugar

147

Always use at least three kinds of fish, in equal parts or other-wise to suit your taste; the three we list are traditional, but any other fresh-water fish will do. Filet the fish, putting aside the heads and bones. Slice the carrots in rounds, the onions in rings. Grind the raw fish quite fine, alternating pieces of the three different kinds. Add one raw egg for each pound of fish. Add salt, pepper, and sugar. Shape this mixture into balls.

Put carrots, onions, fish heads, and bones into enough water to cover them well. Bring to a boil and boil for twenty minutes or so, replenishing with hot water if the fish doesn't stay covered. Add the fish balls, turn the heat down, and let the whole thing simmer for thirty to forty minutes.

Discard the fish heads and bones. Pack fish balls, carrots, and any onions that are left intact in hot, sterilized jars, and fill them nearly full with the broth.

Process pint jars in a pressure-canner for a half hour and quart jars for forty minutes.

8

FREEZING

The discovery of freezing has changed our eating habits in the last thirty or forty years more than any other related innovation. When we lower the temperature to well below freezing point and prevent air from penetrating the food, we retard the natural process of decay; and many of you who have never tried this simple method of preservation will be able to do so easily by following the simple guidelines outlined in this chapter.

Freezing can be as easy as storing for certain foods, or may require just a few additional steps when preparing others. The greatest problem in freezing is to decide what foods to freeze. We hope to provide suggestions you can adapt to your family tastes, habits, and special circumstances. Of course, the best foods to freeze are those that retain most of their natural qualities, taste, texture, and looks. Luckily, there are many, and we recommend you freeze these products rather than those that are affected by extreme changes in temperature.

Your freezer can be a precious vault rather than a convenient catch-all closet. Unless you already own a large freezer, consider buying a fairly small one, especially if you don't live in a very isolated spot, and reserve its use only for foods that cannot be preserved successfully by any other means. Above all, make the best use of your freezer. Keep it stocked at all times and rotate its contents frequently, taking full advantage of the variety in diet this method of preservation provides.

If you don't own a freezer but are planning to buy one, remember that the way in which the manufacturer calculates cubic feet is often misleading, so that very often the amount of food you can actually freeze is overstated; he has considered only solid cubic volume, as if you were to freeze one solid mass of food instead of many different foods separately packed, many of which have irregular shapes and therefore occupy considerably more space. And though it may be a little more expensive, we suggest you buy an upright freezer rather than the chest type; it provides easier storage and accessibility and occupies less floor space. However, it consumes more electricity.

A reminder, especially for city folks. Very often in the summer the freezer should be set at a lower temperature than zero degrees Fahrenheit, as the power companies these days sometimes cut down the electricity supply by 5 per cent or even 10 per cent. In fact this is becoming the rule all year round. Because of the power shortage, the energy supply in many parts of the country has already been cut down at least 3 per cent, although this decrease in power has been buried at the bottom of the news about energy supplies and shortages.

• CONTAINERS •

A large number of containers on the market are made especially for freezing. The most satisfactory are those of rigid plastic. They can be reused, are available in different sizes and shapes, are easily sealed and opened, and are, of course, unbreakable. For small-sized vegetables or fruits, you may wish to use plastic bags. If you do, and if you want to use plastic food bags that have been accumulating in your kitchen, make sure they are sturdy (not the thin type) and that you wash and dry them before using. While you are washing them, test if the bags are waterproof by filling them with water. If they have any holes, discard them. Enclose these bags in cartons so that they will not be accidentally pierced as you shift around the other foods in your freezer.

150

You can also use aluminum, tin, any other metal (provided it is rustproof), or glass. You can reuse any empty food jars you happen to have, provided they can be sealed so that they are airtight and that both jar and cover are absolutely clean. (Smell the cover to make sure that odor from the previous food stored in the jar has not lingered on.) However, never use glass containers for anything that has been packed in water or any watery substance as the glass will break when the liquid expands. Of course, you'll have to be more careful in shifting glass jars, as glass becomes even more fragile when frozen. Do not use wax cartons, unless you are preserving food for a very short time, and even then, never use them for foods that contain liquid.

For oddly shaped and large packages of foods it is advisable to use sheets of heavy aluminum foil, or if that is too expensive, heavy film plastic, polyethylene, or any good freezer tape. Or, you may prefer to use heavy plastic film and to make a bag by sealing three sides first with a warm iron. Do not use the iron directly on the plastic (place a sheet of heavy paper over it), and keep the iron rather cool so that the plastic will not melt and bunch up. Also, before sealing, check the dryness of the plastic, inside, and check the entire bag after sealing it to make sure you have not left open spaces. You can use this sealing method also for the fourth side of a plastic bag, but it is much easier to just twirl the top of the bag around your finger, fold, and then close it with a metal "twist." It is also advisable to squeeze out as much air as possible before sealing or closing the bag. The advantages of using a metal twist instead of the hot sealing are that the bag can be reused; and also you can take out only a portion of its contents, then close it again and put it back in the freezer.

• PACKING •

The secret of proper freezing is to act quickly, both in preparing the food and in packing and freezing it. To speed up the freezing process, always pack cold food into cold containers.

The reason for acting quickly, especially with vegetables and fruits, is that the enzyme action that has brought produce to the ripe stage continues after picking, into the decaying process. So the quicker you prepare, cool, and freeze the food, the better it will be nutritionally. The enzyme action is slowed down to a minimum when the food is frozen, although a minor amount of such activity continues even then.

Because liquids expand when they become frozen, a little space—referred to as head space—must be left at the top of the containers when packing foods that are preserved in liquid or solid foods or those that have a high liquid content. If the food is in pieces, so that each piece has room to expand within the container, head space is usually not necessary. Otherwise, the general rule is to leave about one-half inch for pint-size containers and one inch for the quart size. Increase the space if the containers have a narrow opening. We shall not specify if head space is needed, unless a space larger than usual is required for specific foods.

Use your judgment about packing foods. Do not compress them so much that you could bruise them, especially if they are delicate foods, but don't pack them too loosely because the amount of air in the package should be minimal. You need to leave head space for foods that will expand while freezing, but once foods are frozen, there should be very little air left in each package.

• LABELING •

When freezing food, it is especially important to label each package or container with the date on which you pack it, the specific food, type of packing, or any other bit of information you are likely to forget when you take it out for use. Have ready a notebook or large chart (such as we have recommended before for other processing), and hang it on a nearby wall. Repeat on it the same information, plus the number of packages you put in the freezer. Cross out the packages you take out of the freezer and use so that you will always know how well you are supplied.

• TEMPERATURE •

If your freezer has a temperature regulator—and most new freezers have one—lower it to a temperature five or six degrees below zero and keep the temperature at this level for twenty-four hours. For normal storage temperature, zero is sufficient.

152

Distribute the new packages to be frozen in the coldest part of your freezer, in one layer and with a little air space between packages, to allow circulation and to quicken the freezing process.

• POWER FAILURE •

This is definitely the major hazard in freezing.

Should your freezer, due to malfunctioning, cause the temperature to rise, or should it break down completely, or should there be a power failure in your neighborhood, you will have to take quick steps to try to avoid the spoilage of food. If your freezer is full, and fairly large, the food should stay frozen for about forty-eight hours. If it is half full it will not stay frozen longer than twenty-four hours. (In smaller freezers food thaws more quickly.) Try not to open the door unless it is absolutely necessary, so that you won't allow the warm air inside.

If the power failure lasts longer and you can buy a sufficient quantity of dry ice, place a lot of it in pieces on top of your packaged foods after insulating your food by inserting heavy cardboard or planks of wood on top of the packages. Do not handle dry ice with your bare hands or you will burn yourself. Use heavy gloves.

If foods are partially or totally thawed before your freezer can start operating again, refreeze only the foods that still have some ice crystals on them. If the process of thawing has gone beyond the crystals stage, discard eggs, milk, and fish, and use the rest of the food (or at least cook it) as soon as possible. If your refrigerator is functioning, refrigerate the food but use all of it within a couple of days. However, it is preferable not to refreeze any fruits or vegetables even if only partially thawed, as their quality deteriorates more easily than that of other foods. If you are in doubt as to which foods to try to save and which to discard, discard them, especially if their looks are affected or if they are beginning to smell.

Another word of caution about something few people ever seem to consider. This concerns commercially frozen foods you have bought in a store. One never knows, really, if the frozen food one buys has been thawed and refrozen. Even if the quality

153

of the food has not been greatly affected in terms of looks, safety, or taste, a good part of the nutrients will have escaped if the food packages have been allowed to thaw even partially. The same thing can happen in your own home, with food you have frozen yourself. If you leave home for more than two days, check your freezer upon your return, and check with your neighbors to make sure there hasn't been a blackout during your absence, or your food will have thawed and refrozen itself without your being aware of it.

Many new freezers come provided with an alarm that goes off in case of power failure or malfunctioning of the unit. If your freezer does not have one, you can buy an alarm at your dealer or at some hardware stores. It is a good investment.

• A FEW GENERAL SUGGESTIONS •

Your freezer space is precious and should be used to the best advantage. So, before you start freezing anything, assess your family's preferences, and try to judge in advance how much to freeze. It is always surprising to see how bulky food seems to become when you try to stuff it in the freezer.

Don't underestimate your refrigerator. Many leftovers are more suited for the refrigerator than for the freezer. Remember that cooked food, for the most part, can be stored in the refrigerator for several days without spoiling. So, if you decide to double the recipe of a favorite dish (or a particularly difficult dish to prepare), don't forget you can also refrigerate it and serve it again four or five days later. Besides, the idea of freezing prepared foods is not always good, not only in terms of extra bulk in your freezer, but also because there are some disadvantages in freezing some of these favorites.

For example, the flavor of most herbs and spices tends to disappear, but pepper gains considerably in bitterness. Potatoes, onions, pasta, and starches in general, when incorporated in a dish you freeze, become tasteless and soggy.

Whenever possible, if you are cooking dishes that contain these ingredients, make two batches, one for immediate consumption and the other for freezing. Don't add salt, pepper, spices, herbs, or starches to the portion you are going to freeze, and label the package accordingly, so that you will remember to add these ingredients when rewarming the dish.

If you have a fairly large quantity of any product to freeze, do not put it in the freezer all at once, or you may bring up the temperature and partly defrost the rest of the food. Freeze it in relatively small batches while preparing the rest, or place it first in the refrigerator to cool before you freeze it.

• MEAT •

Very few people know that most meats should undergo an aging period to improve their quality and acquire sufficient tenderness. Until refrigeration modified this process, the animal was simply skinned, eviscerated, and left hanging in a cool place for a few days. Modern technology has invented more precise and more sanitary ways to accomplish this, but the basic method is frequently the same. Refrigeration during this aging period also prolongs the time between slaughtering and eating (or freezing), and the whole animal, or half, is kept under refrigeration, at a temperature of about 35 degrees Fahrenheit for as long as one month. Because of the added expense for refrigerated storage and because of the shrinkage (and consequent weight loss) caused by minor dehydration while aging, this meat is more expensive and increasingly hard to find, as fewer meat producers find it profitable to provide this aged meat for which there is less and less demand from individual consumers. They prefer to reserve it only for sale to top-grade restaurants. Furthermore, many people have been shying away from aged meat because most cuts of meat acquire a darker color with aging, and the texture becomes more compact, leading many consumers to erroneously believe that the meat is not fit to eat.

So the private consumer is left with practically no choice, a state of affairs that, in part, he has brought upon himself by preferring to buy "fresh" meat, believing that the best meat must look bright red as proof of fresh slaughtering. He has also unwittingly provoked the butcher's unlawful but still widespread practice of adding fresh blood to the cuts of meat so neatly packaged with the added liquid, which makes the meat look even

155

"fresher" and at the same time increases its weight and therefore its cost.

To obviate the purely visual drawback, some companies have discovered another way of aging meat by exposing it to ultraviolet or other types of rays. This minimizes discoloration. However, meat aged by this means is not easily available.

Because we don't usually slaughter our own animals, there is very little we can do to improve the taste and tenderness of the meat we purchase. But, since the process of aging works also, though to a minor extent, for cuts of meat as well as for the whole animal, what we can do is buy the meat, leave it in our refrigerator for a few days, and then freeze it (or cook it). This will improve only moderately the tenderness and taste of low-grade quality meat, but the improvement will be more noticeable for better-grade meat. Most of us have at one time or another had to contend with a tough piece of meat, so it may be worth your while giving all your meats this simple aging treatment. Of course, toughness in meats can be caused either by extreme freshness, or because the animal was too old. If the meat you purchased was from an aged animal, there is little you can do about softening the texture of the meat, unless you choose to rely on those meat tenderizers that are likely to soften your insides as well.

Buying meat regularly from the same butcher or in the same store, once you have found someone reliable, can save you a lot of money in the future, as it is very discouraging and wasteful to freeze meat for months, and then discover it is almost too tough to eat. However, should this happen to you with one cut of meat out of a larger amount you have bought at the same time, thaw the rest in the refrigerator and leave it there a few days before cooking it. Unless the toughness was caused by the age of the animal, you may still succeed in improving the quality of the rest of that unfortunate purchase.

When labeling your packages before freezing, it is a good precaution to mark the origin of your purchase, so that you'll easily be able to distinguish any cuts that may have been frozen too fresh.

This process of aging does not apply to pork, which should be frozen immediately, nor does it apply to ground and variety meats. The meat that should be aged is the lean meat of larger animals. A shorter aging period is advisable for lamb and similar animals.

— BEEF, VEAL, LAMB, AND PORK —

Except for the vegetarians among you, meat is often the main provision in a home freezer. And rightly so, for meat of almost all kinds is perhaps the product that freezes best and most retains its natural properties when thawed, as you have undoubtedly already found out.

If you have a large family, you may wish to investigate the possibilities of buying meat in bulk. More often than not, if you buy a whole side of beef, let's say, the butchering is done by the supplier, and for a nominal sum he can also pack it for you, so all you have to do is put it in your freezer. We don't recommend that you cut the meat yourself unless you are experienced. Aside from the physical difficulty of cutting and sawing, meat must be cut according to specific directions and is a job best left to the professionals. Of course, this caution does not apply to simple jobs, such as halving a large steak or cutting pieces for stew from a large chunk of meat.

However, before you decide to buy meat in bulk, we must point out that, while this type of purchase at first glance seems to afford a considerable saving, the actual weight is less than it appears because the meat has to be trimmed. Before embarking on such a project, find out exactly what types of meat the particular portion you are planning to buy will yield, or you may find yourself with a disproportionate amount of ground and stew meat, and your original saving may almost disappear.

For the average purchase of meat, it is preferable to leave the meat in fairly large pieces, as they occupy less space in your freezer, and suffer less from possible surface dehydration or freezer burn. Trim away excess fat and remove the bones from the pieces of meat that don't need to be cooked with the bone attached. You can use the bones to make stock, which you then can freeze (see Index). Aside from occupying precious space, the jagged edges of bones can easily tear through the package and expose the meat to freezer burn, which is the very thing you must try to avoid when freezing any product. For those cuts of meat that must retain the bones, it is a good precaution to crumple some plastic film or freezer paper and place it on top of the bone before wrapping the meat.

The meat should either be wrapped in freezer paper or in plastic film or plastic bags. If you use freezer wrapper, squeeze out as much air as possible and tape the ends; and squeeze out the air from bags also, then seal the openings either with tape or, preferably, with metal "twists" so that you can reuse the bag. Separate cutlets or thin slices by a sheet of polyethylene in between, so that they'll be easier to thaw, and use the desired amount and replace what you don't need in the bag or package for further freezing. Ground meat you plan to use for hamburgers can be shaped into patties and each patty should also be separated in the same way.

If you buy meat that has already been packed in paper or plastic trays covered with plastic film it is advisable to re-wrap it, unless you plan to use it within a few days as this packaging does not provide sufficient protection for prolonged freezing.

Beef and lamb in large chunks and steaks keep up to one year, provided the temperature is kept at zero. Decrease this maximum storage period by about two months for smaller pieces, and two months more for ground meat. Liver and heart freeze for up to four months.

Veal keeps about two months less than beef and lamb. Veal liver or heart keeps up to three months.

Pork can be frozen for six months if in large chunks, four months if ground or in sausage form. Bacon will keep three months; liver and heart for two months.

Other variety meats keep as follows: tongue, four months; kidneys, three months; sweetbreads, brains, and tripe, one month. Tripe should be cooked before freezing, so you might prefer to can it or pickle it instead.

• POULTRY •

Whole poultry keeps in the freezer a little longer than cut poultry, but you may want to sacrifice the extra period of safe storage and freeze birds whole only when you plan to roast them, as a whole chicken or turkey occupies much more space than when cut in pieces. Roasters should be trussed for easier wrapping. If packed in sturdy plastic bags (which is perhaps the easiest way), squeeze the air out of the bags before sealing. It is not recommended to stuff any bird before freezing, as the safe freezing period would be reduced to about two months. Freeze giblets separately, as they have a shorter storage span than the bird itself.

It is easier to halve or quarter broilers or fryers before packing. Fryers may be cut even smaller: Each breast half can be halved and the legs can be separated into thighs and drumsticks. Particular care should be taken in wrapping or packing cut poultry, as the bones can easily pierce holes and readmit the air you squeezed out, producing freezer burn. Use very sturdy polyethylene bags or wrap first in freezer paper, then put in bags.

The storage periods for chicken and turkey are as follows: whole, one year; parts, about seven or eight months; smaller pieces, about five months; giblets, about three months.

Duck or geese can be stored for six to eight months. Oil glands should be removed from duck and geese before freezing, or they'll impart a bitter taste to the entire bird.

• WILD GAME BIRDS •

Treat these as poultry, but if you have a hunter in the house who provides you with these delicacies, take special care to eviscerate the birds as soon as possible after they have been killed.

The need for aging before eating applies to game even more than to other types of meat. After the birds have been bled and emptied, they should be hung from their beaks in a cool place, their feathers still on, for about a week or their meat will be too tough. After this period, pluck the feathers, cut off feet and head (although the brain is considered a true delicacy), and pack as whole poultry for freezing.

People who have never tasted game birds that have been aged may be repelled by the idea of leaving them hanging for a whole week. The true gourmets, however, enjoy a real treat, that of tasting game birds at their best. In fact, gourmet hunters believe game birds should be hung from their beaks until they fall to the ground and the beak remains attached to the hook, a process that takes about two weeks or longer. This may be overdoing things a bit, though we have tasted game aged this long and found the meat really tender and tasty. We believe that for most birds of medium size one week is the right aging period; a day or two can be added for larger birds. The temperature in the cool place should be well above freezing, but no higher than 50 degrees Fahrenheit.

Skin, eviscerate, and bleed small game animals, then chop off head, cut up, and pack as chicken. We believe that a few days in a cool place after eviscerating but before skinning helps to tenderize the meat and improve its taste. Hang animal by the hind feet and check the eyes after a couple of days, as the eyes are the first part to visibly decompose; when they begin to lose their clear look and firmness, skin the animal and prepare it for freezing. For small to medium rabbits or hare, a period of three to four days should be long enough. Larger rabbits have tougher meat so, if possible, they should be aged about five days.

Don't expect to be able to cook this type of game as you would cook chicken or other meats; the meat has a different texture, almost no fat, and a tougher composition. Marinating the meat for a couple of days as it thaws, if you have frozen it, helps to tenderize it and removes some of the gamey taste. Soak the bird in some dry red wine and about one-fourth this amount of vinegar, add spices, and make sure the liquid covers the meat.

If you have a hunter in the family who might bring home big game (deer, elk, and related species) the best thing for you to do is to arrange to bring the animal to a nearby freezer plant, which will skin it, cut it, and prepare it for your freezer, as to do this yourself would be a very difficult job. Both young and not-so-young animals have rather tough meat if not aged, so these animals should be aged for about one month. The professional butcher who is going to cut and prepare the animal can usually take care of aging it as well, though you may have to convince him that that is what you want, since he will find it easier to freeze the animal immediately.

160

It is very important, however, that the hunter in your family knows how to bleed, eviscerate, and clean the animal while he is still in the woods before bringing it home. The sooner this is done, the tastier the meat. Otherwise, big game meat tends to acquire a rather strong taste, most of which is caused by delay in cleaning. After the animal has been bled and emptied, don't worry if you can't take it to the butcher for a day or so. Leave it in a cool place, hanging if possible.

• FISH •

Fish that has not been prepared in advance but comes to you directly (and quickly!) from the ocean, lake, or brook must be cleaned immediately. Chop off the heads of larger fish, after removing the entrails. To clean the fish, insert the point of a scissors into the aperture near the tail, cut open up to near the head, and scoop out all the insides. Then remove the scales by holding the fish by the tail and running a sharp knife toward the head with a scraping motion. (Some fish, such as trout, have no scales, so they don't need to be scraped.) Now wash the fish under running water, removing all the blood from the inside. Remove the gills with scissors, wash again, and pat dry. Delicate fish, or medium-size fish, can be cooked with the head still on. In this way it retains all its juices and the meat doesn't fall off. Freeze the fish without an outer wrapper, then pack and seal as soon as it is frozen.

Freeze small fish spread out on trays, then seal them into a plastic bag, or place them in a rigid container, cover with water, leaving some head space, and keep in horizontal position until the water freezes.

Lean fish will keep up to a year, at zero temperature. Lean fish include, among others, bass, blowfish, cod, flounder, fluke, haddock, halibut, perch, pickerel, pike, porgy, red snapper, smelt, snook, sole, swordfish, trout, and whiting.

Fatty fish can be stored in the freezer up to six months at zero. The most common varieties are bonito, carp, catfish, eels, herring, mackerel, millet, pompano, salmon, shad, squid, striped bass, tuna, and whitefish.

· SEAFOOD ·

Lobsters must be boiled before freezing, about fifteen minutes if medium size, ten if smaller. It is preferable to freeze small lobsters weighing up to two pounds, as the larger ones are frequently tough.

After cooking, split in half, remove the sac behind the head, devein, and place the two halves together again. Wrap in freezer paper tightly and freeze. You can also remove them from their shells, if you need extra freezer space, though this tends to make the meat tougher.

Soft-shelled crabs don't need to be cooked in advance, but they must be cleaned thoroughly. Cut off the head and squeeze each crab to remove the green liquid behind the eyes, which is bitter. Remove the rest of the soft shell with scissors. Pack in layers, separating each layer from the next with a sheet of plastic. Wrap and seal.

Handle oysters and clams with the utmost quickness. Wash them thoroughly several times both in running water and in a bath. Open the shells with sharp knife or place in lukewarm oven until they open by themselves. Put aside the liquor, wash them in a very mild salted solution with water, then drain. Package in rigid containers, in their own liquor to which you can add water, if insufficient. Cover completely with liquid, but leave head space.

· FRUITS AND VEGETABLES ·

With the possible exception of meat, seasonal fruits and vegetables are the most rewarding products you can freeze, especially if you grow them yourself. The advantage of freezing them is that the taste and quality of most fruits and vegetables are only slightly altered by this process. For the most part, fruits can be used just thawed, as if they were fresh, and jams and dried fruits are best for making pies. Remember also that many fruits and vegetables can be stored successfully in other ways, so freeze only those that turn out best if frozen. Save the frozen vegetables only for side dishes, since you can use dried vegetables for soups, stews, and casseroles. Most root vegetables, for example, keep very easily if stored in a vegetable cellar, and need not take up space in a freezer.

So many varieties of fruits and vegetables grow in the United States that we will mention only those that are fairly common in most of the country. We suggest you contact the local agricultural services in your state for more precise information as to the best varieties suitable for freezing in your locality. At the end of this chapter is a list of foods, including fruits and vegetables, that we do not recommend for freezing for one reason or another.

If properly prepared and packed, fruits and vegetables can be satisfactorily stored in your freezer for ten to twelve months (except for citrus fruit, which should not be stored longer than six months), so you can have a whole year's supply to carry you over until the next growing season.

Most vegetables and some fruits need blanching before they are frozen. Whenever possible, steaming rather than boiling is preferable, as vitamins are better retained by that method. Check again the chapter on canning for a description of steamers, and follow those general guidelines for freezing. Specific instructions for steaming as well as blanching in water are given for each fruit or vegetable under the separate listings, but here are some general directions.

When steaming, always make sure that there is sufficient water at the bottom and that it is boiling. The water should not reach the bottom of the steaming basket, however.

If it is not possible to steam, you can boil foods in a small quantity of water, or no water at all if they contain a large amount of natural moisture, as does spinach.

As you prepare the products and pack them, start freezing as you go. Don't wait till you finish packing the whole batch before freezing them; speed is of the essence if you want to preserve all nutrients. The first step is to cool your cooked fruits and vegetables by plunging the containers into a tub filled with large chunks of ice. (Ice cubes are little help and melt too fast.) An easy way to make large blocks of ice is to freeze water previously in a few of your plastic containers or any other type except glass.

— FRUITS —

It is best to freeze fruits in their natural state—that is, without adding any sweetener. They are hence natural and more versatile; when you take them out of the freezer, you can use them in any way you want. Unfortunately, the number of fruits that can be packed in this fashion is relatively small, but you may wish to experiment with other fruits yourself and perhaps succeed in widening the possibilities. Perhaps the best thing would be for you to freeze one container in dry, unsweetened pack, while you are freezing the rest of the batch in the more conventional way. The looks of that particular fruit when frozen in its natural state may have suffered, but if the quality and flavor suit you and if you don't mind the slightly altered look of the fruit, you may decide to omit sugar in the future. A good rule, though, is to use up unsweetened fruit more quickly than the rest, since it usually cannot stand long storage.

Most of the fruits that are to be frozen without sweeteners, however, will need the addition of ascorbic acid (see Index) in order to preserve their looks. Lemon juice can also be used, but it may render the fruit too sour and it is not generally as effective as ascorbic acid. Some fruits, such as citrus fruit and certain berries, contain enough vitamin C so that you may omit this addition or use it in a much smaller quantity.

The amount of ascorbic acid to be added will not be specified under individual listings; so we are not very scientific about this, and you don't have to be too precise either. Within limits, there is no risk involved in eating too much vitamin C, so you are only adding this nutrient to the fruit you freeze, aside from helping the fruit retain its appearance and texture.

You can pack in their natural state (sometimes in water pack) most berries, such as blueberries, currants, gooseberries, cranberries, and blackberries; as well as figs, pineapples, plums, grapes, and rhubarb.

All fruits, except berries if fairly clean, must be washed thoroughly but gently before packing, especially if they have been sprayed with pesticides or other harmful substances. Immerse whole fruit (before cutting) in ice water, a little at a time.

164

Move it about with your hands, taking care not to bruise it. If fruit needs a really thorough washing, either repeat (changing the water) or place colander with fruit under gently running water. Soft or delicate types of fruit, such as some kinds of berries, do best just submerged in water rather than standing under running water. Do not keep in water longer than necessary, or you will risk waterlogging the fruit, thereby losing flavor and nutrients. Allow the fruit to dry spread out on a clean cloth or, for fruit that doesn't bruise easily, pat it dry with cloth to speed up drying.

As we mentioned before, most fruits tend to darken when peeled or during the freezing process. To avoid such discoloration, there are a few anti-oxidants you can use, but ascorbic acid is by far the best. Some preparations you can buy in powder form at specialized stores also contain citric acid, and some are sold in tablets. We would recommend your buying genuine ascorbic acid; the other preparations sometimes contain sweetening agents of dubious nature, and the tablets often contain other substances that may leave a sediment. Most drugstores carry ascorbic acid in powder, or you can find it in stores that specialize in freezing equipment.

Unless otherwise indicated, dissolve the ascorbic acid in a small quantity of water, but make the solution at the last moment so that it won't lose its potency. In case you are going to use it in syrup and you have made your syrup in advance, add the ascorbic acid directly to the syrup at the last moment, stir, and use.

There are just a few ways to pack fruit. The correct method and amount of anti-oxidant to use follow:

(1) *Unsweetened, or natural*: A solution of about one-half teaspoon of ascorbic acid is usually mixed in about one pint of water and sprinkled on the fruit, and the fruit gently mixed so that the anti-oxidant can be well distributed. The fruit may be whole or cut. If it is not too big, we usually prefer it uncut. Head space is not necessary if there is a little space between the fruit.

(2) *Dry sugar pack*: Anti-oxidant solution (see above) is sprinkled on the fruit as for unsweetened fruit, then the sugar is sprinkled directly on the fruit. The fruit is then mixed and packed. The amount of sugar depends on the fruit. The sugar tends to draw out the juice from the fruit in just a few minutes, and the sugar then acts as a preserving agent. We prefer our fruits as natural as possible, and tend to stay low on the amount of sugar. Beyond this minimum amount, which is approximately five tablespoons per pound of fruit, it is a question of taste. Only a little head space is necessary with this method.

(3) *Syrup pack*: A syrup, usually made by using three cups of sugar for each quart of water, is added when packing the fruit. For most fruits we use a lower percentage of sweetener, about two-and-a-half cups of sugar. But we often use half sugar and half honey, or corn syrup, or less of a percentage of honey— that is, one-and-a-half cups of sugar and one cup of honey or corn syrup. Ascorbic acid can be stirred directly into the syrup. Leave at least an inch of head space for each quart, less for a pint, more for a tall, narrow container.

(4) *Water pack*: Pour clear, cold water on the fruit after stirring anti-oxidant into the water. Leave head space as for syrup pack.

(5) *Fruit juice*, crushed fruit, or purée: Anti-oxidant is stirred directly into fruit juice, or dissolved in a little water, then sprinkled on fruit. Leave head space as for syrup pack.

Fruits that are packed in any liquid may tend to float when they are being frozen. To avoid this, crumple a piece of aluminum foil or stiff freezer paper and place it on top of the liquid, which should always cover the fruit. Then cover and freeze.

166

We will now list, alphabetically, the kinds of fruits that can successfully be frozen, with our preferences as to the kind of packing. This does not mean that they cannot or should not be frozen in other ways. Whenever possible, we omit any sweet additions.

Apples

Peel and core. Slice into twelve crescents if medium size, sixteen if large. As you slice them, sprinkle immediately with a strong ascorbic-acid solution, since they tend to darken quickly. Or, you can dip them in water and strong ascorbic-acid solution as you peel them, but don't leave in water too long. Pack and freeze as you go.

For applesauce, slice without peeling. Add one cup of water for each three quarts of apples—more if you prefer looser sauce, less if you like your sauce firm. Simmer until tender. Then force through strainer or food mill, and sweeten to taste. No antioxidant solution is needed.

Apricots

We prefer them unpeeled, but in order to prevent the skin from becoming tough during the freezing process, plunge whole apricots in boiling water for half a minute, then immediately chill in ice water. Halve and pit, then pack in syrup adding strong ascorbic-acid solution.

Make apricot purée by plunging whole apricots in boiling water for half a minute, then peel, quarter, and pass through a sieve or food mill. Add a strong ascorbic-acid solution and about six tablespoons of sugar for each quart of pulp.

Avocados

Halve and pit. Sprinkle each half thoroughly with lemon juice or strong ascorbic-acid solution or mixture of both. Wrap each half completely, leaving no air space, in aluminum foil or freezer wrap. Do not store longer than two months if you prepare them in this way.

For longer storage, scoop out and mash the pulp, mix thoroughly with ascorbic acid or lemon juice, and pack immediately.

167

Bananas

They are difficult to freeze, but you may wish to try it since there is no other way to preserve them. Some varieties don't freeze well, so experiment before freezing in quantity. Act very quickly because bananas darken almost as soon as you mash them. Before you mash them, prepare a mixture of one-half cup of sugar mixed with two teaspoons of ascorbic-acid solution for each three cups of purée. Now mash bananas and immediately mix with sugar. Be sure to defrost unopened, in refrigerator.

Do not store more than three months.

Berries

Pack unsweetened (except strawberries), leaving a little head space.

Cherries

Pack whole, unsweetened, after sprinkling with a little ascorbic-acid solution. No head space necessary.

Cherries, Sour

Pack whole, adding two cups of sugar for each two pounds of cherries if they are very sour, less if sweeter. No head space necessary.

Grapefruits

Like other citrus fruits, it is best to freeze the juice. Grapefruits can be frozen in sections too, provided you remove all seeds and membrane, add sugar and very little ascorbic acid. We prefer storing the whole fruits (see chapter on storing).

For juice, don't press oil from rind, which adds bitterness. Add instead a small amount of ascorbic acid and stir. Allow head space.

Grapes

Their consistency is similar to that of berries (see Berries), but sprinkle with stronger ascorbic-acid solution.

Mangoes

Peel, pit, and slice or cube. Add ascorbic-acid solution and pack as they are, with a little head space.

Melons (and Watermelons)

Cube or shape into balls by using potato gadget. Pack in rigid containers either in light syrup mixed with ascorbic acid or in fresh orange juice, plus a little ascorbic acid. We prefer the latter method. And don't omit the crumpled tin foil on top, to keep melons submerged while freezing.

Nectarines

Many people prefer not to peel them. But if you mind the slight toughness of the skin in the finished product, proceed as with apricots. Halve or quarter if you are going to add syrup and slice for dry pack. And don't forget the ascorbic-acid solution.

Oranges

See Grapefruits, but omit anti-oxidant.

Peaches

Peel without immersing in boiling water, or fruits will look odd after thawing. Halve or slice and immediately plunge into ice water to which you have added ascorbic acid. This water pack is best for peaches.

Pears

This fruit does not freeze very well. But if you still want to freeze them, try a small batch first and see if you like them. Like some other fruits, they darken very fast. Peel, cut in halves or quarters, core, and immediately dunk in one gallon of cold water with two teaspoons of ascorbic acid. Pack in syrup.

Persimmons

They must be *very* ripe, when the fruit is extremely soft and the skin translucent. Cut into crescent sections. Remove all the whitish filaments that tend to give this fruit a tongue-puckering taste. Scrape fruit off the skin, sprinkle with strong ascorbic-acid solution, and dry pack without sugar, leaving head space. For varieties that are not very sweet you may wish to add some sugar, or preferably honey—honey and persimmon go very well together. You will obtain better results if you purée first.

169

Pineapple

It freezes very well. Slices can be sprinkled with ascorbic-acid solution, then separated by cellophane sheets and packed as they are.

Plums

Pack the whole fruit directly as is. The skin may break while freezing, but we don't mind. If you plan to serve uncooked, when thawing you may wish to dip frozen fruit in cold water for about ten seconds, and peel it then, if you like.

Rhubarb

Cut stems, sprinkle with anti-oxidant solution, and pack.

Strawberries

Among the best fruits to freeze, they can be frozen whole, although this tends to alter their taste slightly. The best way is either to crush them slightly or cut them in half (you may want to quarter the ones that are very large). Sprinkle them with ascorbic-acid solution, then with three-quarters cup of sugar for each quart strawberries. Fold over gently until sugar is dissolved and their own juice is mixing with the sugar. A little head space is needed.

— VEGETABLES —

As with fruits, the best vegetables to freeze are those you can put up as soon after picking as possible. They should be tender and most of them should be picked before they become too large. They should be washed, unless they have their own pods, and all vegetables should be blanched before being stored in the freezer. To avoid this step would be an expensive mistake, because you would then eat a product largely devoid of vitamins and minerals. Proper blanching curtails the enzyme action, which the vegetables require during their growth but which continues after maturation unless it is almost entirely stopped by blanching. Underblanching is like no blanching at all, so you might as well save yourself the trouble. And overblanching, while stopping the enzyme action (or slowing it down considerably), will produce soggy, sometimes discolored vegetables. The most important thing about freezing vegetables is to be very accurate in your blanching time.

This process is done in two ways, either by plunging vegetables in a large amount of rapidly boiling water for a few minutes (specified for each vegetable) or by steaming them.

It is not advisable to blanch more than one pound of vegetables at a time, except small vegetables, such as peas and beans (for which amounts can be doubled), but make sure you replace the evaporated water as needed, since you will probably do several batches once you start the job. Add the vegetables only when the water is boiling furiously and not before. For steam blanching, start counting time when the water at the bottom of the pot is boiling, then cover tightly.

Some vegetables, such as pumpkin, sweet potatoes, and winter squash, can be cooked in the oven. They can also be cooked in pots, but again we prefer partial or total baking in the oven to retain vitamins and minerals.

As with fruits, it is important to freeze the vegetables as quickly as possible after preparation. The cooling period should be started immediately upon removing the vegetables from the fire, since this will stop the cooking process. The head space specified for other foods goes for vegetables as well. If the pieces are not compact, no head space is needed. If they are compact or in a purée, leave about one-half inch for pint-size containers, one inch for quart size, and more if the containers are tall and narrow.

Following, in alphabetical order, are vegetables that freeze well. We have either omitted or given brief explanations for the ones that we think should be preserved in some other way.

Artichokes

Only very small artichokes can be frozen satisfactorily. This means you can only freeze the ones you grow yourself, as they are otherwise almost impossible to find in this size. They should be compact, the leaves should still be tender and unopened, and the choke should not have formed yet.

Remove outermost leaves and discard (or use in soups).

Leave about one inch of stem, and cut across the top of the artichoke. Boil with the juice of one lemon for each two quarts of water added to prevent discoloration, to which these vegetables are particularly prone. For very small artichokes, blanching time is two minutes. If they are larger (but again, don't try to freeze artichokes that are larger than an egg) increase time to four minutes. Cool immediately and drain by placing them upside down on cloth. As they tend to dry up if frozen directly in a container, it is best to wrap them individually in cellophane or freezer wrap and then place them into a rigid container. Though they can be frozen for a longer time, it is best to use them within four months.

Asparagus

Separate the asparagus according to thickness of stalk into small, medium, and large, and blanch separately. Cut the woody portion until you have lengths of about five or six inches. You can use the rest of the stalks in soups or other dishes.

Blanch, in water, large spears four minutes, medium three, and small two. To steam blanch, increase timing by one minute each, but tie asparagus in bunches with thread and place in steamer, tips up. Untie while cooling and draining, but if you re-tie them before packing you'll find it much easier to steam them again when you are ready to eat them.

Beans, Green

Select stringless beans, still tender and not too large. Leave whole or cut in half after removing stems. If you prefer to leave them whole but sizes differ, blanch separately, adding one minute to the blanching time for the larger size. We do not recommend cutting vegetables as they lose some of the nutrients they contain with each cut.

Blanch in water three minutes, or steam blanch for four minutes.

Beans, Shell

Except for lima beans, other types are better preserved and are more nutritious if dried.

172

It is best to freeze only select beans, and we suggest the following test to determine which beans to freeze and which to cook immediately.

Stir one cup of salt in about one gallon of water at room temperature. Add shelled beans and stir again to allow the sinkers to sink and the floaters to float. The floaters are your choice. Lift them out with a strainer and proceed to blanch them, saving the very large ones and the sinkers for cooking, and using only small and medium beans for freezing.

Blanch, in water, medium beans three minutes and smaller beans two minutes. For steam blanching, add one minute to each.

Beet Greens

While beets don't freeze well, by no means discard the beet greens, because in terms of nutrition they are the best part of this vegetable. And they can be frozen very well.

Select tender leaves and wash thoroughly both in running water and by immersion. Blanch in boiling water for two minutes. Drain by pressing in cloth. If you prefer chopped beet greens, they can be cut with scissors, either before or after blanching.

Broccoli

Choose broccoli that have fairly thin, tender stalks. Trim part of the stems if needed, then cut lengthwise, trying to make uniform pieces. If some stems are thicker than others, slit once or twice and leave flowerlet whole.

Blanch the larger pieces in water four minutes, the medium three, and the small two.

If steam blanching add one minute to each.

Brussels Sprouts

Remove outer leaves before washing. Trim stems, select according to size, and blanch large heads in water five minutes, medium four, and small two.

If steam blanching add one minute to each.

Carrots

The only carrots that freeze well are the very young ones. If you grow your own, pick them when they are very small. That way you can freeze them whole, without scraping them; a thorough washing is sufficient.

If the carrots you have are longer than three or four inches, scrape them gently, since the best nutrients are on the outer edge, and cut in uniform sizes, either in halves or quarters, depending on their thickness. Remove the internal part if at all woody.

According to size, blanch in water three and a half minutes if whole, three if cut.

When steam blanching add two minutes to each.

Cauliflower

Cut the head into flowerlets of uniform size but not too small. About two inches across the flowerlet is the best. You may wish to slit the stems once to help uniform blanching. Add the juice of one lemon to each gallon of boiling water, as this vegetable tends to discolor. (There is no need for lemon juice if you are blanching the purple variety, which usually turns green during cooking, unfortunately.)

Blanch pieces in water for four minutes. Add or subtract one minute if larger or smaller.

Although blanching in steam is often not recommended because of discoloration, this can of course be done with the purple variety. Add one minute to the above method. But since we prefer steam blanching, we have successfully steamed and frozen our cauliflowers with little or no discoloration by mixing a little lemon juice with one or two tablespoons of water and sprinkling the flowerlets on all sides before steaming.

Celery

We do not recommend freezing celery. It loses its crispness and can only be used for cooking. However, if you wish to add chunks of celery to your cooked dishes, choose the green variety of celery and use only the medium stems (the heart is too soft and

174

leafy, the outer stems are too tough and stringy), cut in one-inch lengths, water blanch three minutes or steam blanch four minutes.

Collard Greens

See Beet Greens.

Corn

Choose only sweet corn at the best time of year. Test with thumbnail or sharp pointed tool: If the milk oozes out, this is the best corn for freezing. Remove husks and silk.

If you wish to freeze the corn on the cob, blanch in water about six or seven minutes for large ears, five for medium, and three or four for small. After cooling, draining, and wiping dry, wrap individually with tin foil or freezer wrapper.

If you wish to freeze corn on the cob for a short period (no longer than two months) choose husks that have in no way been opened, gather each tip together with string or metal twist, place the cobs separately in the coldest part of your freezer, and after freezing place a few ears in a plastic bag, which you will seal as usual. To thaw, place corn in cold water before husking.

To save space, corn can be frozen in kernels. Proceed as above, cooking the corn on the cob. After cooling, remove the kernels with a sharp-pronged fork. Leave a little head space.

Eggplant

Select firm eggplant, no larger than medium size. Peel and cut in half-inch slices. If blanching in water, add two teaspoons of ascorbic acid per gallon of water and blanch for four minutes.

To steam blanch, cook for five minutes and add ascorbic acid to the cooling water (or sprinkle before steaming, as for cauliflower).

Pack by inserting cellophane between slices if you wish to thaw quickly.

Kale

Follow instructions for beet greens, but blanch one minute.

175

Mushrooms

These are not particularly good when frozen, as they tend to become rubbery and lose some of their taste. Dried mushrooms (see Index) are infinitely tastier.

However, if you freeze them, blanch them in water to which you have added two tablespoons of lemon juice per quart. They are best if blanched either whole (if small) or halved, but not sliced, as they become soggy. Leave in boiling water three minutes, then drain after cooling.

You need not worry about a loss of nutrients when dealing with mushrooms, since they are very low in vitamins, so you'll hardly lose any if you cut them. Of course, they are also very low in calories, and for some of us this is a great advantage!

Mustard Greens

See Beet Greens.

Okra

Choose only young pods, as the small, tender ones have very little of that gummy, slimy texture peculiar to older pods. Remove the stems and outer rims near the stem with a small, sharp knife, trying to give that end of the pods a conical shape. This is done so as not to disturb the inner juices that are so nutritious. Sort according to size. Blanch large pods in water three minutes, medium three, and small one. For steam blanching add one minute. After cooling, pat dry with cloth.

Onions

Freeze only pearl onions, whole. Blanch by boiling for three minutes, then cool and dry. Chopped onions can also be frozen, but they become rather soggy and tend to lose their taste when frozen. Then they can only be used for cooking. Chop and plunge in boiling water for less than a minute.

Peas

It is most important that you pick very tender peas, as the more mature peas are better left to commercial freezing enterprises.

At home they don't freeze well. Fortunately, for most dishes the small, tender peas are infinitely superior to the larger ones. Save those for drying, or use fresh large peas in soups and stews.

Shell and dip in boiling water for one minute, or just half a minute if very small. Double the time for steaming.

Blackeye peas are cooked by the same method, but double the blanching time.

You can also use the same test as for beans in choosing the best peas for freezing, but if you select very small peas, this is not necessary.

Peppers, Sweet or Hot

Sweet peppers don't have to be blanched before freezing, although some sources suggest blanching. A blanched pepper, however, tends to become soggy and waterlogged. The hard, unporous skin may be a deterrent to enzymatic action. But since you should not freeze them whole, except hot peppers, which are smaller, what happens to those vitamins and minerals if you freeze them without blanching? We solved the problem by blanching the peppers that we intend to cook later and we freeze without blanching those we wish to eat raw. And, purely for visual pleasure, we mix the colors whenever possible and freeze green and red peppers together.

Remove crown and seeds, after quartering, then blanch peppers, halved, in boiling water three minutes. Increase to five if steaming.

You can freeze rings for salads without blanching and blanch the other peppers.

Do not seed or cut hot peppers. Just stem and freeze.

Potatoes

Only fully cooked and peeled potatoes can be frozen successfully, although it does seem impractical to freeze potatoes, which store so well for so long.

And French fries are so awful when frozen that we don't recommend them. But if you insist, fry them until almost done, and store in freezer no longer than two months as they pick up a rancid taste very quickly. After freezing, fry them again quickly in deep fat.

Potatoes, Sweet

Cook thoroughly before freezing. The preferred method is to bake them in the oven until done. To freeze whole, in halves, or in slices, cool after baking by putting them in a bowl in ice water, peel, halve or slice, and dip each piece individually in ascorbic-acid solution or in a mixture of one-half cup lemon juice per each quart of water. You can also purée them, and prevent oxidation by adding two teaspoons of orange or lemon juice to each pound of purée. Leave head space when packing.

Pumpkin or Winter Squash

Cook fully before freezing, either by boiling, steaming, or (preferably) baking after peeling and removing seeds. Since it has to be mashed before packing, you can cut it in small pieces so it will cook faster. Cool by placing bowl in ice water, stirring to hasten the cooling process. Cooling a small quantity at a time also hastens the cooling period. Leave head space when packing.

Spinach

Wash thoroughly under running water and by immersion. Blanch in water one minute if leaves are tender, two minutes if leaves are tougher or larger. Squeeze dry by making a ball and pressing between your hands, but save water for cooking soups, etc.

Use tougher leaves for chopped spinach, cutting with scissors or putting through food chopper after blanching, before cooling in bowl. This also helps remove some of the water.

Squash, Acorn

Halve and remove seeds, brush abundantly with butter or good-quality oil, and bake until tender. Let cool at room temperature, then wrap each half in tin foil or freezer paper.

Freezing, though, seems superfluous, since acorn squash, like most hard-rind types of squash, can be stored in a root cellar or other cool place.

Squash, Summer

Select rather small squash. Without peeling, but after removing hard portion at both ends, cut into half-inch slices. Blanch in water three minutes, in steam four. After cooling, dry by patting with cloth.

Swiss Chard

See Spinach. Freeze stems separately, like celery.

Tomatoes

These cannot be frozen whole, as their skin cracks and their taste is altered. There are so many more satisfactory ways to preserve tomatoes that we suggest you freeze only tomato purée and juice; especially tomato juice, since cooked purée can be preserved in many other satisfactory ways.

For tomato juice, choose very ripe tomatoes, trim, and core. Simmer each quart for about ten minutes. Press through fine mesh sieve or food mill, or place double layer of cheesecloth on strainer and force pulp through. Cool immediately by placing bowl in ice water. Pour into containers or jars, allowing plenty of head space. Add salt, pepper, lemon juice, or other spices after you thaw in refrigerator.

Turnip Greens

See Spinach.

Wild Greens

Freeze dandelion, pokeweed, sorrel, and such as you do spinach.

Zucchini

See Summer Squash.

• MISCELLANY •

— BAKED GOODS —

Baked goods can be preserved for a long period of time and thaw rather quickly. Most unbaked products don't give very good results and can only be frozen for a relatively short period of time, so freeze only baked goods. Breads, cookies, and biscuits of any type give satisfactory results. Pies and cakes can also be frozen successfully if they are prepared as if you planned to serve them immediately. Leave pies in their metal trays, and if you have other metal pie plates of the same size, put an empty one on top of the pie, seal all around with freezer tape, and freeze in horizontal position. (Make sure you don't use any of those pie trays from commercially baked pies that have holes at the bottom.) For cakes, add the icing when you are ready to serve.

Allow any baked product to cool completely before freezing.

Breads, pies, and all baked goods except cakes can be thawed very quickly by placing them in moderate oven for ten to twenty minutes, depending on size. Bread slices can be sawed off and toasted immediately.

— CONCENTRATED BROTHS —

It is very easy to make good soups if you have prepared in advance a concentrated broth and frozen it. This can be done by continuing to cook any stock you may have made with meat or chicken. Simply strain the broth that has cooked. Allow to cool (or speed up process by placing in freezer for an hour or so), skim fat, and continue to cook by simmering very gently, partly covered, until a lot of the moisture has evaporated. It can be reduced to half the original amount, one quarter, or less. Allow to cool, then package in rigid containers, leaving head space, and freeze. Label properly as to type of broth and amount of water to add when ready to reconstitute. If you plan to use only small quantities of this consommé at a time, you can freeze in ice-cube trays, then put the blocks in a plastic bag. You can use the same procedure for vegetable broths.

— Dairy Products —

Milk

Only homogenized milk can be frozen, in its own container provided it's still sealed. Store no longer than three months.

Cream

We suggest you don't attempt to freeze cream. Only very heavy cream can be frozen, and only if pasteurized, but the result is not satisfactory. If you wish, you may freeze (uncovered, on a tray) little mounds of cream you have previously whipped, either sweetened or natural. When the mounds are ready, wrap each blob separately, then pack in rigid container.

Butter

It must be made of pasteurized sweet cream, or it won't last very long in your freezer. Sweet butter can be stored for up to one year, and salted butter five to six months, since the salt speeds up the process of rancidity in fats. Leave the butter in the same package in which you bought it, but overwrap with freezer paper.

Cheese

Some cheeses freeze well, others don't. As a rule, we don't see much reason to freeze anything but fresh cheese, whose life is rather short-spanned otherwise. But there are a few cheeses that cannot be frozen. Of the most common, cream cheese, ricotta, or creamed cottage cheese cannot be frozen, but we suggest you try this method with other fresh cheeses.

Most other cheeses can be stored so easily elsewhere that you may prefer using your valuable freezer space for other foods. If you would like to try it, though, wrap cheese in family-size portions, and double-wrap if it is particularly strong-smelling. Freeze only a small portion of each type of cheese the first time you attempt it, as some qualities may separate or crumble, their consistency may change, or they may lose some of their flavor.

Leave head space when packing fresh cheeses for freezing.

Ice Cream

Try to purchase (or pack, if you make it yourself) in plastic containers, rather than cartons. Commercially manufactured ice cream can be stored up to four months if made with high-fat cream, for only two months if with low-fat. If you wish to preserve ice cream in waxed cartons for more than two months, overwrap before storing in freezer, or repack in plastic containers.

Eggs

Although it is not impossible to freeze eggs, they should be shelled first, then lightly beaten. We remind you that other methods of preserving eggs (see Index) in their shell will keep them longer and are more successful.

• FOODS NOT RECOMMENDED FOR FREEZING •

So many foods can be frozen successfully that we haven't even attempted to list them all. So it is perhaps more practical to list here those foods that give poor results. They don't turn out well because their appearance, flavor, and texture undergo considerable change during the process of freezing, but they are safe to eat.

Bananas that have not been puréed and treated
Cabbage, whole and unchopped
Celery (see exception in this chapter)
Cheese toppings for casseroles
Cheeses (check dairy products in this chapter for exceptions)
Cloves and many other spices (cooked in a dish)
Cream, unpasteurized
Crumb toppings for casseroles
Egg whites
Eggs, hard-cooked
Fried foods of any sort
Garlic
Herbs
Milk, unpasteurized
Onions, except pearl onions or chopped onions for cooking
Peppers, in cooked dishes
Potatoes
Rutabagas
Sauces containing milk, cheese, or with a high fat content
Sauces thickened with flour or cornstarch
Starches, such as pasta, rice, etc., in cooked dishes
Turnips
Vegetables, raw, especially salad greens

To this list we would also add salt when it is used in dishes that contain fatty substances of any kind, as it tends to quicken the process of rancidity.

You can, of course, still freeze these dishes, but we suggest you cut their storage time in half if you do.

JAMS, JELLIES, SYRUPS, AND ASSORTED CONFECTIONS

It's hard to think of sugar as a preservative, so distinct in taste and association is it from salt or vinegar, but it is acid-stimulating and a very efficient preservative. You will need lots of sugar (or sugarlike sweeteners) to work your way through this chapter, which will show you how to preserve with it a cornucopia of fruits, vegetables, nuts, and other kernels.

The only two pieces of specialized equipment that you will probably want on hand are a jelly thermometer and a jelly bag. The thermometer will be an advantage if you plan to make either jelly or candy. The proper thermometer is a heavy-duty one of heatproof glass with an attachment for fastening it to the side of a kettle and a horizontal, clockfacelike dial for you to determine the heat of boiling liquids.

When using the disk-and-screwband type of jar for jams or jellies, fill your jars up to overflowing, then let out any air bubbles that formed by sliding a knife blade in and around the edges. Then, quickly, slide on the inside disk, scooping off a bit of the jelly or jam as you do it. Fit on the screwband top and screw it down tight to force out any air that may have remained inside.

You can, with a little dexterity, fashion a fairly airtight seal with tin foil or heavy-duty wax paper, tying it down firmly all around with wire, string, stout rubber bands, or decorative ribbon. You should, however, lessen your storing time if you use this kind of seal.

Since there are some old-country home preservers who don't feel they are really "putting things up" unless they put a paraffin topping over their marmalades, a few directions for it follow. Such paraffin sealing is not necessary, however, if you use Mason or Ball jars.

Handle paraffin with great care and keep a small metal teapot for this use alone.

Buy paraffin in blocks. Break it into small pieces into a teapot, put the teapot on the rack in the water-bath canner, and add water to the kettle halfway up the sides of the teapot. Boil until paraffin has melted sufficiently to pour. This is safer than heating the paraffin in a small pot directly on the fire; it may take slightly longer to reach pouring consistency, but the danger of fire is considerably reduced.

Now pour a small quantity of the runny paraffin directly on top of the jelly or jam in the glass (which you should not fill to overflowing). Tilt the glass this way and that so that the wax runs all over and adheres to the edges of the glass. Let that thin layer harden, then repeat with a second thin layer, so that it runs all over and forms a complete seal.

Remember, don't use paraffin so hot that it will melt the food you are sealing with it.

Cooking jams or jellies by the clock is folly; it is impossible to accurately state the exact amount of time they will take, for the acid content of the fruit and a number of other factors are influential. An undercooked jam or jelly will ferment, because the moisture has not sufficiently evaporated. A preserve that is overcooked will be hard or crystallized or too sweet; its flavor, appearance, and texture will suffer.

The jelly thermometer will be useful to you since boiling jelly should be allowed to reach 220 degrees Fahrenheit, and jams a degree or so higher, but you will still want to use the "sheet test" to ascertain the precise moment to stop cooking a jam or jelly. Dip a cold metal spoon in the cooking mixture, then hold it a foot or so above the kettle, turning it sideways so the liquid runs off the side. If the liquid coats the spoon and forms a thin sheet as it falls off, your jelly is cooked.

Or pour a tablespoonful into a saucer and put it into the freezing compartment of your refrigerator for a minute or so. If the liquid solidifies to the proper consistency, your jelly is done. But making one or two batches of jelly will make you feel more secure about your judgment, and you will have the satisfaction of cooking by "eye" and by "feel." The testing of a clear jelly is more imperative than the testing of jam since consistency is more crucial a matter, but you should test both.

In all recipes for specific jellies or jams (into which category we have put both marmalades and conserves), you will notice that specified times are always qualified. With the aid of your sheet test, you can for future reference write in the exact number of minutes you boil each fruit as you make the recipe.

Jelly bags are absolutely essential to the home jelly-maker. They can be purchased ready-made, but you can make them very easily. A jelly bag is only a drawstring bag made of muslin or several thicknesses of cheesecloth. You put the fruit pulp in, draw the strings closed, and suspend the bag to drip over a bowl or kettle. You don't need to make a drawstring top if the bag is long enough to knot the top over some means of suspension.

Scales will be useful (see Index). Spoons should be of wood.

You will want on hand such kitchen utensils as dippers, skimmers, spatulas, knives, mashers, sieves, pots, pans; and, of course, a number of jelly glasses or jars (that can be sterilized) with airtight lids as well as a supply of wax paper and tin foil.

A marble-top kitchen table is especially good for the making of some candies. Formica tops will do as well, or in the absence of either marble or Formica, a large china platter.

Pectin is the substance, present in ripe fruits, that forms a jelly when it combines with sugar and acid. Some fruits have more pectin than others. Apples, for example, are the prime suppliers of this vital colloid in this country, with citrus fruit and grapes probably running a close second. If you make a jelly from a non-fruit (a vegetable, herb, flower, or other plant) or even some fruits, you will need to add pectin in some form. Commercial pectin is sold in liquid or powdered form, but you can make your own.

Use hard, tart apples of the cooking variety. You can even use fallen apples, provided they are ripe and relieved of any bruised spots. Remove the stems and chop or slice thinly. Don't pare or core them. Put apples into saucepan and add five cups of water for each two pounds of apples. Bring to a boil and continue to boil on a high flame for twenty minutes. Remove from fire and pour into a dampened jelly bag. Let it drip at its own speed, without your pressing or squeezing too much, until all the liquid has come out, then put the juice aside.

Now measure the pulp left in the jelly bag. In a saucepan combine the pulp with an equal volume of water, bring to a boil, and boil for twenty minutes. Strain as before.

Combine the two juices in a shallow saucepan or skillet, wide enough so that the liquid is no more than two inches deep. Bring the combined juice to a boil and continue to boil rapidly for at least a half-hour, or until the liquid has been reduced two-thirds, or is one-third of its previous volume.

You can use this liquid pectin immediately, or you can pour it into hot, sterilized jars, cover tightly, and store in a cool place. It will keep for months.

The addition of sugar is one of the best and surest ways of preserving foods for short or longer periods of time, at home or commercially. (Or the addition of another sweetening agent.) So accustomed is the American palate to the taste of food sweetened with sugar that we are no longer able to take pleasure from the natural flavors of all good foods thus sweetened. Cane sugar is the most widely used, though the product of the sugar beet is sometimes used by the food industries as a sweetener.

You may prefer to substitute honey for sugar. If you do so in the recipes that follow, keep in mind that honey is a more concentrated sweetener and that you'll need between half and two-thirds as much, depending on the quality of your honey. Consider also that its flavor is far from identical to that of sugar. Moreover, honey is already liquid (some brands are more liquid than others) and hence does not have to be made into a syrup as does sugar. On the other hand, the density of honey varies and to some of the more viscous varieties you will want to add water. Honey is hygroscopic, which means it takes on moisture, an argument for the substitution of honey in baking, since it keeps fresh better than sugar. And honey does not go through the complicated refining processes that bring lily-white sugar to our tables in a granulated form, but is a pure, natural product.

You may want to substitute corn syrup, molasses, or maple syrup for sugar in your cooking and preserving. These syrups behave more like honey than like sugar in cooking, but consider nevertheless how they may affect taste and color before you try them out.

Avoid all copper pots, even tin-coated. Stainless steel is best but aluminum is also good, provided you don't use aluminum containers to ferment the fruit as this may affect the color of your syrup. Avoid also enameled pots as they tend to retain heat too long, and you may not be able to regulate the temperature of the syrup.

• JAMS, MARMALADES, AND CONSERVES •

The preparation of jams and these related treats is a bit simpler than making jellies and less time-consuming because you don't go through the jelly-bag dripping process, which sometimes stretches jelly-making out over two days. On the other hand, because you don't strain the juice from your fruit (or vegetable), you must select the fruits with even more care than for jelly-making. Generally speaking, you will want fruits that are sound and perfectly ripe, for their color and general appearance are more important in jams.

Jam-making is basically a two-step process: First clean and prepare the fruit, slicing, peeling, coring, pitting, or whatever, then soften it, if necessary, by mashing or soaking or a little boiling in water. Secondly, you add the sugar and cook to thicken. During this cooking the fruit gives up some of its moisture and combines with the sugar; and the natural pectin in the fruit provides some jellying. It isn't crucial to remove the jam or conserve from the heat at any particular moment, as it is with jelly.

Some home jam-makers prefer to use commercial pectin because the cooking time is reduced, and it seems to maintain the color and flavor of the fruit better. The addition of pectin dictates the use of more sugar. Others cut their sugar with salt, claiming that you use about half the amount of sugar that way, and that no one can detect the salt after the jams have been stored for several weeks.

The recipes that follow embrace all these methods and provide, we hope, a satisfying variety of foods. If you are more adventurous than we have been in putting different fruits together in jams, we'd like to hear about your most successful effects.

— APPLE GINGER JAM —

This recipe comes to us from friends in England, where it is a popular concomitant to high tea.

> *approx. 4 lbs. apples*　*2 tsp. powdered ginger*
> *1 cup water*　*(or 1 tbs. ginger root)*
> *sugar*　*juice and grated rind*
> *of 1 lemon*

Peel and core apples. Boil in the water until soft. Then strain the applesauce through a coarse sieve and weigh it. Add three-quarters cup of sugar for each pound of sauce. Bring to a boil again and skim. Stir in the ginger, lemon juice, and rind. Now boil without stirring until the right consistency has been reached. Pour into sterilized jars and cover tightly.

189

— APPLE PEAR CONSERVE —

4 cups sugar   *juice of 1 large lemon*
3 cups pared, chopped pears   *1½ cups chopped walnuts*
3 cups pared, chopped apples   *(or hazelnuts)*

Put all ingredients except nuts into a pot. Cook slowly for about twenty minutes. Add walnuts, stir in, then pour into hot jars and seal immediately. You may substitute peaches for the pears in this conserve.

— APRICOT JAM —

This is one of the best of jams and simple to make.

Wash and drain apricots and halve them. If very ripe, pass through a sieve directly; if not ripe, place in a pot, add a little water, and cook for a few minutes before straining. Add two-thirds the amount of sugar and cook to the proper consistency before sealing in jars.

You can add to this jam some of the seeds from inside the pits of the apricots. Boil for twenty minutes, slice, and put them into the jars just before pouring in the jam.

— BANANA AND APPLE JAM —

Peel and core three-fourths of a pound of yellow apples and two pounds of bananas. Cut both into thin slices. Add about two tablespoons of water and one tablespoon of lemon juice, and simmer slowly until you can easily mash the pulp with a fork. Now strain the mixture, weigh it, and add two-thirds the amount of sugar or a little less. Simmer another half-hour; pour into jars.

— BEET PRESERVE —

approx. 4 lbs. beets   *1 tbs. grated ginger root*
2½ lbs. sugar   *(or ½ tbs. powdered ginger)*
juice and rinds of 2 lemons   *handful of walnuts or almonds, peeled and chopped (optional)*

Scrub unpeeled beets under running water, then slice thin. In water to cover, simmer them about fifteen minutes. Add sugar, lemon juice and rinds, and the ginger and stir in. Bring to a boil, then simmer for about an hour or until sufficiently thickened. Add nuts (if desired) for the last five minutes or so of cooking. Pour into sterilized jars and seal tightly.

— Blackberry and Apple Jam —

1 lb. peeled, cored apples   grated rind of 1 lemon
½ cup water   pinch of cinnamon
1 lb. blackberries   2 lbs. sugar

Put apples and water in a pot and simmer, stirring meanwhile, until they begin to soften. Add blackberries, lemon, and cinnamon and cook gently until all the fruit is soft. Stir in sugar and boil rapidly until the jam has thickened. Pour into sterilized jars and seal tightly.

— Blackberry-Whortleberry Jam —

6 cups blackberries
water
1 cup whortleberries, ripe and green
7 cups sugar
6 ozs. liquid pectin

Pick over and wash the blackberries, removing stems and caps. Crush and combine with water in saucepan. Bring to a boil, then lower heat and simmer, covered, for five minutes. Put through a coarse sieve, discarding seeds. Pick over and wash whortleberries. Combine with the pulp of the blackberries, then add water until it measures four cups. Add sugar and stir over heat. Then let it come to a boil and cook for a minute or so while you continue stirring. Remove from heat, stir in pectin, then skim and stir for five or six minutes more. Pour into jars, seal, and store.

— Blueberry Preserve —

1 qt. blueberries
½ cup water
4½ cups sugar
grated rind and juice of 1 lemon

Stem and wash blueberries. Add all the rest of the ingredients and bring slowly to a boil, stirring constantly. Then cook at a boil for an additional three or four minutes, skimming. Pour into jars, let cool, and seal tightly.

— CANTALOUPE JAM —

The cantaloupe, or muskmelon, is an obliging fruit growing all over this country in several varieties differing chiefly in size. The casaba or honeydew melon might also be treated in this way.

2½ lbs. ripe melon, peeled and diced
2½ cups sugar
grated rind of 1 orange or tangerine
(or ½ tsp. vanilla)

Put cantaloupe, mixed with sugar, in a bowl, cover, and leave in the refrigerator (or a cool place) for a day and a night. Drain off the liquid and boil it over medium heat for five or six minutes. Put back the cantaloupe and rind or vanilla and simmer, stirring occasionally, until jam has thickened. Pour into warm jars and seal tightly.

— CARROT JAM —

2 lbs. carrots
3 cups water
juice of 1 lemon
1 lb. sugar
½ tsp. freshly grated ginger
(or ¼ tsp. powdered ginger)

Choose medium-size carrots. Scrape and grate them and cook in two cups of the water, together with the lemon juice, until tender. Separately, make a syrup with the sugar and the rest of the water, add it to the carrots and cook, over low heat, stirring constantly, for about fifteen minutes or until it is of the right jam consistency. Stir in the ginger just before filling the jars. Seal tightly.

— CHESTNUT JAM I —

This chestnut jam from Italy differs somewhat from the one that follows, which is from France.

2 lbs. chestnuts
fresh fennel, or anise seeds
1 lb. sugar
brandy

Peel outer skin off chestnuts, put in a pot with enough water to cover and a handful of fennel. Boil slowly for fifteen minutes or until nuts are tender. Remove from fire and peel inner skin, reserving the cooking water. Purée nuts by passing through a sieve. Take one-half cup of the reserved cooking water, add a pound of sugar to it, stir in the chestnut purée, and boil on a slow fire, stirring constantly, for a half hour. Remove from heat, cool to lukewarm. Add a jigger of brandy for each pound of jam. Mix well and put in jars. Seal tightly.

— Chestnut Jam II —

2 lbs. shelled chestnuts
milk
water
sugar
2 vanilla beans

Boil chestnuts until soft in a mixture of half milk, half water. Purée them in your blender (or other device), then weigh or measure the purée. Add an equal amount of sugar, the vanilla beans, and a half cup or so of water. Warm slowly, stirring constantly. Jam is done when it comes away from the bottom of the pan if stirred with a skimmer. Put into sterilized jars and seal tightly.

— Cherry Kipper —

The hardest part here is pitting the cherries; it must be done by hand, carefully, so as to preserve their shape and the integrity of their skins.

cherries
cider vinegar
sugar
cinnamon sticks

When you have the cherries all pitted, put them into a crock and cover them with vinegar. Put on the lid and let stand for three days. Then drain and measure the cherries. For each cup of fruit add a cup of sugar. Mix gently and let sit for three more days, stirring once or twice each day. Now distribute the fruit into very clean jars, add half a stick of cinnamon to each jar, and seal with ordinary screw-caps. No paraffin is necessary, and the cherries will keep for months in a cool place (or even in open jars or bowls in the refrigerator).

— CRANBERRY CONSERVE —

For each cup of chopped cranberries you'll need:

> _1 cup water_
> _1½ cups sugar_
> _½ cup raisins_
> _pinch of salt_
> _1 large orange_

Wash and drain fresh-picked cranberries. Chop them and add water, sugar, raisins, and salt. Peel oranges and slice rinds (removing white portion) into narrow strips. Remove orange seeds and the coarse parts of the skin and veins. Add to the rest of the mixture. Bring to a boil and then simmer until it thickens, or about half an hour. Let cool a bit and pour into warm jars. Cover tightly.

— CUCUMBER JAM —

Our British friends do extravagant things with cucumbers.

> _3 lbs. cucumbers_   _½ cup crystallized ginger_
> _3 lbs. sugar_   _(or 1 tbs. ginger root_
> _grated peel and juice_   _or 1 tsp. powdered ginger)_
> _of 2 lemons_   _brandy_

Wash cucumbers and slice but do not peel. Spread on flat surface, sprinkle with the sugar, and let stand twenty-four hours. Add lemon and ginger, put in a pot, and boil gently for an hour. Then raise heat and boil until ready to set. Pour into warm jars and put a few drops of brandy on top of each jar. Besides helping to preserve the jam, the liqueur improves its flavor. Seal tightly.

— CURRANT AND RASPBERRY JAM —

Combine fruits in ratio of one pound of raspberries to four pounds of currants. Cover with water in a pot and simmer until softened, stirring. Strain through a rather fine sieve and weigh the sauce. For each two pounds add one and a quarter cups of sugar. Cook over a slow fire, stirring constantly. When the jam has thickened, in ten to twenty minutes, remove from fire and cool to lukewarm. Seal tightly in jars.

— FIG JAM —

Figs are considered ripe for jam when they begin to ooze their milk from the bottom of the fruit. Ripe figs need very little sugar.

ripe figs

sugar

water

cinnamon, powdered or crushed

Peel figs and weigh them. Put them in a pot with one third their weight in sugar. Add a half cup of water for each pound of mixture and bring it to a boil. Add the cinnamon and let boil over a low fire for fifteen or twenty minutes, until the jam thickens. Remove from fire and pour into jars. Let cool slightly, then close tightly.

— FOREVER FRUIT —

This is a splendid mishmash of pineapple, dark cherries, peaches, and apricots, preserved with nothing but sugar. It should not be kept "forever," but for a few months it can safely be left out of the refrigerator and scooped up to spill on ice cream, pudding, or some other bland dessert. Or it can be eaten with meats and vegetables as an interesting accompaniment.

The fruit you can keep "forever" in this way does not have to be restricted to these four, and the order of combining is no hard and fast rule either. For a beautiful sauce, for four weeks, put 1 cup of fresh pineapple chunks and 1 cup of sugar, 1 cup of dark cherries, pitted, and 1 cup of sugar, 1 cup of quartered peaches, peeled, and half a cup of sugar, and 1 cup of halved apricots

195

and half a cup of sugar into a crock and cover with a plate, a week apart. Stir after each addition, then re-cover the pot to sit another week. Eat Forever Fruit shortly after the addition of the apricots. We see no reason why you couldn't just keep adding, for several more weeks, any fruit you happen to have around in excess. Just use some more sugar with each addition.

— Four-Fruit Jam —

This dish, distant cousin to Forever Fruit, comes to us from Guinea, in West Africa.

4 large oranges
1 large grapefruit
3 medium-size lemons
8 bananas
5 cups sugar

Peel and slice or dice the citrus fruit, discarding the seeds, peel and slice the bananas next (so they won't turn dark). In a large saucepan combine the fruits and the sugar; cook over medium heat, uncovered, to the right consistency, or about forty minutes. Pour into warm jars and seal tightly.

— Grape Conserve —

Gather purple (Concord) grapes for this. For each two pounds you'll need:

1 orange
½ cup nuts, any kind
½ cup raisins
3 cups sugar

Wash and drain the grapes and remove the skins by squeezing the fruit out. Save the skins. In a saucepan, bring the grape pulp to a boil and then simmer until the seeds show. Remove from the fire and pass through a sieve, discarding the seeds. Peel the orange, seed and string it, then chop both pulp and rind. Peel and chop the nuts. Combine all the ingredients but the grape skins in a saucepan. Bring to a boil, then simmer, stirring constantly, until jam thickens. The skins may be added during the last fifteen minutes of cooking. Pour into jars and seal tightly.

— Green Gooseberry Jam —

This is for gooseberries that haven't begun to ripen. Wash and dry the berries; remove their tops and tails. Measure an equal weight of sugar as berries and combine it in a pot with a cup of water to the pound of sugar. Bring to a boil and cook rapidly for fifteen minutes or to the right consistency. Remove from heat and stir a little longer before pouring into warm jars. Seal tightly when cool.

— Red Gooseberry Jam —

Use the hairy type of gooseberries, which have just turned red. Wash and dry the berries; remove their tops and tails. Put sugar equal to the weight of the gooseberries in a pot and add water, only enough to dissolve the sugar. Heat and stir until boiling, then skim well. Add gooseberries, boil them for ten minutes, and remove from fire. Cover and let stand overnight. Then bring to a boil again and boil rapidly until the jam is clear and a little thickened. Pour into warm jars, let cool, and cover tightly.

— Ground-Cherry Preserve —

The ground cherry, also known as the strawberry tomato and the winter cherry, is a species that may be dying out. It grows in the Mississippi Valley and other parts of the American Midwest. It is strongly entrenched in the nostalgic childhood memory of many a transplanted Midwesterner, one of whom gave us this recipe:

1 lb. ground cherries, husked
½ lb. sugar
grated rind of 1 orange or lemon

Combine the fruit and sugar over medium heat and cook slowly for about twenty minutes, or until the right consistency is obtained. Add the citrus rind and seal in sterilized jars.

— Kumquat Marmalade —

12 kumquats
1 medium-size orange
sugar
juice of 2 lemons

Wash the kumquats, slice very thin, and remove seeds. Peel the orange, remove seeds and strings, and chop both pulp and rind. Add three cups of sugar for each cup of combined fruit and let stand, covered, overnight in a cool place. Then put in a pot, bring to a boil, and simmer, uncovered, until the rinds are soft. Add lemon juice and one cup of sugar for each cup of cooked fruit and liquid and boil again until marmalade has thickened. Pour into warm jars, let cool, and cover tightly.

— Green Mango Jam —

Choose hard, green mangoes and grate them, without peeling them, working all around until you reach the seeds, which you will discard. Add equal amount of sugar and one-fourth the amount of honey. Peel and chop two limes for every pound of mango pulp. Mix all ingredients and bring to a slow boil, simmering them while you stir constantly for about fifteen minutes or until the jam appears to have the right consistency. Put into jars and seal when cool.

— Peach or Plum Jam —

Wash the ripe fruit; remove pit and stem. Put in a pot without water and heat over medium fire, stirring once in a while to crush the fruit, for ten minutes. Press fruit through a sieve and measure it. Add three-quarters its weight of sugar, bring to a boil, and cook for about half an hour, or until good jam consistency is achieved. Seal into clean, warm jars.

— Sweet and Sour Pepper Jam —

This jam is made with sweet peppers, either red or green, or both. It is excellent with cold cuts, or cold boiled meats, with any type of soft or semi-soft cheese, or in omelets.

For every ten large peppers you will need:

2 tsp. salt

1 lb. sugar

1½ cups cider vinegar

Wash peppers, stem, and slice open. Remove seeds and chop fine. Spread on a wide, flat surface and sprinkle with salt. Let stand three or four hours, then rinse thoroughly in cold, running water. Put peppers in a saucepan with the sugar and vinegar. Bring to a boil, then simmer until thickened, stirring frequently. Pour into warm jars and seal.

— Persimmon Jam —

Use very ripe persimmons, making sure the fruit is absolutely ripe, by which we mean extremely soft and barely held together by the skin, which should have become nearly transparent. If you don't grow your own persimmons, the fruit you buy cannot be sold at its peak, so it is usually quite unripe and a light orange in color. Leave it at room temperature for a few days at least, or until it darkens and becomes really soft. To eat or make jam out of an unripe persimmon can be a disaster, but if you wait until the fruit is really ripe, you will have a rare delicacy.

For each three pounds of fruit you will need:

1 lb. sugar

¾ cup water

grated rind and juice of ½ lemon

Remove stems and crowns; quarter the fruit and remove seeds (if any) and white filament, but leave on skin. Cut in chunks and, separately, bring water and sugar to a boil; after a couple of minutes, add the persimmons and simmer for about twenty minutes, stirring often. Then add the lemon, stir well, and boil until it has reached the right consistency. Pour into hot jars and seal when cool.

— Sweet Potato Paste —

(Dulce de Batata)

The following is a specialty from Argentina.

Wash five pounds of sweet potatoes or yams and boil them in their jackets until almost done. Then put aside the water in which they have boiled, peel, and pass them through a sieve. Weigh the pulp and for each pound measure one pint of the water (adding more if needed) and 1½ cups of sugar. Make a syrup with the water and sugar by boiling it a few minutes, then add two vanilla beans (finely crushed) or a quarter teaspoon of vanilla extract, and two tablespoons of lemon juice. Stir well, add the potatoes, and simmer until the mixture reaches a consistency considerably thicker than that of the average jam.

You can, when adding the vanilla and lemon, grate about half a teaspoon of nutmeg into the syrup, or twice that amount of fresh ginger root.

— Pumpkin Jam —

For every two pounds of pumpkin meat you will need three-quarters of a pound of sugar and the rind of one lemon. Peel and remove seeds and slice the meat very thin. Put in a pot with grated lemon rind and sugar. Cook for two hours, or until mixture reaches jamlike consistency, over a medium flame, stirring frequently and scraping the bottom of the pot. Pour into sterilized jars and seal tightly.

— Pumpkin-Pistachio Jam —

2 lbs. sliced pumpkin meat
¾ lb. sugar
½ cup orange blossom water or rose water
1 tbs. chopped pistachios

Proceed as with pumpkin jam but add the orange blossom or rose water when cooking the pumpkin meat. Mix the pistachios in well just before removing from the fire.

200

— QUINCE JAM —

5 lbs. quinces

sugar

Wash the fruit and rub it dry. Place in a large saucepan, cover with water, bring to a boil, and cook, covered, for forty-five minutes or until tender. Drain, peel, cut up, and put through a sieve or good grinder or blender. Add three-quarters cup of sugar for each cup of purée. Place over a slow flame and simmer, stirring often, until the jam has thickened. Pour into warm jars and cover tightly.

— RASPBERRY JAM (UNCOOKED) —

Here is a jam you can make without boiling. For every four pounds of ripe raspberries, use five pounds of sugar. Put the raspberries, washed and picked over, in a pot over a slow fire. Bring almost to a boil and add the sugar. Stir to dissolve the sugar but don't allow to boil. Pour into warm jars and cover tightly immediately. If the fruit is at just the right stage of ripeness, its flavor will be preserved intact.

— RHUBARB JAM —

For each pound of rhubarb stalks you will need:

½ cup water

2 lbs. sugar

grated peel of 2 oranges, or of 1 orange and 1 lemon

Wash and drain the rhubarb, then cut it into cubes. Place in a saucepan with the water, sugar, and citrus peel. Bring to a boil and then simmer constantly until the jam thickens, or about half an hour. Let cool slightly, pour into warm jars, and cover tightly.

— ROSE-HIP JAM —

Pick the roses yourself so you will know they are fresh; the flowers can be either in buds or in full bloom or a few of both. Scatter the petals in your drawers or put them aside for the making of rose-petal jam. Chop or grind the hips, trying to remove as many seeds as you can. You may want to finish the process in a blender, adding just enough water for the blender to be effective. When you remove from the blender, add two-thirds the volume of honey, mix well, and pour into sterilized jars. Cover and put the jars into a water bath. Boil for fifteen minutes, then let kettle cool for five minutes before removing jars. Check covers for air-sealing and store in a dark, cool place.

— ROSE-PETAL* JAM —

wild roses, preferably
water
honey
lemon juice

Pick a large quantity of rose petals. Wash and drain and set to work immediately so the petals won't wilt. Cut off whitish tips (if necessary). Chop and measure the chopped petals. Put into a saucepan half that amount of water and half that amount of honey. Stir, and when the water and honey have merged, add the petals and one teaspoon of lemon juice for each two cups of crushed petals. Bring to a slow boil and then simmer until jam thickens, or about a half-hour. Pour into warm jars and cover tightly.

— STRAWBERRY JAM —

Gather ripe wild or cultivated strawberries, wash, and hull them. For each pound you will want three-fourths of a cup of sugar. Grease the bottom of a pot with unsalted butter or margarine and layer the strawberries and sugar into the pot. Put the pot on very slow heat, stirring gently once in a while, without breaking up the berries. Then bring to a boil and cook for a very short time, until the jam sets. Pour into warm jars, let cool, and cover tightly.

* You don't have to limit yourself to rose petals in making jam from flowers. Try, for example, jasmine, orange, or rosemary blossoms.

— TANGERINE MARMALADE —

tangerines
sugar
lemon juice

Peel the tangerines and remove all traces of white strings and skin from both peeling and pulp; remove the seeds without losing any of the juice. Put tangerine sections into a bowl and weigh them. In a saucepan, add to the fruit an equal amount of sugar plus one tablespoon of lemon juice for each pound of tangerines. Bring to a vigorous boil and cook, stirring often, until done. It may take as long as three hours, because of the high moisture content of tangerines. When sufficiently thickened, pour into warm jars and seal.

Orange marmalade can be made the same way.

— THREE-FRUIT MARMALADE —

This citrus delight comes from the United Kingdom.

2 large oranges
2 grapefruit
2 lemons
water
3½ lbs. sugar

Wash the fruit but don't peel. Drain and cut each fruit into six or eight wedges, then slice the wedges thin. Combine in a large kettle, add enough water to cover, and stir until blended. Let stand in the refrigerator or a cool place for two or three days, stirring once or twice each day. Then cook over slow heat for half an hour. Stir in sugar, bring to a boil, and cook another fifteen or twenty minutes, stirring constantly. Skim occasionally and when it has reached marmalade consistency, pour into warm jars. Cover tightly.

— GREEN-TOMATO MARMALADE —

Use completely green tomatoes. For each two pounds you'll need:

1 tsp. salt

3 lemons

1 lb. sugar

Wash green tomatoes and drain. Coarsely chop the tomatoes and sprinkle them with salt. Peel the lemons thinly, and slice the rind into thin, short strips and boil them in a little water until tender. Slice the lemon pulp, after discarding seeds and white part, and place in saucepan. Bring to a boil and immediately add chopped tomatoes, lemon rinds, and sugar. Simmer about a half-hour, or until marmalade thickens. Pour into warm jars and cover tightly.

— WATERMELON JAM —

watermelon

vanilla beans

lemons

sugar

rum

Peel watermelon, leaving some of the white part, deseed, and cut into slices about two inches thick. Weigh slices and measure out four pounds of sugar for every five pounds of melon pulp. Leave the melon in a bowl with three or four vanilla beans and two lemons cut in thin slices. After a day and a night, add sugar, remove vanilla beans, and cook very slowly for eight to ten hours, or until it thickens sufficiently. Before taking jam from the heat, add a cup or so of rum and let it boil a few minutes more. Seal tightly in warm jars.

— WATERMELON AND ORANGE JAM —

For each two pounds of cut-up watermelon, you will need:

3½ lbs. sugar

1 or 2 lemon slices

water

3 lbs. skinned, deseeded oranges

Peel and remove seeds from watermelon; cut flesh into squares. Add one and one-half pounds of sugar and leave standing for two or three hours. Then put on fire, add lemon slices, and cook slowly for about an hour. Remove lemon. Meanwhile, peel oranges and destring them, until you have three pounds of pulp. Quarter the oranges and cut the peel of two of them into thin strips. Put oranges and peel strips into one and one-half cups of water, to which you have added two pounds of sugar. Boil for about an hour, or until thickened. When the two jams are cooked, combine them and then pour into jars and seal.

· JELLIES ·

For jelly-making, use fruit that is firm and unblemished, mixing if you wish under-ripe and just ripe but never over-ripe fruit. The under-ripe fruit contains more natural pectin, while the ripe will contribute more flavor. The process is divided roughly into three steps: first, softening the fruit and extracting the juice; second, evaporating the moisture; and third, combining the juice with the sugar.

1.   Pick over and wash the fruit. Crush berries and soft fruits, then cook them for about ten minutes, to soften. Harder fruits will need the addition of water and longer cooking, about twenty-five minutes for most. Wring out your jelly bag in hot water before putting in the fruit. If you are working toward a clear jelly, don't ever really squeeze the fruit inside the bag, though you may shift it about from time to time.

2.   Boil the juice on high heat for a short time, skimming carefully during this period. Be sure to use a large kettle, deep enough to forfend the jelly's boiling over after the sugar has been added. About five minutes is usually enough for this step. Then add the sugar and (if you're using it) the pectin.

3.   Now you are ready for the final step, the actual cooking, when the sugar and the fruit combine. This is done over lower (though still boiling) heat. It continues until the sheet test tells you the mixture is ready to jell. Continue to skim off foam if necessary.

Different fruits may be treated in different manners. Roughly, you use the same amount of sugar as fruit, though this varies somewhat from recipe to recipe. But you can make up your own jellies by adhering to the general directions. If you have not hurried the dripping by squeezing and pummeling the bag, and if you have skimmed well, you will unfailingly achieve a beautiful clear jelly, which, unless you're directed otherwise, you may improve in color and flavor by leaving in the light of a sunny window for a few days before putting away on your canning selves.

Combining wine or liqueur with fruit juice in making a jelly or a jam is a refinement that you may want to experiment with on your own. Imagine the flavors melding—Tokay apple jelly, for example, or Cognac orange. If using a liqueur, add just a few drops as you pour the jelly into the jelly glasses. Should you choose to combine a lighter wine with the fruit juice in larger ratio, just remember that you will then have to cook the juice a bit longer for it to arrive at the moment when it passes the sheet test and begins to jell.

— APPLE JELLY —

Quarter the apples and remove the stems. Leave the seeds and core in and the skin on. Cover them with water. Simmer, covered, to the mushy stage. Put into a jelly bag and let drip. Boil the juice for about five minutes to reduce. For each cup of juice you now have, add a cup of sugar. Bring back to a boil and boil until the liquid passes the sheet test, about fifteen minutes. Skim off the foam while you boil. Pour into hot, sterilized jelly glasses and seal.

— APPLE-MINT JELLY —

Add to your supplies a handful of mint leaves plus either some mint extract or some green food coloring. Then proceed as above, choosing apples that are not very pink or red. Add a few drops of extract or food coloring just before you test the boiling liquid for doneness. And put several fresh mint leaves into each jelly glass before you fill them.

Mint is not the only herb you may combine with apple jelly; try it with savory, tarragon, sage, or others. But do not expect to change the color of your jelly by the addition of any herb.

— Beach-Plum Jelly —

The beach-plum makes a handsomely colored jelly that is much sought after by Cape Cod tourists.

Stem but do not peel or pit the plums; put in a saucepan and add enough water to cover. Cook them, covered, for about five minutes, then crush with a potato masher. Continue cooking until they are mushy, stirring from time to time. Put into a moistened jelly bag and let drip thoroughly. Reduce the juice a little (boiling about five minutes), then measure it. Add to it an equal volume of sugar, bring rapidly to a boil, then simmer until the liquid tests done, about forty minutes. Seal into jars while hot.

— Beet and Grape Jelly —

Use red grapes, about one and a half times as much weight as beets. Peel the beets and slice them very thin. Pass the grapes through a sieve, then discard the peel and seeds. Put the beets in a heavy pan and pour enough grape pulp on them to cover them in a layer about two inches deep. Cover the pot partially and simmer the mixture for four or five hours. Then pass through a jelly bag or a sieve and let cool. Pour into sterilized jars and seal.

— Cactus Jelly —

Use under-ripe cactus (prickly pears) except for a few ripe ones to give color to the jelly. Brush with vegetable brush under running cold water. Quarter and place in saucepan with enough water to cover. Boil until very tender. Mash with a potato masher and pour both liquid and pulp into a jelly bag to drip. Measure juice and for each two and one-half cups of juice add one three-ounce package of powdered pectin. Bring to a full boil, stirring constantly. Add three or four tablespoons of lemon or lime juice and about one and a half times the volume of sugar as your measured juice. Bring again to a full boil and keep boiling for three minutes, or until it tests done. Pour into warm jars and cover tightly.

— Four-Fruit Jelly —

Take equal quantities of ripe strawberries, raspberries, currants, and red cherries. Wash all and pit the cherries carefully so as not to lose any of the skin and juice. Crush them and soften the fruit on light heat for a few minutes. Put the fruit into a jelly bag, squeeze it lightly, and let it drip. Reduce the juice a bit by boiling for five or ten minutes, skimming foam. Then measure the juice, add an equal volume of sugar and boil again, until it tests done, or about twenty minutes. Seal in sterilized jars.

This is a very pretty, very delicious jelly.

— Grape Jelly —

Pick the ripest purple grapes you can find and let them sit, picked, in the sun for a day or two before you use them. Add a few that are not quite ripe when you start to make the jelly. Put all the grapes into a pot and heat to not quite boiling. Mash with a potato masher and boil gently until they are very soft and mushy. Now pour them into a jelly bag and let drip. Measure the juice when it has finished dripping through, and then boil it for five or ten minutes, skimming. Add an equal measure of sugar, bring it back to a boil, and continue boiling until jelly tests done, about ten or fifteen minutes more. Seal tightly in jars.

— Guava Jelly —

Wash and drain green guavas and remove stems. Slice the fruit thin, place in a saucepan with enough water to barely cover, and bring to a boil. Cook until fruit is very soft. Pour into a jelly bag and let drip. Then measure the juice, and boil for five or ten minutes. Add the same amount of sugar, bring back to a boil, and cook until the jelly passes the sheet test. Pour into warm jars and cover tightly.

— Mint Jelly —

Pick a few handfuls of mint, the top leaves of young plants if possible. Wash it, chop it fine, and measure its volume. Put it in a saucepan with water to cover and one-quarter as much sugar as the mint measured. Stir and let stand for four or five hours. Then bring to a boil, let cool for fifteen minutes, and strain out the leaves. Add apple juice in the same amount as the mint originally measured plus half as much volume of sugar; bring the liquid to a boil and cook it until it thickens, or about twenty minutes. Pour into warm jars and cover tightly.

This jelly will not be the green color expected of mint jelly unless you add a few drops of green food coloring, or of mint extract, during the last boiling.

— ORANGE JELLY —

Grate the rinds of four sweet oranges and two lemons. Add half a pound of sugar, a cup of water, and boil all together for a few minutes, until it almost candies, stirring constantly. Stir in three ounces of liquid pectin, then boil again, skimming foam, until it tests ready to jelly. Seal into warm jelly glasses.

— PARADISE JELLY —

This delectable jelly combines the juices of apples, quinces, and cranberries in ratios of twice as many apples as quinces and half as many cranberries as quinces.

Pick over the cranberries; peel the quinces and slice them (leave the core and seeds in); quarter the apples but don't peel or core or remove seeds. Combine the fruits, cover with water, and simmer until they are all soft. Put into jelly bag and let drip. Measure juice, then boil about ten minutes, skimming the foam. Then add sugar, a cup for each cup of measured juice, bring to a boil again, and continue to boil until the jelly tests done. Pour into jelly glasses, cool, seal, and store.

— RASPBERRY-GERANIUM JELLY —

With a rose geranium plant, and some fresh, ripe red raspberries, you can make this beautiful jelly that is a most exotic taste combination.

Pick a handful of the geranium leaves and wash both raspberries and the leaves. Put wet berries in a kettle, heat to boiling, and mash them with a potato masher into mush. Pour the mush into jelly bag and let drip. Measure the juice, then boil it, uncovered, for ten minutes, skimming foam. Add an equal measure of sugar, and boil about five minutes longer, skimming. Test for doneness. When it is ready to jell, put a geranium leaf into each clean warm jar and pour the jelly in. Let cool and seal tightly. Put in bright sunlight for a while and admire the bright ruby color.

— RHUBARB JELLY —

Wash your rhubarb stalks, then cut up and put them through a food grinder (or blender) and then into a jelly bag. Let drip, possibly overnight. For two cups of juice, add an ounce or two of powdered pectin. Bring to a boil and boil for five minutes, skimming foam. Add about one and a half times the amount of sugar as rhubarb juice and bring to a boil again, stirring constantly. Boil a few more minutes, until liquid passes sheet test. Cool and seal in warm, sterilized jars.

— TOMATO JELLY —

Start by pulling out of your pantry one of the pint containers of tomato sauce you have already made (see Chapter 13). Add to it the juice of three or four lemons, one cup of sugar, and a tablespoon of Worcestershire sauce. Boil this mixture for about five minutes. Now add about three ounces of liquid pectin, bring back to a boil, and cook another minute or two. Remove from the fire and stir and skim off foam as the jelly cools. Seal tightly in warm, sterilized jars.

This jelly is both sweeter and spicier than traditional tomato aspic, but it may be used in the same ways.

— WINEBERRY JELLY —

The fruit of the wild grapevine or the currant is sometimes called wineberry. When it is ripe, see how many you can gather before the birds get them all.

Wash the berries and crush them with a potato masher. Cook them for a few minutes until just tender, then let them drip through a jelly bag. It might be a good idea with this jelly to put the liquid through another clean jelly bag. Now measure your juice, add an equal volume of sugar, and boil until the liquid passes the sheet test, probably about ten minutes. Just before

210

pouring jelly into glasses, add some white framboise liqueur, about a teaspoon to the pint of juice, stirring it in well.

• CANDY AND OTHER CONFECTIONS •

For making candy you will need no specialized tools other than those already mentioned. Even the "candy thermometer," which is identical to the "jelly thermometer," is not essential if you learn to recognize the following different stages when cooking sugar.

1. *Caramelized Stage*: Sugar is caramelized by heating over a low heat until it melts. It is caramelized when it has become completely liquid, is viscous, and brown in color.

2. *Thread Stage*: Dip a metal spoon into the cooking mixture and lift it up over the vessel and turn it on its side. The liquid should run off in a thread.

3. *Soft-Ball Stage*: Dip a metal spoon into the cooking mixture and drop a few drops of it into a cup of cold water. If it forms a flat circle, it has reached the soft-ball stage.

4. *Firm-Ball Stage*: Drop a few drops of the cooking mixture into cold water. If it forms a round ball that is rather firm but can be flattened with your finger, it is now in the firm-ball stage.

5. *Hard-Ball Stage*: Drop some of the liquid from a metal spoon into cold water. It will form a hard, round ball that holds its shape, yet can be molded somewhat with your fingers, if it is in the hard-ball stage.

6. *Crack Stage*: If the liquid falling into cold water immediately becomes brittle, the sugar is at the crack stage, but the ball will be plastic when removed from water.

7. *Hard-Crack Stage*: At hard-crack stage, the ball that the dipped-out liquid forms will be brittle both in cold water and when removed from it.

The only danger in candy-making is that if you look away from it for a few seconds and your heat is perhaps a bit higher than you thought, it can boil over. To insure against that, use a deep saucepan and also butter it all around the top inch of the pan. If smoothness is desired, you can add a teaspoonful or so of corn syrup to any mixture while it is cooking. Never beat the candy until it has cooled somewhat.

— Bourbon (or Brandy) Balls —

1 lb. vanilla wafers,
graham crackers, or
biscuits of any type

1 cup pecans, walnuts, or
hazelnuts, or a mixture
of all, finely chopped

2 tsp. powdered cocoa
or carob powder

½ cup light corn syrup

¼ cup bourbon, or brandy

⅛ tsp. vanilla extract
(or ½ vanilla bean, crushed)

confectioner's sugar

Crush the wafers or biscuits fine with mortar and pestle or use a rolling pin or empty large bottle (putting a sheet of paper between bottle and wafers). Place the crumbs in a bowl, add all the ingredients except the sugar, and mix thoroughly. Sprinkle some sugar on your hands, spoon out the mixture into one hand —approximately one tablespoon at a time—and shape into balls. Spread the balls on a platter and allow their surface to dry for about two hours. Roll into confectioner's sugar, store in tin can or airtight container, separating the layers with wax paper. Cover tightly and store in a cool place.

— Butterscotch —

6 cups brown sugar
2 cups cold water
½ tsp. salt

⅛ tsp. cream of tartar
1½ cups melted butter
2 tsp. lemon extract
½ tsp. vanilla

In a large saucepan, mix sugar with water and salt until dissolved, then cook over medium flame, stirring frequently. When it comes to a boil, add cream of tartar, mix in, and stop stirring. Lower heat, cover pan, and let simmer for ten or twelve minutes. Uncover, raise heat, and cook until caramelized stage is reached (310 degrees Fahrenheit on candy thermometer). Remove mixture from fire, pour melted butter and the extracts into it, and mix well. Then pour into well-buttered shallow pan. Smooth top with well-greased spatula and allow to cool for about half an hour. Then cut with a sharp knife into pieces about 3″ x 1″ or into small squares. If the butterscotch seems too soft when you start to cut, let it cool somewhat longer. Or, let it become completely cold, then cut it with well-greased scissors. Wrap each piece in wax paper or tin foil and store in an airtight container in a cool, dry place.

— CANDIED CHERRIES —

2 cups sugar
1 cup water
2 cups fresh cherries, pitted, unstemmed

Boil sugar and water in a deep pot until candy thermometer reads 230 degrees Fahrenheit or the syrup forms a thread when lifted in a metal spoon. Add the cherries and bring to a boil again, then let cool a little. Wet a shallow pan with cold water; lift cherries by their stems, and put them in the pan. Boil syrup five minutes longer, then pour it over the cherries. Now put them in the sun under a cheesecloth or muslin tent (so that the cloth does not touch the cherries) and leave them there for several hours. When the syrup looks well set, transfer the cherries to a double layer of cheesecloth spread on a rack or strainer and allow to dry another few hours. When the surface of the fruit looks entirely dry, store in tightly covered jars.

— CARAMELS —

2 cups sugar   1 tbs. butter
1 cup light corn syrup   ¼ tsp. salt
2 cups milk   1 tsp. vanilla extract

Prepare a well-greased shallow pan and set aside. In a saucepan, blend well the sugar, syrup, and one cup of the milk. Put the rest of the milk in a small pot and start warming it on a very low flame. Then put the saucepan on high heat and cook, stirring frequently, until the candy thermometer reads about 245 degrees Fahrenheit or a few drops in water form a firm ball. Pour the scalded milk in very slowly and stir gently as you pour. Add the butter and salt and continue cooking until the mixture reaches firm-ball stage again. Remove from fire and stir in vanilla. Pour immediately into pan and let cool. When the caramel is cool, using a wet knife, cut into squares. But don't separate until absolutely cold. Store in any container.

— CHESTNUT PASTE —

1 lb. chestnuts
½ cup milk
1 cup sugar
½ tsp. vanilla extract
brandy

Peel chestnuts and put them in a saucepan with just enough water to cover. Boil them until tender, then remove the second skin, drain, and place in a bowl. Add the milk and press the chestnuts with a spoon so as to make a rather thick paste. In a small pot, add a very little water to the sugar and cook until it caramelizes. Pour this slowly on the paste while with the other hand you "work" the paste so that the sugar is thoroughly mixed in. Then add the vanilla extract and continue to knead. While the mixture is still warm, put it in jars with a few drops of brandy on top of each jar.

When the paste is still warm it will seem too loose, but it will cool off to the right consistency.

— Fondant —

Fondant, which originated in France, is the base for many desserts, candies, and other sweets. It is what is inside chocolate creams and outside bonbons. With the addition of a little oil of peppermint, it forms the base of chocolate peppermints; and if made with maple sugar instead of white, it is the principal stuff of maple creams. If you have sugar maples on your land, and you sugar off every spring, you will no doubt want to make your fondant of maple sugar; if you have to buy maple sugar, perhaps you will want to use it for part of the sugar that you put into fondant. Either way, since so much time and patience are required, make fondant in a fairly large amount and put it away.

9 cups sugar

3 cups water

¼ tsp. baking powder

Heat sugar and water on a slow flame until the sugar is melted. Then wipe a damp cloth around a knife or spatula and clean the sugary mixture off the sides of the pan. Mix in the baking powder, then bring to a boil and cook until soft-ball stage or until candy thermometer reads 240 degrees Fahrenheit. Remove from heat and in five minutes pour onto a cold, buttered (or moistened with cold water) surface, where you can beat with a wooden spoon. When the mixture turns white, knead it with your hands as if it were dough until it is completely smooth. Again, as if it were dough, you can leave it for an hour under a damp cloth, then knead it again. Or, you can store it immediately, being sure that it occupies nearly all the space of the air-tight container you put it in, so that it won't dry out and harden. It will keep practically forever. And you can use part of it from time to time to experiment with adding different flavorings or liqueurs to create different kinds of candies.

— HALVAH —

Halvah comes to us from the Middle East. It is both a scrumptious delicacy and an excellent way to preserve some nuts or seeds.

¾ cup butter

2 cups flour

½ cup honey

½ cup walnuts and almonds
or sesame, sunflower, or pumpkin seeds

You may combine several different kinds of nuts and/or seeds and you may chop them up coarsely or grind them finely; or, particularly in the case of sesame seeds, leave them whole.

Melt the butter and stir in the flour. Then cook this mixture over a very low flame, stirring frequently, until a light caramel color forms. Meanwhile, caramelize the honey separately until it reaches the thread stage (or slides off a spoon dipped into it, forming a thin thread). Combine the two substances and blend them thoroughly, adding the chopped nuts or seeds as you stir. Then pour the halvah onto a moistened flat surface or greased platter; press it into a thick rectangle with a wet knife. Cut it into bars before it is completely cool. When cold, wrap the pieces in wax paper or tin foil.

— LEMON CURD —

4 lemons

½ cup unsalted butter

1 cup sugar

3 eggs

Grate the rinds and squeeze the lemons. Melt butter and sugar in a pan; beat the eggs and stir them into the butter and sugar. Now stir in the lemon peel and juice. Cook very gently, either in the top of a double boiler or over *very* low heat, stirring constantly, for fifteen or twenty minutes, or until mixture has thickened. Never let it come close to a boil (or it will curdle). Pour into pots and seal tightly. It will keep a few days at room temperature, much longer under refrigeration.

216

This is more a pudding than a candy, a very sweet and delicious dessert.

— MAPLE CREAMS —

Butter a shallow pan. Melt maple-sugar fondant and pour it into the pan an inch or more thick. Immediately cover with chopped nuts and chopped candied fruits, angelica, or candied rinds. Or, simply place whole candied cherries or halved walnuts or pecans or whole almonds on top, pressing them gently to make them sink in a little, about one and one-half inches apart. Allow to cool, then wet a sharp knife and slice into squares. But don't separate the squares until the fondant is completely cold. Store in an airtight container, layering with wax paper.

— FROZEN MAPLE-SUGAR PUDDING —

By name this is a pudding, but it is sweet enough to find a place among the candies.

3 egg yolks	1 cup heavy cream
1 cup grated maple sugar	½ tsp. vanilla extract
1 tsp. cinnamon	1 cup candied fruits
1 cup milk	and/or nuts
	1 cup whipped cream

Beat the yolks with the sugar and cinnamon until light. Heat the milk to boiling and pour in, beating as you pour. Then put into double boiler over medium heat and stir until the custard coats the spoon. Let cool and add the cream and vanilla. Now put into your freezing compartment. When the pudding is partially frozen, stir in the fruits and nuts; then continue freezing. Serve the pudding with whipped cream on top.

— MARRONS GLACÉS —

3 cups large chestnuts	3 cups sugar
water	or half sugar/half soft honey
	or half sugar/half corn syrup
salt	½ vanilla bean, crushed
1 tbs. sugar	or ¼ tsp. vanilla extract

Boil chestnuts in lightly salted water to cover for twenty minutes. Drain and peel, taking care not to break the nuts. Use the same amount of water, to which you have added a tablespoon of sugar, and boil the chestnuts again until they are tender. Drain. In a separate pot, mix the three cups of sweetening with a cup and a half of water and the vanilla, and bring to a boil. Let cook without stirring until candy thermometer reads 300 degrees Fahrenheit, or syrup reaches hard-crack stage. Add chestnuts and leave them in syrup five minutes. Remove nuts carefully, making sure not to break them, and reserving syrup. Put the chestnuts on a flat sieve and leave them in a warm place overnight.

The next day, heat the syrup, and when it is hot, dip the chestnuts again, leaving them in for five minutes. Drain and let dry overnight or longer. When the surface of the nuts looks crystallized and dry, wrap them individually in tin foil, making sure you use enough to overlap and then twist on the ends, as in wrapping candy. Place in an airtight container and store in a cool, dry place.

If during the process you break a few chestnuts, proceed with the pieces in the same manner, but at the end warm up the syrup once more, put the pieces of nuts in a jar, and cover them with the warm syrup. Seal tightly. This syrup can be used as topping for parfaits, for coupe aux marrons, or for garnishing practically any dessert.

— MILK PASTE —
(*Dulce de Leche*)

Dulce de leche, while used in many South American countries, is by far the most ubiquitous ingredient in Argentine desserts. Singly or with other ingredients, it is used as a cake layer or icing; as candy, just by itself; as a filler for chocolate candy; as a coating or filler in crunchy-type candy; as a pudding in a softer version; and, on the breakfast table, as a spread for bread.

It has a very distinctive flavor (perhaps too sweet for some palates), a rather thick texture, and an appealing pale tan color. You may wish to add it to your shelf of preserves, where it will keep almost indefinitely.

To four quarts of whole milk add three and one-half cups of sugar and one-eighth teaspoon bicarbonate of soda (baking soda). Stir the bicarbonate into the milk and bring slowly to a boil; then add the sugar, stir to dissolve it, and continue to boil over medium flame. Stir constantly until the mixture begins to change color, then again stir constantly when the color really changes. When the consistency is that of a rather thick jam and the color is a blond tan, remove from fire, add one tablespoon of unsalted butter, mix well, and continue stirring occasionally until lukewarm.

Use immediately, or pour into jars before it solidifies, and store.

— CANDIED MINT LEAVES —

Pick some whole, large, perfect mint leaves. Wash thoroughly but gently so as not to tear or crush them. Let dry. Beat the white of an egg slightly, and with a soft brush, wet each leaf thoroughly on both sides with the egg. Sprinkle the leaves with sugar or chocolate powder or carob powder. Preheat your oven to 200 degrees Fahrenheit and put the leaves in on a baking sheet in one layer. If they seem to be drying too fast (and curling), keep the oven door slightly open. When the leaves look dry and crystallized, let them cool, then pack in an airtight container layered between wax paper.

— MOLASSES CANDY —

Squares of this mouth-watering confection were the object of many a trip to the "penny-candy store" of many an American childhood.

1 tsp. butter	1 tbs. water
1 cup molasses	½ cup sugar
	¼ tsp. baking soda

Butter a large shallow pan and put it aside. Melt the butter in a heavy saucepan, add the molasses, water, and sugar, and stir. Bring to a boil and cook, stirring from time to time until nearly done, then stir constantly until syrup reaches the hard-ball stage. Remove from heat, stir in the baking soda, and pour into the greased pan. When cool enough to handle, pull the candy (the way you would taffy) until light-colored and porous. Work with fingertips and thumbs. When it begins to harden, stretch to a thick cord and cut into pieces with buttered scissors. Let cool on a greased surface. Then wrap in wax paper and store in an airtight container.

— NUT BRITTLE —

Use any kind of nuts you like, one kind separately or a mixture of two or more. If you use almonds, chestnuts, or hazelnuts, remove skin by plunging into boiling water first. And, if you have gathered fresh nuts, dry them before making this candy. Butter a shallow pan and set it aside.

For each cup of shelled, skinned nuts you'll need:

2 cups sugar or
1 cup sugar and 1 scant cup honey, or
¾ cup honey

To the sweetening, add enough water to make a thick paste. Heat in a skillet, stirring constantly, until it turns syrupy and light brown. Add the nuts and cook a few more minutes, lowering the flame. Remove from fire and pour onto the pan to half-inch thickness. Allow to cool for half an hour, then with a wet knife, cut into squares. But don't remove from pan until completely cold. Put into airtight container in layers separated by wax paper. Cover tightly and store in a cool place.

— CANDIED ORANGE OR LEMON PEEL —

Peel fruits so that very little white is left on the rinds. Cut them in even squares of a half-inch or smaller. Or, you may cut the entire fruits into quarters and *then* remove the peels; this will allow you to cut the quarter peels into shapes like flowers, hearts, stars, etc., in case you want to use them as decorations.

Put the rinds in a bowl under dripping faucet for a day or two, to rid them of bitterness. After this put the peels into a pot of water (three times the volume of water as orange peel) and bring to a boil. Cook about fifteen minutes, or until the rinds can be easily pierced with a toothpick. Don't overcook. Then plunge peels into cold water and drain. Now weigh the rinds. Combine an equal weight of sugar with just enough water to make a paste, to which you add the rinds. Cook over medium heat, stirring frequently. When the syrup has thickened to your satisfaction, cool a little. Pour rinds and syrup into warm jars, cover tightly, and store in a cool place.

— Peach Paste —

Choose very ripe peaches. Plunge them into boiling water, then into cold water. Peel and remove stems. Cut in pieces and discard pits. Press the flesh through a coarse sieve into a bowl and weigh. In a saucepan, bring peach pulp to a boil, stirring constantly. When it boils, add sugar in three-quarters of the weight of the peach pulp. Cook, stirring, about ten minutes, or until thickened. Remove from heat and line a shallow pan with wax paper. Spread the paste over it, about a half-inch thick. Smooth top with a wet spatula and put pan in oven at no more than 150 degrees Fahrenheit with the door ajar for a few hours.

When the paste has dried on one side, line another pan with wax paper, flip the paste into the new pan, and repeat the procedure, drying the other side.

If you want to use this paste as a sandwich filler, cut it into sandwich-size squares and store in layers, separated by wax paper, in an airtight container in a cool place.

For candy, cut it into small squares or rectangles and roll each piece in sugar.

Apricot paste, which is also excellent, is made in the same way.

— Peanut Amber —

After you have candied your orange peels, you may want to go a step further and use up some of your excess peanut supply, too, and at the same time make an attractive and toothsome gift for festive occasions.

1 lb. candied orange peel, cut up fine	*2 cups shredded coconut*
	1 tsp. vanilla extract
2 cans condensed milk	*1 cup peanuts, shelled*

Combine all ingredients, stirring well to distribute the nuts evenly. Press into a greased fudge pan and bake at 275 degrees Fahrenheit for half an hour. Let cool and take out in teaspoonfuls, rolling each into a ball.

You may want to coat the balls by rolling them then in confectioner's sugar.

221

— QUINCE PASTE —

Peel, core, and chop quinces until you have about a quart of cut-up fruit, reserving the parings. Now add a little water to the skins and cook for about fifteen minutes. Remove the skins and add half a pound of sugar to the water and boil until a thick syrup stage is reached, skimming foam off as necessary. Add the cut-up quince meat, and simmer, stirring and crushing the fruit, until you have a thick, pasty substance. Line a fudge pan with wax paper and spread the paste in it to cool. Now proceed as with Peach Paste.

— CRYSTALLIZED ROSE PETALS —

Wash and drain rose petals. Dry them gently with a soft cloth, trying not to crush or scratch them. Dip them one by one in beaten egg white, making sure they are completely coated. Let them drip a little, then cover them on both sides with sugar, being careful to coat completely. Put on wax paper on a tray to dry in the sun, or in a slow oven (200 degrees Fahrenheit at the most, with the door open). When they look crystallized, let them cool. Store them in an airtight container, layered between wax paper.

— DIPPED STRAWBERRIES —

Strawberries dipped in fondant are a joy forever. You can, of course, preserve any other berries in the same way, but there is something so elegant about a fondant-dipped strawberry. For a quart of berries, use a cup of fondant. Make sure the berries are perfect, fresh, and ripe and leave their stems and fruit-leaves on.

Wash and dry the berries thoroughly. Melt the fondant in the top of a double boiler. Hold each berry by its stem and adjoining leaves and dip it into the fondant to coat all over up to your fingers. Then lift it out and circulate it upside down in the air to let the sugar mixture cover a bit more of the berry and dry. When it has dried, rearrange the leaves.

One dipped strawberry on top of a serving of plain ice cream or sherbet or pudding makes a Lucullian dessert.

222

— Salt-Water Taffy —

1 cup corn syrup	*1 tbs. water*
1 cup sugar	*1 tbs. vinegar*
1 tbs. butter	*1 tsp. vanilla extract*

Combine all ingredients and bring to a boil in a saucepan. Stir once in a while, to prevent candy from burning. When it reaches hard-ball stage, remove from heat and pour onto a buttered or moistened surface to cool. As soon as you can handle it, pull it: With your two hands in opposition (or better still, with two people facing each other) pull the mass of candy into a long rope, then when it becomes thin in the middle, double it back upon itself and pull it out again and again until it hardens. When it is cold and brittle, chop or snap it into pieces.

— English Toffee —

2 cups sugar	*½ cup salted butter*
⅛ tsp. baking powder	*2 tsp. rum*
1 cup cream	*few drops vanilla extract (optional)*

Mix sugar and baking powder and put in a saucepan. Add cream and mix well, then bring to a boil and cook for a few minutes, stirring. Add butter and keep stirring until the syrup reaches the medium-hard stage or the candy thermometer reads 290 degrees Fahrenheit. But just before it gets to this point add the rum and vanilla. Immediately pour into a shallow, well-buttered pan to the thickness of about an inch, smoothing the top with a wet spatula. Let cool for about half an hour, then cut into squares, using a wet knife. When completely cold, wrap individual pieces in wax paper or tin foil. Store in an airtight container in a cool place.

— TORRONE —
(*Italian Nougat*)

This is a complicated sweet to make, but it is worth trying, if only to "preserve" a rather large quantity of nuts practically forever. It's a two-person job, ideally.

To make about three and one-half pounds of torrone you will need:

butter for greasing	*3 egg whites*
1½ cups light-colored honey	*½ cup shelled pistachio nuts,*
1½ lbs. shelled almonds	*or 1½ tsp. candied orange peel,*
¾ lb. shelled hazelnuts	*chopped coarsely*
1½ cups sugar	*1 tsp. grated lemon rind*
3 or 4 tbs. water	

Before you start, butter a shallow pan and put it aside.

Melt honey in top of double boiler, stirring, until it has caramelized or reached hard-ball stage. Meanwhile, drop almonds into hot water for a couple of minutes, remove them, peel, and place them in an oven preheated to 350 degrees Fahrenheit together with the hazelnuts, to toast them lightly. About fifteen minutes before the honey has reached the caramelizing point, mix the sugar with three or four tablespoons of water— enough to make a thick paste—and place in a small saucepan. Let the syrup boil, without stirring, until caramelized. While one person is doing this, another can beat the egg whites stiff and fold them into the honey slowly, stirring constantly. This will change the color and texture of the honey; the result should be a fluffy, white mixture.

Now add the caramelized sugar a little at a time to the honey and continue stirring. Cook until the mixture passes the hard-ball test, or just a few minutes longer. Meanwhile the helper can remove the nuts from the oven and rub the hazelnuts gently against the mesh of a strainer to remove the flaky skin. Add the nuts, with the pistachios or orange rind, and the grated lemon rind, to the candy mixture. Mix well and fast, before the mixture begins to harden.

Put the candy into your well-buttered shallow pan, spreading to two-inch thickness, smoothing with a buttered spatula. Let cool for at least a half-hour. If you would like the candy to be very hard, put a buttered board on top of it, with weights on top, and let it cool in that fashion. Cut into squares with a wet knife before it has completely cooled—or you won't be able to cut it at all. Wrap the separate pieces and store in a cool place.

If you wish an even softer candy than the medium soft follow the above procedure (minus the weighting) then add one egg yolk to the three egg whites, and shorten the cooking time by a few minutes at each step; that is, cook honey and sugar, both when they are separate and when combined, until they just begin to caramelize. But make sure the caramelizing has started, or you'll have another confection, but not torrone. Then try to work faster as you mix everything together.

— Candied Violets —

violet blossoms
egg white, beaten
vanilla extract
sugar

Wash and drain the blossoms, remove stems, and then let dry for a short time, not long enough to wilt. Beat egg white, not too stiff, add a few drops of vanilla, and dip blossoms carefully into it. Let the violets drip a little, then coat them entirely with sugar, handling with great care. Place on a tray on wax paper. Try to open the flowers up with your fingers or with a toothpick, then add a little sugar to the insides. Dry in the sun or in a slow oven (no more than 200 degrees Fahrenheit) with the door open. Store in an airtight container layered between wax paper.

Eat the candied violets like candy, decorate a cake or other dessert with them, or give them as gifts.

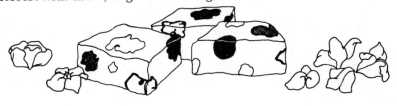

225

· CONCENTRATED SYRUPS ·

It will be a pleasant surprise for many of you to learn that making fruit syrups is actually easier than making jams or jellies. The tools you need are the same, the time you actually spend making them is minimal, and aside from the fruit you decide to turn into syrup, the main ingredient is sugar.

There are a few rules about which you must be absolutely rigorous. The bottles you use must be perfectly clean and dry. Even one drop of water left in the bottle may spoil its contents. When you are ready to make syrup and prepare the bottles, after washing them with a mild detergent and rinsing them well, drain them upside down for about an hour, then put them in a warm place and leave them until completely dry. Look at the bottles carefully in a strong light before using them, to make sure no water or even steam is still inside.

Use good corks, also perfectly clean and dry, and sterilized, which you can do by boiling them in water for ten minutes, then allowing them to dry without touching them with your hands, their smaller ends up.

We presume and recommend that you use bottles for syrups, rather than jars. They are designed for easy pouring and the portion at the top is so small that this helps in their preservation. Of course, you can also use large-necked jars, provided they can be sealed perfectly, and in this case you can use a long-handled spoon to remove the syrup.

To make syrups, the fruits have to be allowed to ferment for a while before you make the actual syrup. This is essential for the majority of fruits, especially those high in pectin. Fermentation takes place in about twenty-four to forty-eight hours for most fruits, longer for others, and it is actually only a first stage of fermentation, as opposed to the wine-making process, for example. The fruit is crushed or cut up and put in wide bowls. As the pectin comes to the surface and forms a film, this film must be broken two or three times to allow fermentation to continue. When the first cycle of fermentation is over, the fruit is strained through a fine-mesh sieve or a strong but loosely woven cloth, or even a jelly bag. Using cloth or a jelly bag is perhaps best because you can squeeze out the last portion of the juice at the end, by gathering the cloth and pressing gently with your hands at the top of the cloth "ball" that contains the fruit. Most syrups are bottled when cold, or at least lukewarm. Should the recipe call for the syrup to be bottled while hot, make sure you warm up the bottles before pouring in the hot liquid. Always wait until the syrup has cooled completely before corking the bottles. (For the best method of corking, see Chapter 10.)

A word of caution. Undercooking the fruit juice means shortening its storing time and perhaps endangering its quality, so that you may have to throw out the entire batch. Overcooking it would caramelize the syrup and make it too thick and hard to dissolve as well as give it a burnt taste.

Should the syrup turn cloudy after it has been bottled, it means the fruit should have fermented a little longer. Reboil its contents, adding a little water as some will evaporate as you boil it, then bottle again. The syrup will not keep very long at this point, so enjoy it quickly, and keep it under refrigeration.

Most of the syrups will last a couple of years, some even longer, provided you have followed these steps scrupulously. However, while labeling the bottles with the name of the fruit, it is advisable to add the date so that you can keep track of the bottles that should be used first.

One or two tablespoons of syrup for each tumbler of water is the average proportion when serving. Pour the syrup first into each glass, then the water or plain soda, stir well, and add one or two ice cubes. In the summer you may wish to make your drink more refreshing by adding a couple of fresh mint leaves, or a slice of orange or lemon.

In the winter these syrups make an excellent and warming drink if you mix them with boiling water. If you wish you can add a few strips of lemon peel, twisted, to the water you put up to boil, and perhaps a few drops of lemon juice to each glass or cup of syrup. A touch of brandy, or (even better) rum, makes this drink even tastier and will warm you up even more quickly. To make your own carbonated water, add one teaspoon of bicarbonate of soda (baking soda) and one teaspoon of tartaric acid or citric acid to each quart bottle of water. Cork tightly and turn

227

the bottle upside down several times. Refrigerate. It is better to make one bottle at a time and use it quickly, or it will turn flat.

— ORIGINAL ORZATA —
(*Almond and Barley Syrup*)

A very ancient drink still widely used in certain countries in the Middle East and North Africa, as well as in Greece and Italy, is almond (or almond and barley) syrup and water. Its origin is not known. Perhaps it was brought to Italy sometime during the Arab occupation of Sicily a thousand years ago, or imported later from Greece or Turkey. In Italy it took the name of *orzata* from the Italian *orzo,* which means barley and is still called that, although it is now more commonly made without barley. Somehow, as the centuries went by, in Italy barley came to be used more for horses than for humans, and perhaps during the refined period of the Renaissance barley was no longer considered fashionable for human consumption, so the syrup started to be made without it. Nevertheless the *orzata* kept its name and its popularity. We still believe the original recipe is by far tastier and healthier, but we are going to share both recipes with you.

1¾ cups barley
6 cups water
1 cup almonds
10 bitter almonds
3 cups sugar or, preferably, 2 cups sugar, ½ cup honey

Boil the barley in the water until mixture is half the original amount, stirring occasionally. Let cool. Grind the peeled almonds in blender, adding a little water, until coarsely chopped. (Peeling almonds is easily done if you pour some boiling water on them and soak them for a few minutes.) Then immediately finish pounding them by hand in a mortar, with a pestle, adding a few drops of water as you pound. The addition of water is important, not only to prevent the nuts from becoming almond oil, but because this liquid mixture is the main flavor in your syrup. Originally, of course, the almonds were pounded only in the mortar, and all the flavor and nutrients remained in the liquid. When you have really crushed them, add them to the barley, mix well,

228

and filter everything into a pot, to which you then add the sugar and honey. Boil for twenty minutes, let cool, and bottle. Store in a cool place.

— ORZATA WITHOUT BARLEY —
(Almond Syrup)

1 qt. water
½ lb. almonds
30 bitter almonds
4 cups sugar or, preferably, 2 cups sugar, 1 cup honey
6 tbs. orange-blossom water, or 3 tbs. rose water

Pour enough boiling water on almonds to cover them. After a few minutes, peel them and pound them in a mortar, adding water a little at a time (or chop the nuts coarsely with a little water in blender first, then finish in mortar). It is important to keep adding a little water as you pound, so that the juice you squeeze out will not become almond oil and the almond flavor will be retained. Two or three times, as you are working the almonds, pour the milky liquid into a pot, filtering it through muslin, then continue pounding with a little more water until the nuts are totally ground. Add sugar and honey to the liquid in the pot, add the whitish liquid (if you have not used the whole quart of water, add the balance now), and bring to a boil. Remove from fire as soon as it boils quickly. Let cool, add orange blossom or rose water, mix well, then bottle, and store in cool place.

Orzata can be used like any other syrup, or you can use it in its concentrated form as an ice-cream sauce, dessert filling, in your pancake batter or cakes. It can also be substituted for any desserts that call for vanilla.

Don't be surprised if it turns cloudy when you add water. This is normal, as with mint liqueur.

— CHERRY SYRUPS —
Sour Cherry Syrup I

Spread very ripe sour cherries in the sun for a whole day (the sun must be strong), then wipe them with a slightly damp cloth but don't wash them. Remove stems and pits, then put them in a pot. Pit them over the pot in which you'll cook them, so as not to waste any of their delicious juice. After about twelve hours, add two and a third cups of sugar for each pound of juice. Simmer very slowly for twenty minutes, skimming the syrup at the end, let cool, and bottle without removing the fruit.

Sour Cherry Syrup II

Again using very ripe sour cherries, clean them and remove the stems. Crush them a bit and allow to rest forty-eight hours in a crock or pot, stirring them twice a day. The container should be kept covered with a clean cloth. Remove the pits, or leave them, as they can be removed as you eat the cherries in the syrup. Just remove about five or six pits for each pound of the fruit and mash them in a mortar (be careful if using a blender or you may ruin the blades) until they form a fairly smooth paste. Mix the paste with the cherries and boil gently for a few minutes. Remove from fire, cover the pot, and let rest overnight. Then measure the juice and place it on the fire again, adding two and a third cups of sugar for each pound of the juice. Allow to boil exactly five minutes, stirring constantly. Skim at the end. Bottle when cool, leaving the cherries in the syrup.

Sweet Cherry Syrup

Make as you would Sour Cherry Syrup I, but cut down amount of sugar to equal cherry juice in weight.

— GRAPE SYRUP —
(or Must Syrup)

A little more lengthy to prepare than the preceding ones, this syrup is well worth the trouble; but it is advisable to make a fairly large quantity, as you may not want to repeat it often.

Use about ten pounds of different varieties of grapes, all ripe, all sweet varieties. Wash carefully, drain, remove the fruits from the stems, then put the grapes in a crock or several crocks or bowls, crushing them thoroughly with your hands. Cover the containers with a folded cloth and let rest, undisturbed, for six days. Strain through a sieve, squeezing as much of the juice as you can. In a pot, mix the juice with about two and a quarter cups of sugar for each pound of juice (a little more if the grapes are not very sweet) and cook over moderate fire, stirring constantly for ten minutes, skimming as it boils. Allow to cool. If the syrup you have obtained is a little cloudy, filter through a funnel into which you have placed a cotton ball. Repeat if needed. Bottle when cool.

It should keep about one year. If you would like to preserve it for a longer period of time, add one tablespoon of citric acid for each quart of syrup. The yield of this syrup is rather low, about two and one-half quarts.

— GRENADINE —

An old-time favorite in most southern European countries, this is the only syrup that has been introduced into this country (usually imported from France and rather expensive) in its classic form. Aside from its use in desserts, ice creams, and fruit cups, it is often used as an ingredient in cocktails, especially non-alcoholic "cocktails"; and your children are probably familiar with it if they have ever had a "Shirley Temple" or similar drink in restaurants while you were having real cocktails before dinner. This children's drink is usually made by adding grenadine to ginger ale or plain soda, a maraschino cherry, and sometimes a slice of orange.

Originally grenadine was made with pomegranate (hence its name), but now it is often made with red currants or red raspberries. In fact, there is even a pathetic "modern" version of it given in some reputable European cookbooks that contains no fruit of any kind, just sugar and coloring agents. We suspect this version was invented during World War II, when it was difficult to find fresh berries or pomegranates (or dangerous to go out and pick them).

True Grenadine

Remove seeds from pomegranates, making sure you discard all traces of the whitish film that holds them together. Press the seeds through a sieve and gather their juice in a pot. Or, crush the seeds (or grains) in a bowl, and strain later. Cover the bowl or pot with cloth and allow the crushed fruit or juice to stand for at least twenty-four hours, mixing it every few hours. Add two and one-half cups of sugar to each quart of juice into a pot, bring to a boil, and boil for exactly fifteen minutes. Skim the foam from the surface and bottle immediately into warm bottles. Let cool before corking tightly. Store in a cool, dark place.

Grenadine II
(*Red Currants or Raspberries Syrup*)

This is now more frequently used, perhaps because pomegranates are so difficult to find.

Put the currants or raspberries in a wide bowl and crush them. Let the fruit stand for a few days in the bowl, which you will cover with a clean cloth and mix thoroughly a couple of times a day. The fermentation process is finished when the bubbles stop and no more fruit floats to the surface. Now filter the juice, and add one tablespoon of citric acid (in powder or liquid, not in tablets) and two and two-thirds cups of sugar for each pound of the juice. Bring to a boil, stirring constantly, and boil for three minutes. Skim the foam from the surface and remove from fire. Bottle when cool.

An excellent syrup is also made by combining equal parts of currants and raspberries, using the above method.

— LEMON SYRUP —

For each two cups of lemon juice, you'll need two cups of sugar and one cup of honey. Squeeze the juice and put in a bowl covered with cloth, letting it rest until a thin film is formed on the surface. Filter through muslin and add the sugar and honey, having removed the lemon juice to a pot. Bring to a slow boil and simmer, stirring frequently, for six minutes, skimming the foam. Remove from fire, and bottle when lukewarm.

You can use about one-third lime juice instead of the same quantity of lemon juice, add to the rest of the lemon juice, mix well, and proceed as above, reducing the amount of sugar and honey slightly.

— MINT SYRUP —

3 cups mint leaves, loosely packed
2 cups water
3 cups sugar

Choose medium-size mint leaves as they tend to have the strongest aroma. Put them into the water and leave them to soak for five or six hours. Bring the water to a boil and simmer, covered, for fifteen minutes. Strain out the leaves, squeezing them, and discard. Make a syrup of the water and sugar, leaving it on the heat just long enough to dissolve the sugar.

— ORANGE SYRUP —

This is bound to become one of your children's favorites.

8 juice oranges   2 lbs. sugar
2 juicy lemons   2 cups water

Grate the rind of four oranges and the two lemons into a bowl. Boil the water, pour it on the grated rind, and allow to cool. Cover and refrigerate. Squeeze the juice of all fruits, pour it into another bowl and leave in a warm place, covered with cloth, for about forty-eight hours or until it stops fermenting. The fermentation shows itself as a dense foam, which you should skim as it rises. When the fermentation is over, filter into a pot, add the sugar and the water with the grated rind, which you will also filter, and bring to a boil, cooking for five minutes, stirring constantly. Bottle immediately, cork when cool.

Some people believe that, in order to obtain absolute perfection and preserve this syrup for years, it is better to use the canning process at this point. When you have securely corked the bottles, tie the corks with a strong string, crosswise, then around the indentation of the neck. Wrap them in rags and put in a large pot or cauldron, which you will fill with enough water to reach the neck of the bottles. Bring to a boil and boil for thirty minutes. Allow the syrup to cool in the pot, then dry the bottles, label, and cork tightly. It is advisable to coat the tops with semi-liquid paraffin or sealing wax.

— Pine Shoots Syrup —

This is a very ancient, thirst-quenching drink from the Alps, pre-pared in most European countries that make up the Alpine zone, although it is by now impossible to determine its origin. It is also used as a cough syrup in its concentrated form.

In the spring, when pine trees have new shoots, cut only the tender, pale-green tips, making sure you pick only the lateral twigs and not the very tip of the branch, so as not to impair the growth of the tree. Weigh the pine shoots, then weigh the same amount of sugar (or, preferably, half sugar, half honey, but the honey should be rather liquid and not the dense, thick type). Press them into a glass jar, alternating layers of pine shoots and sugar and honey, and keep pressing down the shoots as you fill the jar, so that some of their aroma will ooze out. Cover and place in the sun until the sugar has melted and the shoots float. Strain into another jar or bottle and seal tightly. Keep in a dark, cool place.

If you wish to use it as a drink, instead of diluting it with plain water or soda, try ginger ale. It's delicious. Use very sparingly, as it has a powerful aroma. Or, you can mix it with mint syrup or mint liqueur.

As a cough syrup, or to help your digestion, one or two tea-spoons at night will prove effective.

— Rose Petal Syrup —

For seven ounces of fragrant rose petals (any color) boil an equal weight of water, put the petals in a warm jar, and pour the boiling water over them. Close the jar and, when it has cooled, filter into a pot and add three-fourths cup of sugar. Bring to a slow boil and simmer a few minutes, or until the sugar has melted completely. Bottle immediately but cork when cool.

Should you find it impossible to buy or make rose water, this is a reasonably good substitute, but remember that it is very sweet.

— "Seedy" Syrup —

Peel edible, ripe seeds and dry them in the hot sun for a few hours or in a very slow oven for about one hour. For each hundred large seeds, measure three cups of sugar. Chop the seeds, then pound them in a mortar, adding the juice of one or two lemons a little at a time to help make the paste of the right consistency, which should be rather thick. Stuff small, self-sealing jars with the paste, and store.

Dilute in cold or hot water, according to the season, when you are ready to use it as a drink.

For added flavor, you may crush a vanilla bean together with the paste, or add a few drops of vanilla extract.

Working the paste with a little heavy cream makes a delicious sauce for desserts, fruit cups, or ice creams.

— TAMARIND SYRUP —

This is one of the most thirst-quenching of all drinks, and for this reason is widely used in hot climates. The taste is pleasantly tart, and it is reputed to have excellent digestive qualities, as well as a very mild laxative effect. Try it on your children; if they don't like prune juice, the chances are that they'll really go for this one!

It is especially delicious and refreshing served with fresh mint leaves, lightly crushed.

If you cannot find the fruit, and would like to taste the syrup, you might be able to find it in a specialty store, particularly one that specializes in imports from Italy, Greece, or the Middle East, where it may be sold as tamarind extract. Or, you may try a specialty store that imports from India, where the tree originated (as the last portion of the name implies) and is used in a variety of ways.

Add one cup of tamarind fruit to three and one-half cups of water and simmer, covered, for about twenty minutes, stirring occasionally, or until the fruit seems really cooked. Remove from fire, allow to cool some, then filter through cloth into a larger pot, squeezing the peel and pits of the fruit as much as you can. Filter again with funnel and cotton ball, weigh the mixture, and add a little less than twice its weight of sugar. Bring again to a slow boil and simmer very slowly for about fifteen minutes, skimming the liquid. Bottle when cool.

WINES, LIQUEURS, AND SPIRIT-PRESERVED FOODS

· WINEMAKING ·

The making of wine is not nearly as mysterious or as difficult as you may imagine, nor do you need any complicated equipment to make your own wine. Moreover, what better way could there possibly be for you to preserve those opulent quantities of spring blossoms, the berries of early summer, the fruits of mid- and late summer, and the vegetables that mature in the fall?

Winemaking in the home kitchen lends itself to any season of the year, even the winter when you may decide to turn into wine some of those cold-stored potatoes or parsnips that are obviously going to last until way past the season of your new crop. All these wines are as delicate and flavorful as any you can buy, and some of them, like parsnip wine, are so unusual that you'd be hard put to find them in most stores.

You will need corks, bottles, crocks, mashers, and cheesecloth or muslin. With the cloth you will fashion a jelly bag, or some contrivance for straining out the solids at the end of the first fermentation period, with the help of rubber bands, string, and a towel rack to suspend it from. Make sure the corks are made of the wood of the cork tree; plastic, metal, and other such materials do not serve as well as cork. The corks should be of good quality, springy to the touch (test them by squeezing them between your fingers). A good-quality cork also precludes that unpleasant taste of cork you sometimes find in wines.

To ferment the fruit you'll need some tubs, vats, and basins of fairly large size; the size, of course, will depend on the quantity of wine you intend to make. The best material is wood, and if you choose wooden containers they should be not only perfectly clean but, preferably, should be used exclusively for this purpose. Large plastic tubs are often used today and since, when properly washed, they don't retain smell and taste, they can be used for different purposes. Those large country crocks are also good for winemaking, but you should inspect them to make sure in advance that the glaze inside is still intact. Avoid bare, uncoated metal (except stainless steel) for either fermentation or storing.

For bottling use glass bottles with the usual narrow necks, preferably those that are tinted green or brown to keep the light out. Should you have at hand only clear glass bottles, you can use them too, but don't forget to store them in the dark. The only other item you will need is an unmarked calendar or book in which you can make notes as to the dates of the various steps plus, of course, the final date on which you bottled the wine.

It might be a good idea to equip yourself with a fermentation lock (also called an air lock). It will ensure the escape of carbon

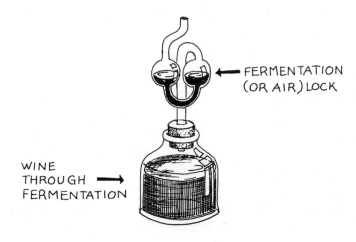

FERMENTATION (OR AIR) LOCK

WINE THROUGH FERMENTATION

dioxide during the first fermentation period and keep out the oxygen. If, however, you can invent a cover for the container you use for fermentation that will yield the same effect, you won't need a fermentation lock.

There are two or three stages of fermentation in wine. The first fermentation is the most obvious, and it is sometimes called tumultuous fermentation. Don't expect great upheaval and roiling in your container. You can actually hear the sound of fermentation, but it's more like a whisper or a sigh, and it is barely visible. In fact, you may be in doubt about the end of this period (and the times given in the following pages are of necessity only approximate). To make sure, just bend down and listen to your wine: If it has stopped whispering, it is time to rack it, or siphon it off into bottles, and then leave it stand for its second (or quiescent) fermentation.

Most wines are bottled after the second fermentation, which may go on for a while even after the wine has been bottled. You can tell when the second fermentation is over by examining the wine closely (without shaking the bottle): If there are no more bubbles climbing up inside, fermentation has stopped.

Fermentation, the essence of winemaking, is simply a chemical change brought about by the action of a ferment (such as yeast) on a liquid containing some form of sugar. Wine-yeast cells are present in the skins of nearly all fruits when they are ripe, but they are found in the greatest quantity in the skins of grapes. Hence, wines made from grapes are usually produced without the addition of commercial yeast, whereas many other kinds of wine are most successfully made with the addition of commercial yeast. Many wines for which grapes are not the basis are improved by the addition, at some stage of their making, of a certain quantity of raisins.

Sugar, some moisture, and an even temperature of about seventy to seventy-two degrees Fahrenheit turn most fruits, and some vegetables and grains, into alcohol. Substituting honey for sugar (as you may already have done in baking and preserving) is permissible, but the quantity should be reduced, since honey is sweeter than sugar: About half to two-thirds of the amount of sugar called for should give you the same results.

Otherwise, the development of your wine will be the same. Of course, if you use honey instead of sugar, you'll be making mead rather than wine.

A few wines need clearing, but this step is optional, since a cloudy wine is equal in taste and nutritive quality to a wine that has not been cleared. Most wines, if made properly, are naturally clear. If, for aesthetic reasons, you want to clear a cloudy wine, you can use either of two methods. Add one small stick of charcoal to each bottle when the second fermentation starts. Or, insert a few small pieces of baked or brittle eggshells. Do not add more than a few pieces, as their cleaning strength is so powerful that if you use more you will have a colorless wine. Consider that one eggshell can clear a whole gallon of wine. Of the two methods, we prefer the latter, because it is completely tasteless, but if you like a woody taste to your wine, you can choose the charcoal.

In all the recipes that follow you will be instructed to "cork loosely" or "cork tightly." During the second fermentation period the bottles should be loosely corked, and the final sealing (corking them tightly) should not be done until this second fermentation period is over.

When you siphon the wine into a bottle, fill it really up to the top, so that when you insert the cork you actually displace a little of the wine, which will spill out of the bottle as you ease the tip of the cork into it. For this first corking the cork should be forced in only about half an inch. Thus you create a vacuum that allows no air between the liquid and the seal. While this second period of fermentation is going on, at a very slow rate, you *may* get a bit of cork-popping, as there may be enough action left in the wine to blow the corks out of the bottles, but probably not to excess. Should this happen, just recork loosely again and wait until the second fermentation is over. It is very important to cork the bottles loosely during this time, because if you sealed the bottles instead, they might explode.

To cork tightly, force the corks down into the necks of the bottles as far as you can, preferably level with the top of the bottle if possible, so that you'll need a corkscrew to open it. You may want to help this final corking by using a small hammer, but be careful not to shatter the bottle. Put a thick cardboard between the hammer and the cork and hammer the cork in by tapping it several times. For prolonged storage it is a good idea to seal the top of the cork with paraffin, since corks are porous and their flexibility is affected by changes in temperature and changes in the moisture content of the air. Remember to scrape off all the paraffin before you open the bottle, to avoid unsightly floating specks of grease in the glasses.

— APPLE WINE, OR CIDER —

In the United States cider is traditionally made from apples, though it can be made from pears as well. Hard cider is fermented in the same way as wine; actually, it is wine. So we can rightfully call this beverage apple wine.

No yeast is necessary, as the skins of the apples provide enough to provoke fermentation.

Use only unblemished apples, perfectly ripe. Then pound the fruit to a pulp, or grind it. Press out all the juice, with the help of a potato masher, then pass it through a cloth or jelly bag, squeezing it dry. The juice should now be put into a barrel or other container and allowed to ferment at a temperature of sixty-five to seventy-five degrees Fahrenheit. Leave uncovered, except for a cloth you will throw on top to prevent dust from falling in, and let it stand undisturbed for as long as it hisses. When first fermentation has stopped, draw the cider off into a clean barrel or other container, leaving the sediment at the bottom of the previous container.

Cover the barrel or container with a plank of wood or any other material except metal, and after four or five days open it and allow to ferment a second time, just covered with cloth. When the second fermentation has stopped completely, siphon into bottles and cork it. Store in your wine cellar, if you have one. You can drink it at any time from this moment on, but real cider experts say it is at its best only after two years.

— Apricot Wine —

6 lbs. apricots,
stoned but not peeled

3 qts. water

1½ cups white raisins,
coarsely chopped

5 cups sugar

1 yeast cake or

1 envelope dry yeast

Boil the apricots gently in the water until tender. Allow to cool some, then remove to fermenting container and break the fruit with a potato masher or similar instrument, without really crushing it. Add raisins and sugar and stir well. When the liquid is lukewarm, crumble or sprinkle the yeast on the surface and let stand in a warm place, covered with cloth. Allow to ferment for three weeks, stirring once a day.

Now strain through muslin or jelly bag, squeezing out as much of the juice as you can. Let liquid settle a couple of days before siphoning into bottles. Cork loosely until no more bubble action is visible inside the bottles. Cork tightly and store at least three months before drinking. Aging it longer will improve its taste.

If you would like to make a spicy apricot wine, add half a cup of chopped, candied ginger during the first fermentation period and allow to ferment four weeks instead of three, then proceed as above, but age this wine longer before drinking it.

— Beet Wine —

You can make a nice red wine from beets. Since beets are naturally sweet, the amount of sugar required is considerably less than for most other wines.

9 or 10 medium-size beets

3 qts. water

2 cups sugar

1 cup dark raisins, chopped

2 tbs. wheat germ, or ½ cup
cracked wheat, or half of both

1 tbs. freshly grated ginger
root, or 1 tsp. powdered ginger

grated rind of 1 lemon

a few peppercorns

1 package dry yeast

2 slices whole wheat bread,
toasted dark

Scrub the beets without peeling them, remove tips and stems. Put the water in a pot, grate the beets into it, and boil for one hour, covered. When cool enough to handle, strain them through muslin or jelly bag, squeezing out all the liquid. Add all other ingredients except yeast and toast, stir until the sugar is completely dissolved. Make a paste of the yeast with a few drops of warm water, and spread it on the toast, then float the toast on the surface of the liquid, yeast side down. Allow to ferment in a warm place for at least two weeks, stirring several times during the first two hours, then once a day. Strain again through muslin or folded cheesecloth (you may have to strain twice, the second time through filter paper or folded muslin or cheesecloth). Allow to settle another two or three days, then siphon into bottles and cork loosely until the second fermentation is over. Cork tightly and store.

Do not use for at least six months.

— CRABAPPLE WINE —

Those hardy trees produce those nice little fruits in abundance, and if you've made your season's quota of crabapple jelly, turn the surplus into good wine.

4 qts. crabapples
2 qts. water
1 cup white raisins, chopped
½ package yeast
3 cups sugar

Slice the apples thinly, without peeling or coring them. Soak them in lukewarm water together with the raisins and yeast and let ferment in a warm place, stirring daily, for two weeks. Strain through muslin or jelly bag, squeezing well so that you'll gather all the liquid. Stir in the sugar and let stand, at the same warm temperature for another two weeks, undisturbed this time. Strain again through muslin or folded cheesecloth, let the liquid decant for twenty-four hours, then siphon into bottles and cork loosely. When fermentation has ceased, cork tightly and store for at least six months before using.

242

— CRANBERRY WINE —

4 qts. water
7 cups sugar
4 qts. cranberries, chopped
½ cup white raisins, chopped
½ package yeast

Bring half the water and all the sugar to a boil. Pour hot over the cranberries and raisins, add the rest of the cool water, sprinkle the yeast on top, and let ferment two weeks in a warm place, stirring daily. Strain and squeeze the fruit through muslin or jelly bag and let ferment another week, undisturbed. Siphon into bottles and cork lightly. Second fermentation (or rather, third fermentation, in this case) may take longer than for other fruits, so check the bottles thoroughly before corking tightly. This wine matures slowly, so don't use it for several months.

— DANDELION WINE —

Probably next to elderberry, the homemade wine most often heard about—at least in the northeastern part of the United States—is made of dandelions. Dandelions grow profusely practically everywhere.

There are many ways to make dandelion wine, in combination with other fruits or flowers, but use only the blossom, removing the green stuff at its base, or the wine will turn out bitter. We give here the most common recipe from which you can make your own variations.

3 qts. dandelions
(heads of blossoms only,
picked when fully open)
3 qts. water
2 lemons and 2 oranges,
peeled and sliced

½ cup white raisins, chopped
4 cups sugar
1 package dry yeast

As soon as possible after you've gathered the flowers, put them in a crock or bowl, then boil the water and pour it over them. Cover with cloth and allow to stand in a warm place for about a week, stirring occasionally. Strain the dandelions through muslin or jelly bag, squeezing out all the liquid, mix fruit and sugar

243

into the liquid, sprinkle the yeast on top, and let ferment, stirring every day, at warm room temperature for about two weeks. Strain again, discarding the solids, and allow to settle for a couple of days. Siphon into bottles, corking loosely, and allow to go through second fermentation, which should take about two months. But make sure this second stage is over before you cork tightly. Store for several months before drinking.

Should you resist temptation and not drink this wine for a year, don't be surprised if at the time of the next blossoming season, it turns cloudy. Nature makes it ferment once more, but its quality is not impaired.

— DATE WINE —

2 lemons, peeled, then sliced

1 orange, peeled, then sliced

2 lbs. unpitted dates

6 cups water

1½ cups sugar

1 package dry yeast

Chop lemon and orange rinds, halve the dates. Soak these ingredients in water for twenty-four hours in a warm place. Now warm the rest of the water, stir in the sugar, and when the water is almost hot, pour it over the dates. When lukewarm, add the juice from the lemons and orange, crush the dates with a masher, then sprinkle the yeast over the surface of the liquid and allow to ferment at warm room temperature for about two weeks, stirring once a day. Now strain through muslin or jelly bag, squeezing out all the liquid, and ferment another two weeks, without stirring this time. Cork loosely after siphoning into bottles, and allow second fermentation to stop before corking tightly. Store a few months before using.

— ELDERBERRY WINE —

The elderberry is truly ubiquitous. More widely found even than the dandelion, it is really a weed that grows wild along the sides of roads and even highways. Learn to recognize it and to pick its flowers just after the blossom time of the apple tree, then turn these flowers into one of the two following wines.

I

3 qts. elderberry blossoms,   2 lemons, sliced thin
       without stalks   1 cup dark raisins, chopped
        3 qts. water   1 package dry yeast
        3 cups sugar   1 slice dark toast

Bring blossoms and water to a boil and simmer, covered, for twenty minutes. Cool to lukewarm, then strain through muslin or jelly bag, squeezing all their juice into the rest of the liquid. Stir in sugar, lemons, and raisins. Moisten the yeast and spread it on the toast, then float the toast, yeast side down, on the liquid. Allow to ferment two to three weeks in a warm place, then strain through muslin or folded cheesecloth and let sit another two or three days. Siphon into bottles and cork loosely. When second fermentation has stopped, cork tightly and store for about a year before drinking.

II

You can make a spicier elderberry wine, one that is more suitable for mulling and drinking warm on a winter's eve. Use the same ingredients and the same process but add to the sugar about half a cup of candied ginger, chopped fine, and a dozen peppercorns.

— Grape Wine —

We now come to the most popular wines of all and the most natural, since no addition to the grapes is needed, and natural fermentation occurs without yeast.

To make a dry table wine, choose a grape variety that is not very sweet but rather tart. The most suitable are the grapes that are grown specifically for winemaking but should you find these difficult to obtain, you can use regular table grapes. Just select a tart variety with small fruits so that proportionately you will have more of the skins, which are the essence of fermentation and make a better wine. Grapes that are very ripe will yield a sweeter wine, but if they are slightly underripe, the wine will be drier, perhaps a little tart but pleasantly so, and you'll be able to preserve it longer.

If the grapes have not been sprayed with toxic substances during their growth, it is strongly recommended that you don't wash them. If you are not sure check each bunch carefully, since the spray most commonly used is visible on the leaves and on the grapes even when dry. If you must wash at least a few bunches, do it very quickly, then hang the bunches with thread from a rope or stick placed horizontally across two supports in a well-ventilated place. Blowing a fan in their direction quickens their drying.

Unless you want to experiment first with a small amount of grapes, we suggest you make a considerable amount of wine, or the whole effort may not be worth your while. Of course, should you decide to experiment, you'll have to postpone to the following year the pleasure of making a large batch of your own wine. Thirty pounds of grapes will yield about ten to twelve quarts of wine. Should you decide to make this amount, divide the grapes to be fermented in at least two tubs, instead of using only one large container, where fermentation would take longer and might not turn out right. In a warm but well-ventilated room, crush the grapes thoroughly with a stick or mallet. During fermentation, stir vigorously several times, using a pumping motion, to allow as much oxygen as possible into the must. This quickens the process and increases the alcoholic content.

When first fermentation has completely subsided, siphon the wine into bottles, corking loosely until the second fermentation is over. Then cork tightly and store.

This process makes a good, full-bodied wine that you will be able to enjoy about two months after bottling it tightly, though it will, of course, keep much longer and improve with age.

You have now made real wine, which is considered such if it has a minimum alcoholic content of ten percent, i.e., ten degrees. The span in alcoholic percentage for wine is between ten and fifteen degrees. Stronger wines, such as sherry, madeira, Marsala, and port, have been fortified with brandy or other alcoholic liquid. They are still called wines, since their alcoholic contents have been raised by the addition of an extraneous substance, but they are not wines, technically speaking. By the same token, wines that have been diluted with water are also not pure wines, but semi-wines. You can only preserve and age wines with an alcoholic content of ten percent or higher.

However, after you have finished making your authentic wine in the manner just described, you can make an additional batch, for quicker consumption, in the following way.

This *vinello*, or little wine, is an almost-wine, weaker than the real thing, that usually reaches an alcoholic content of about eight degrees. Because it does not come up to the prescribed ten degrees, it will not keep very long and should be consumed quickly. In a cool place, though, you can preserve it for about two months.

This procedure is common in wine-growing countries, as it is a real waste not to make this little wine after the serious wine-making is done.

When you finish making the real wine, calculate the amount you have just obtained and measure about one-third to one-fourth of this amount of water. Pour it on the remains of the grapes, again crushing and stirring with a stick, but this time crush and stir twice a day, and cover the container with a plank of wood or plastic to help it ferment and to prevent the must from evaporating or turning. After about five or six days, the little wine should be ready to siphon off into bottles. You can also repeat the operation more than once, adding more water (in smaller quantity) until when you taste the third or fourth wine it no longer has sufficient flavor.

Label all your bottles not only with the date, but with the number of times it has been processed: second wine, third wine, or strong wine, medium wine, etc. Keep these bottles separated from the real wine, so as not to be confused, and drink the last little wine first.

Both real wine and little wine will be red. The color is given by the skins and seeds, which contain large quantities of tannin. White wines are produced without using the skins, take longer to ferment and to mature, and are better left to the professionals, since the procedure is more complicated.

— DESSERT WINE —

Serve with dessert or as an after-dinner drink.

The type of grapes, as we said before, should be of a sweet variety, such as Concord.

Crush the grapes with a potato masher in the container in which you will let them ferment. Be sure to break all the skins. For ten pounds of grapes use five cups of sugar, adding it to the grapes a cup at a time while you stir the crushed grapes. Allow to ferment in a warm place for about six weeks, covered with cloth; stir daily and mash the grapes a little more each time you stir. Strain through muslin or jelly bag and put back in a warm place, still covered with cloth, for another two weeks, but leave it completely undisturbed this time. When first fermentation is completely over, siphon off into bottles, and cork lightly until you can see no more fermentation. Then cork tightly and store for two months before drinking.

You can obtain a lighter dessert wine from the following:

10 lbs. grapes

2 qts. water

6 cups sugar

Do not crush the grapes first, but add the water to them and let them ferment for six or seven days in a warm place, undisturbed. Then mash the grapes and stir in the sugar a little at a time as you mix it. Put back in a warm place and stir every day for about six weeks, being sure you really turn over the must as you go along. At this point fermentation should have stopped. Put through a jelly bag or muslin, then leave the wine undisturbed for another week. Siphon into bottles, cork lightly for a few days, then cork tightly and store for at least three months before using.

This wine is lower in alcoholic content than the previous one, but it is a little stronger than *vinello*. Because you have added sugar, though, it can be preserved longer than the *vinello*.

— White Grape and Apple Wine —

Another delicious dessert wine can be made with white grapes and apples, although, for the reasons given previously, the final color is going to be much darker than the white wine you might expect.

> approx. 3 lbs. white grapes   3 qts. water
> 3 lbs. apples, tart, chopped fine   6 cups sugar

Mash the grapes thoroughly, add apples, skin, seeds, and all. Bring the water to a boil, then allow it to cool to lukewarm. Add apples, water, and sugar to grapes; set in a warm place, covered with cloth, for about four weeks. Stir and mash every day during this period. Strain through muslin or jelly bag and let ferment an additional week. Siphon into bottles, cork loosely, and watch for the end of fermentation. Then cork tightly and store for at least six months before using.

— May Wine —

May wine can be made from a number of blossoms—apple, rose, clover, or honeysuckle, just to mention a few. Very often it is made from the flowers of the common field daisy, which grows with great profusion in so many parts of this country in the spring. Blossoms can also be used in combination. The recipe is:

> 1 gallon water   ½ quart May blossoms
> 2 oranges, peeled and sliced   2 cups raisins, chopped
> 2 lemons, peeled and sliced   1 package yeast
> 2 lbs. sugar, white or brown

Bring the water to a boil, add citrus peel and sugar. Stir and allow to come to a second boil, then reduce heat and simmer for ten minutes. Put blossoms in a bowl and pour syrup and peelings over them. Cool to lukewarm, then add the juice of the fruit, the raisins, then the yeast. Cover with cloth and leave in a warm place, stirring once a day, until completion of first fermentation. When the bubbling has stopped, remove to bottles, corking loosely for a few weeks or until second fermentation is over, then cork tightly and store.

Let this wine age for at least three months before drinking.

249

— Parsnip Wine —

The best thing we can think of to do with parsnips is to make. wine with them.

> 4 lbs. parsnips, small size   4 cups sugar
>   7 cups water   2 cloves, cut in pieces
> 1 cup dark raisins, chopped   1 package dry yeast
>   1 cup prunes, pitted and   1 slice whole wheat bread,
>   chopped   toasted dark

Scrub parsnips clean, without peeling. Grate them and boil them in the water for one hour. When you can handle them without burning your hands, strain through a muslin or jelly bag, squeezing all the liquid out. Put the raisins and prunes in the container in which you plan to ferment the wine, pour on them the warm liquid, then stir in the sugar until it is dissolved. Add the cloves and allow to cool some more. Then spread the yeast (previously moistened with a few drops of warm water and reduced to a paste) on the toast, which you will then float, yeast side down, on the surface of the syrupy mixture. Allow to ferment, in a warm place, for two weeks, stirring daily. Strain again through several layers of cheesecloth or folded muslin, and let stand three more days. Siphon into bottles, corking loosely until second fermentation has stopped. Then cork tightly and store.

Allow to mature at least six months before drinking.

— Potato Wine —

Don't peel the potatoes in this recipe, since the skin helps the fermentation of this wine, and choose potatoes of a mealy variety, possibly not new potatoes.

>   4 lbs. potatoes   1 cup prunes, pitted, chopped
>   6 cups sugar   3 oranges
>   4 qts. water   3 lemons
> 1 cup dark raisins, chopped   1 package dry yeast

Scrub the potatoes well, removing all dirt, and slice them thin, but don't peel them. Combine sugar and water and bring to a boil. Pour this liquid over the potatoes, raisins, and prunes and let soak for a few hours. Now slice the oranges and lemons, skin and all, add them to the other ingredients, stir well, sprinkle the yeast on top and let ferment in a warm place for at least two weeks, stirring every few days. Then strain, pressing out all the liquid, and allow a few more days for fermentation to end. Siphon into bottles, cork loosely for second fermentation, then seal and store. Allow to mature a minimum of six months before using.

— Rhubarb Wine —

People who don't like the taste of rhubarb (though they often change their minds when served rhubarb that has been stewed with a good amount of honey), can be easily persuaded if they taste this lovely, yellow-amber wine. If you would prefer a red color, you can add red beets, grated first and then boiled for thirty minutes. The amount of beets should be three-fourths that of rhubarb but, of course, you will have to increase the amount of water proportionately and use a little more yeast in combination with the other ingredients in this more classic New England recipe.

2 gallons water
10 lbs. rhubarb, cut into pieces
7 cups sugar
2 cups white raisins, chopped
rinds of 2 lemons, chopped
1 package dry yeast

Bring the water to a boil and pour over the rhubarb. Let stand three or four days in a warm place, stirring occasionally. Strain out the liquid and squeeze it through muslin or a jelly bag. Add the sugar, raisins, and lemon rinds, stirring well. Sprinkle the yeast on the surface and let stand three more weeks at room temperature. Strain again and let the liquid stand at least twenty-four hours before siphoning it off into bottles. Cork loosely until this period of fermentation has stopped completely. Then cork tightly and store for at least six months before drinking.

251

— RICE WINE —
(Sake)

This wine can only be made with brown rice (or unpolished rice), which can easily be obtained in health-food stores or even in many food markets. It is a milder version of the sake of China and Japan.

2 lbs. brown rice
2 cups white raisins, chopped
5 qts. water
3 cups sugar
1 package dry yeast
1 crushed eggshell

Put first two ingredients in fermentation container, together with two quarts of the water. Bring the rest of the water to a boil, add the sugar, stir until dissolved, then pour it over the rice and raisins. Stir well and continue to stir every few minutes until mixture is lukewarm. Now sprinkle the yeast on the surface and let ferment in a warm place for at least two weeks, preferably for twenty days. During this time you must stir the mixture thoroughly, separating any rice that may have clumped, once a day.

At the end of the first fermentation period, strain and ferment again for another ten days. Siphon into bottles and let go through third fermentation (it may take longer than for other wines) before corking tightly. Leave eggshell in for second period.

It is best not to drink this wine for at least ten months.

• LIQUEURS AND CORDIALS •

A good number of the recipes in this section have been translated and adapted from very old European recipes. The adaptation for the most part concerns the main ingredient, pure alcohol, which cannot be purchased in this country, except for rubbing alcohol, which, of course, is not for internal use. Pure alcohol can be bought freely in many European countries (especially those countries that have a low incidence of alcoholism), so that the majority of the recipes in this section called for the genuine product. Since vodka is tasteless, we have chosen it as the substitute most likely to give the best results. In liqueurs or cordials that called for spirits of wine, the closest alternative is dry sherry or similar types of fortified wine, with alcoholic contents that vary between twenty-five and forty-five degrees and therefore come closest to the original ingredient.

On the subject of vodka, we recommend that you buy the most inexpensive brand you can find, provided that the proof corresponds to the recipe. Check the alcoholic content, usually referred to as "proof." One hundred proof means approximately 50 percent alcohol and 50 percent water; it does *not* designate the percentage of pure alcohol. In the case of vodka, there are at least two different strengths of proof, which simply means that the liquor with the higher proof has been filtered (or processed) two or more times, and the one with the lower proof has been processed only once. Because of the double process, the higher-proof vodka costs more. In the United States the higher proof vodka is usually between 90 and 100, the lower around 80.

We have calibrated the following recipes according to the two types of vodka, specifying "strong vodka" for the 90–100 proof and simply "vodka" for the recipes that originally needed alcohol in lower percentage. In case you have only the weaker vodka available and the recipe calls for the addition of some water, lower the amount of water or dispense with it and you will no doubt obtain a good product, although in some instances you may not be able to preserve it quite as long. The sugar that is often added can be melted either in very little water or even directly in the vodka; you'll just have to stir it until melted,

253

which takes a little longer but is quite easy to do. However, if at all possible, we suggest you use the same alcoholic content specified in the recipe.

For some of these recipes you may substitute other types of alcoholic beverages as the base, but remember, the alcoholic content should remain the same and the taste should be consistent. For example, don't try to substitute sherry for vodka (both taste and alcoholic content are very dissimilar), or don't use gin instead of vodka, because the powerful taste of gin would mask the taste of the other ingredients.

Like sugar, honey, salt, and vinegar, alcohol is an excellent preserver of foods, perhaps better than all others; in addition to preserving, it purifies all substances so that it is also the safest of all methods. Alcohol will keep food for greater lengths of time and almost always enhances the taste of the other ingredients.

Although some of these recipes may seem a bit complicated as you read them, after you try some you'll find that they look more difficult on paper than they actually are. As you read them you will often note that at some point you are advised to leave your bottles in storage for a few days or weeks during the process. It is very important not only to label the bottles with the date on which you should proceed with the next step, but also to keep a notebook or chart in a very conspicuous place that will remind you of the prescribed date.

Alcohol evaporates very easily. As you work on these recipes, don't leave the liquor bottles open more than necessary at any time. Use good-quality corks that seal perfectly—the more resilient the cork, the better. We bang the corks into the bottle with a small hammer covered with a rag until they are level with the neck of the bottle. If we are not satisfied with the quality of our corks, or if we make a liqueur that should be stored for a long time, we prefer to seal the top of the bottle with sealing wax, also covering the surrounding area of the neck. Aside from helping to preserve the contents, this final touch gives our bottles a very professional look. If you don't want to bother with sealing wax, simply dip the top of the bottles in liquid paraffin. Wait until the paraffin has cooled off some but is still fairly liquid and repeat the operation twice, after the first sealing is dry.

Filtering is easily accomplished by inserting into a funnel some fairly thick muslin, or (perhaps the best method) a ball of sterile cotton wool the size of your fist. Press it slightly inside the smaller end of the funnel.

A fairly large funnel is a great timesaver. If filtering of certain liqueurs seems to take too long, fill your funnel and cover it with a shower cap or similar cover so that the alcohol will not evaporate.

To clarify cloudy liqueurs, assemble the following:

1 large sheet filter paper

4 tbs. magnesia alba
(carbonate of magnesium, not the laxative type)

1 large funnel

1 clean shower cap or soft plastic bowl cover with elastic

Measure a square of good-quality filter paper about twelve inches on each side, fold it diagonally, and form a triangle. Fold again to make another triangle. Make sure not to pierce any holes as you fold the paper. Open up the sheet of paper and carefully place inside a large funnel. Then slide the funnel inside a large bottle or large wide-necked jar. Cut excess paper at the outer edges, making sure the "tip" of the paper cone fits well inside the funnel, but again be careful not to break the paper. Place the magnesia inside the filter and gently pour the liqueur filling up the funnel (you can place the bottle and funnel against the corner of a wall, so that it will not tip over), but you must cover the funnel while the liqueur is being slowly filtered so that the alcohol will not evaporate. You can do so either by placing a heavy plate on the funnel or (less dangerous!) by covering it with the shower cap or plastic bowl cover. Allow the liqueur to drip slowly and refill the funnel as needed.

Should the first filtering fail to produce a perfect result, repeat the process again using magnesia and check every few minutes to see when it is time to refill the funnel.

— ANGELICA LIQUEUR —

The fruit of the angelica plant, when squeezed, gives out an oil that is frequently used in various types of commercially made liqueurs and perfumes. Therefore, rare as this plant may be in your area, we included the following recipe. We are not sure of the origin of this liqueur, but we found it and very similar versions in old cookbooks from England, France, and Italy.

2 lbs. angelica stems (if tender) or leaf stalks
2 cups sugar
½ cup water
1 qt. vodka or brandy

The stalks must be very fresh, clean, and chopped coarsely. Add the sugar (previously melted in the warm water) to the vodka or brandy, then add the angelica. Cork the bottle tightly and let stand for at least one month, shaking the bottle once in a while. Then pour (filtering out the angelica) into another bottle, cork tightly again, and store.

Allow to stand another month before using.

— ANISE LIQUEUR —

For this other international favorite, which probably originated in France, the most important ingredient is, of course, the anise seed, which should be of very good quality and preferably of the green variety.

1 quart strong vodka	*1 clove*
3 tbs. anise seeds	*few drops vanilla extract*
1 tbs. coriander seeds	*2 cups water*
1 cinnamon stick	*2 cups sugar*

Put all ingredients, except water and sugar, in tightly closed bottle for three months and label with date. Shake the bottle often during this time.

When ready to proceed, heat the water, adding the sugar, and bring to a boil. Allow to boil for three minutes. When almost cool, add to the bottle and shake well, after corking tightly. Label again with a date thirty days later, and don't forget to shake the bottle every now and then. At this point your home-made "anisette" is almost ready. Filter into a clean bottle with filter paper or cotton ball. You may have to filter twice, but quite probably, since this liqueur tends to become cloudy, you may have to use the method suggested earlier in this chapter to obtain good results. At the end of this step, you are ready to cork the bottle tightly, but you should still store it in a dark place for at least two months before tasting it.

— APRICOT LIQUEUR —

1 lb. ripe apricots
1½ cups sugar
1 qt. strong vodka

Stick the apricots in several places with a sharp needle or toothpick. Put them in jars, cover them with the sugar, then add the vodka. Seal and turn upside down, then again right side up a few times for the first few hours, until all the sugar has dissolved. Remove fruits and store for three months at room temperature. If the liquid has become cloudy, filter or clarify. Bottle and store for at least three more months before using.

— BLUEBERRY LIQUEUR —
(*Giásena*)

This is a specialty from the Venetian Alps, where it is called *giásena*. In Italy it is usually made with very ripe, fresh *mirtilli,* a very close relative of the American blueberries. *Mirtilli* are not cultivated, however, are much smaller and sweeter, and leave your mouth a deep purple-blue even if you eat only a few.

Because of the difference in the taste of the two types of berries, we have raised the amount of sugar in the following recipe. The rest, except for the vodka, of course, is exactly the same. And, should you wish to color it to make it look more like the real thing, you might want to reduce the amount of blueberries by two or three tablespoons and replace them with an equal amount of blackberries.

2 lbs. blueberries
5 tbs. sugar
vodka

If the blueberries have not been sprayed with pesticides and if they look relatively clean, don't wash them, just rub them gently with a damp cloth, remove the stems if you wish (but you can also leave them on), and crush the fruit a little.

Place them in a glass jar or wide-necked bottle, add the sugar and enough vodka to cover. Seal tightly, shake well, and let stand for forty days in a dark place. Label the jar with the date.

Now all you have to do is filter through filter paper or cotton ball, bottle, and cork tightly. Do not use for at least one month.

You can repeat this operation three times over using the same blueberries if you wish to make other batches of this delicious liqueur, but after the third time discard the blueberries.

— CAMOMILE LIQUEUR —

This recipe calls for fresh camomile flowers, the very small, daisy-type flowers that grow on rather tall stems, with feathery leaves not dissimilar to those of daisies.

We have never tried to make this liqueur using dried camomile, which can be found rather easily in many drugstores or health-food stores. If you would like to try it using dry flowers, make sure you buy whole flowers and not camomile powder, and that you cut down the amount given here.

It is one of the easiest liqueurs to make:

> *3 tbs. camomile flowers*
> *2 cups vodka or brandy*
> *2 cups dry white wine*
> *pinch of cinnamon*
> *¾ cup sugar*
> *½ cup honey*

Place all ingredients in a bottle and cork well. Shake the bottle often during the first couple of hours, then let stand three days or longer. If you use fresh flowers, wait until they have all descended to the bottom of the bottle. We prefer to shake the bottle once a day—this does not affect the "descent" of the flowers, as they sink when they have soaked up enough liquid to make them heavy—and we leave the flowers in the bottle at least six days. Then filter through filter paper, muslin, or cotton ball, squeezing all the juice out of the flowers. Bottle and cork tightly. Let stand at least two months before using.

258

— CENTERBE —
(Hundred-Herbs Liqueur)

This ancient Italian favorite, which undoubtedly originated in some medieval monastery, has gradually dropped a few herbs over the centuries but it is still a superb delicacy.

All herbs should be fresh, unless otherwise indicated.

1 qt. strong vodka	*4 juniper berries*
4 leaves mint	*4 dry camomile flowers*
4 leaves cedrina	*(6 or 7 if fresh)*
(Verbena triphylla)	*4 cloves*
4 leaves sage	*½ cinnamon stick*
4 leaves basil	*½ tsp. tea leaves (dry)*
4 bay leaves	*⅛ tsp. saffron (dry)*
4 medium-size leaves	*2½ cups sugar*
from a lemon tree	*1½ cups water*
7 leaves rosemary	

Fill a jar or large-neck bottle with the vodka and add the herbs. Cover tightly and let stand one week in a dark warm place, shaking the bottle daily. Boil the sugar in the water for a few minutes, add to the bottle after it has cooled some, and let stand another three days. Then filter through muslin, filter paper, or cotton ball before bottling. Cork tightly and store in a dark, cool place for at least six months before using.

— CHERRY LIQUEUR —

1 lb. very ripe black cherries
½ cup sugar
2 cups vodka
2 cups kirsch or curaçao

It is better not to wash the cherries, unless they have been sprayed with pesticides. If you want to make sure they are clean, though it's a tedious job, wipe them individually with a damp cloth and allow to dry before proceeding. Remove the stems, place in glass jar and, as you fill it, crush the cherries with a fork or a potato masher, so that the pits will be exposed and the juice can flow out of the cherries. Allow to stand, loosely covered, in a cool, dark place for six to eight hours. Then pour into another glass jar that can be tightly sealed, add sugar and the other liqueurs, seal tightly, and store in a cool, dark place for forty days. At the end of this period, filter and bottle.

Do not use for at least two months.

— SOUR-CHERRY-LEAVES CORDIAL —

If you own or live near a sour-cherry tree, and if you think it might be a European variety, a morello cherry tree, pluck a leaf and bite it. If it has a nice taste not unlike that of the fruit, you can make this delicious drink.

100 sour-cherry leaves, large and green
1 qt. red, dry wine
3⅓ cups sugar (or 2 cups sugar, 1 cup honey)

Clean (wash and dry thoroughly, if needed) the leaves and put them in a crock. Cover them with the wine and close the crock. After ten days, remove the leaves, pour the wine into a pot, add the sugar and honey, and boil for ten minutes. Bottle immediately; cork when cool.

— CURRANT LIQUEUR —

3 cups strong vodka
1½ lbs. red currants
1 lb. sugar
1 cup water

Pour vodka into a wide-necked bottle. Without plucking the currants from their stems, rinse them gently if needed, plop them inside the bottle and cork it. Let stand in a dark place for four days, shaking the bottle often. Then strain the vodka into another bottle, allowing the currants to remain in the first bottle. Mix sugar with one cup warm water and pour over the currants. Cork both bottles, and allow to stand another two or three days. Now pour out of the currant bottle only the syrup, and boil it for two minutes. When cool, pour it once again over the currants, adding the vodka from the second bottle. Cork tightly. Two days later, filter the liqueur only into a clean bottle, cork well, and store. In another jar (of the type that can be sealed) place the currants, then seal. Store in a dark, cool place.

When you serve this liqueur, drop a few currants in each glass. But wait at least two months before using.

— ELDERBERRY CORDIAL —

Gather enough ripe elderberries to make a pint of juice when put through a fine strainer. Add a pint of molasses and boil about twenty minutes, stirring constantly. Let cool and add a pint of brandy, stirring again. Bottle and cork tightly. Store in a cool, dark place.

It is a lovely sauce for desserts or fruit, puddings or creams, and a good cough remedy.

— GINGER EXTRACT —

Take the peel from one large lemon and chop it finely or grate it; add one-third cup fresh ginger root, grated, and let both stand together for ten days in a quart of brandy or whiskey, shaking it once a day.

Strain through fine muslin, filter paper, or cotton ball as you bottle it. Seal tightly and store in a cool place. It will keep almost indefinitely.

Ginger extract is good as the basis of a sauce for fish, poultry, or vegetables. Mixed with water it will make ginger tea.

— GRAPE LIQUEUR —

(*Ratafiá di Uva*)

Put in a bottle one pint grappa or aquavit, half a teaspoon coriander, one cinnamon stick, and four cloves. Cover and shake well. Put aside for ten days; shake it frequently. Then wash and stem one pound of ripe grapes, simmer without any other liquid, stirring until they are broken but still in pieces. Remove to a bowl. When cool, pour into the stored bottle, cork and shake well. After thirty days, filter, add four tablespoons of sugar, bottle, and shake it once a day for a week.

Let stand at least six months before drinking.

261

— HONEY LIQUEUR —

2 cups vodka or Armagnac, or any strong orange liqueur
1½ tbs. slivered bitter orange rind, or 3 tbs. regular orange rind, but bitter orange preferred
¾ lb. honey
1 cup water (increase to 1½ if you use other than vodka)
1 clove
2 cinnamon sticks

Put orange rinds in vodka or other liqueur, close tightly, and allow to stand fifteen days. Then dissolve honey in water and add to the bottle with rinds, together with the other ingredients. Let stand, well corked, for four days, shaking once in a while during the first three days. Filter and bottle.

— JUNIPER LIQUEUR —
(*Or How to Turn Vodka into Gin*)

If you live in a hilly or mountainous region and around September or October you can pick juniper berries, or if you can obtain these delicious berries from a specialty store, here is an excellent liqueur you can make with a taste very similar to that of English gin.

Choose the berries very ripe (toward the end of October in temperate climates) and place one-half cup of berries into a bottle and add three and one-half cups strong vodka. Cork well and label the bottle with the date. Store in warm place and shake well every couple of days. Forty days later bring to a boil three-quarters of a cup sugar and one-half cup of water and boil for five minutes. Allow to cool. Add the vodka from the stored bottle, straining the berries (filtering is best). Cork tightly and do not use for at least six months.

— LEMON LIQUEUR —

1 qt. vodka
4 large lemons
3 or 4 cloves
3 vanilla beans, or ½ tsp. extract
½ cinnamon stick, or ½ tsp. powder
4 tbs. sugar

Wash an empty bottle and then pour into it one-half cup of the vodka. With a very sharp knife, remove only the yellow part of the lemon rind and cut it into thin strips, about two inches long. Drop the strips into the bottle and add cloves, vanilla, and cinnamon. Cork tightly and shake vigorously in all directions. Shake a few times a day for eight days. At the end of this period place four tablespoons of sugar and four of water in a fairly large pot, bring to a boil, and let boil three minutes. Allow to cool. Then pour the vodka from the bottle, straining it and reserving the lemon rind. Shake the bottle to allow all the rind to fall out. With a spoon, press the rinds against the sieve as much as possible, in order to gather all the aroma. Add the rest of the vodka, stir, and filter with filter paper or cotton ball into a clear glass bottle.

Do not drink it for at least three months.

— GREEN LEMON ROSOLIO —

If you happen to have on your land one of those lemon trees whose fruits never seem to reach maturity, this Italian recipe is an excellent way to use them, or you may try some of our other green-lemon recipes (see Index). You can make the same liqueur with two limes and two small yellow lemons. Nothing should go wrong that we can think of, and you may invent your own special brand.

3⅓ cups sugar
1 qt. rain water or spring water (or sterilize by boiling)
3½ cups strong vodka
3 garden lemons, still very green

Mix sugar and water into a bottle and shake often until the sugar is completely dissolved. Into a separate bottle, pour the vodka and add the finely chopped lemon rind, also shaking this bottle once in a while, after corking it tightly. Aften ten days, pour the vodka into a bowl, catching the rinds with a sieve. Squeeze the rinds into the vodka with the help of a spoon. Discard the rinds. If much of the rind has fallen into the vodka, filter it into another bottle. Shake the bottle vigorously and let stand another twenty-four hours. Then combine the liquid of the two bottles, stir or shake well, cork tightly and let stand fifteen days, shaking once in a while. At the end of this period, filter into another bottle, and cork tightly.

Store for at least one month before using.

— PORTUGUESE-STYLE ROSOLIO —

This recipe was imported to Italy from Portugal at least a century ago.

peel of 1 large orange
1 cup sweet sherry, madeira wine, or port
pinch of saffron
1 cup water
1 cup sugar

Peel the orange, cutting only the outer portion of the rind and none of the white substance, which is bitter. Chop it coarsely and place it in a large-necked bottle, together with the sherry (or madeira or port) and the saffron. Mix well by shaking it, and let stand three days. After shaking it, uncork the bottle and cover it with only a piece of strong paper through which you will pierce a few small holes, after tying it with a rubber band around the neck of the bottle. In a separate container, mix water and sugar, stirring so that the sugar will melt thoroughly, and let stand also for three days. On the fourth day, combine both liquids, mix well, cover tightly, and let stand eight days. Strain through clean cloth and then a second time through cotton or a paper filter. Cork tightly.

It keeps for at least one year if placed in a cool spot, but don't be in a hurry to taste it; store for at least two months before drinking.

— MARIGOLD CORDIAL —

We now come to an American recipe of the nineteenth century. It can only be made in the summer or late spring, and you must look around for a great number of marigolds, if you don't grow them yourself. You can make an abundance of marigold cordial if you use the following recipe; you may wish to cut it in half, especially since you will perhaps want to test it first and make sure you like it.

> 2 qts. marigold petals 1 cup honey
> 1 cup raisins 3 qts. water
> rind of 1 orange 1 package yeast
> 1 lb. sugar ½ cup brandy
> 1 tbs. glycerine

Wash and drain marigold petals, and put them in a bowl together with the raisins and the chopped orange rind. Separately, make a syrup with the sugar, honey, and water, and heat until almost boiling, then pour over the petals. When lukewarm, sprinkle a bit of yeast on top, and allow to stand twenty-four hours. Stir well, add half the yeast, and allow to stand another two days, stirring once a day. Strain the solids through muslin or a jelly bag, squeezing out all the liquid, add the brandy, and stir in the rest of the yeast and the glycerine. Bottle and cork loosely until it has stopped fermenting, then cork tightly and do not use for several months.

— MILK LIQUEUR —

The following is a recipe from France, where it was a ladies' favorite in the nineteenth century.

> 2 cups milk
> 1 medium-size lemon
> 6 bitter almonds
> 1 pint strong vodka
> 2 tbs. sugar

Boil the milk if it is not pasteurized. Chop the lemon coarsely, rind and all, then crush the almonds with a mortar and pestle, after removing their skin (which can easily be done by plunging them in boiling water for a few minutes). To make this step easier you can use a food chopper at first but finish the crushing in the mortar, so as not to disperse the precious oils and aroma of the almonds. Place all ingredients, including the sugar and vodka, in a wide-necked bottle or jar, seal, and let stand for fifty days. You may have to filter twice before bottling.

— MINT LIQUEUR —
(*Crème de Menthe*)

5 tbs. fresh mint leaves
25 or 30 anise seeds
1 qt. strong vodka
1½ lbs. sugar
3 cups water

Choose medium-size mint leaves, as they tend to have the strongest aroma. Drop them, together with the anise seeds, in a bottle filled with vodka. Shake well and put in a dark place, corked, for eight days, shaking the bottle a few times a day. On the ninth day bring to a boil the sugar and water, stirring constantly while it boils for two minutes. Remove from fire and allow to cool, then pour the contents of the bottle into the pot, using a fine sieve so that the mint and seeds don't fall in. Stir well.

Don't be surprised if the liquid looks pale. Commercially manufactured mint liqueurs can be either white, like yours, or of an incredible emerald green, which is provided by artificial coloring. We suggest you keep yours genuine without any additives.

Bottle and store in a dark place, unless your bottle is of tinted glass. Do not use for at least three months.

— ORANGE LIQUEUR —

8 large oranges
4 large lemons
1 quart strong vodka
2 cups warm water
2 lbs. sugar

Use a two-quart bottle or two one-quart bottles (but in this case you must carefully divide all the ingredients in half). Remove only the outer rind of oranges and lemons, leaving and discarding as much as possible of the white internal part, which is bitter. Cut in very thin strips, about two inches long. Slip the strips into the bottle with the vodka. Mix the warm water with the sugar and pour into the bottle. Cork well and shake the bottle vigorously, bending it in all directions, so that the rinds are completely exposed to the liquid. Allow to stand for six days, repeating this thorough shaking three times a day, then filter the liqueur into a nice-looking, clear glass bottle. Store orange liqueur at least a few weeks before using, for a better aroma.

— PEACH LIQUEUR —

This is a classic liqueur still frequently made in many countries throughout the world. It is very easy to make.

The next time you eat peaches of any kind, save the pits instead of discarding them. (But don't save them for more than a couple of days, or the taste of this liqueur will be weaker.) With the tip of a pointed knife or stiff brush remove any particles of peach that might adhere to the pits, then place the pits into a large glass jar. Fill up the jar about three-quarters full of pits and pour strong vodka over them, filling up the jar. Cover tightly and store, shaking the jar every day. After forty days, weigh an empty bowl and record the weight. Cover it with a clean cloth kept taut by slipping a strong rubber band around it and pour the vodka from the jar into the bowl. Discard the pits. Weigh the bowl again and subtract its own weight. Cover the bowl with a plate and put a heavy object on the plate to keep it airtight, so that the alcohol will not evaporate. Now that you know the weight of the vodka in the bowl, weigh the same amount of sugar and an equal amount of water, put into a pot, and boil for two minutes. When the syrup is cool, add to the bowl, stir well, bottle in a nice-looking bottle, and cork tightly.

It is best not to use it for at least three months.

— PLUM LIQUEUR I —
(*Prunelle*)

This is a home-made somewhat milder version of the French prunelle.

5 large red or wild plums
1 qt. dry white wine
½ cinnamon stick
1 vanilla bean, crushed
¾ cup sugar
1 cup vodka

Peel plums, mash or chop, and boil in the wine for fifteen minutes. Remove from fire and add cinnamon and vanilla. Cover and let stand in a warm, dark place for three days. Strain or filter, and boil the wine together with the sugar for five minutes. Let cool, add the vodka, stir, and bottle. Store for at least six months before using.

— PLUM LIQUEUR II —

A stronger version of plum liqueur, perhaps closer to the real prunelle, is made by using one and one-half pounds of wild plums, very ripe, or small plums, slightly unripe. Mash as for previous recipe, but leave the pits together with the rest of the fruit. Add the other ingredients called for in the previous recipe, except for the wine, which you'll omit, and store the mixture in large-mouthed jars for forty-five days in a dark place, at room temperature, shaking at least once a day. On the forty-sixth day, pour everything into another jar, straining out the solids; then pour into bottles, filtering the liquid. Store for about a month in a dark place, checking it occasionally. Should the liqueur turn cloudy, clarify it by means of the method described at the beginning of this chapter. Store for at least six months before using.

— QUINCE CORDIAL —

If you have a quince tree in your backyard, either apple quince or pear quince, you can of course make jelly or preserves from it, but you may also want to make some delicious quince cordial.

Select ripe, sound quinces only; remove the fur and grate them. Put the fruit into a jelly bag and press out every drop of the juice.

For every quart of the juice you extract, you will need:

25 or 30 bitter almonds, peeled, or cooked peach kernels
⅔ qt. brandy
1 lb. sugar
12 cloves

The inner part of the peach kernel resembles in taste the bitter almond, but it is slightly poisonous unless it is cooked. If you use it, instead of the bitter almonds, break the hard kernel with a hammer and boil the inner "almond" for fifteen minutes before using it. Then add to all the other ingredients in a stone crock, cover tightly, and leave for a week in a warm place, stirring if a film forms on top. Then filter and bottle, corking tightly.

Store in a cool place at least one year before drinking it.

— ROSE LIQUEUR —

Pick one quart of highly scented roses, preferably red. Don't wash them unless they have been sprayed, in which case, soak them briefly two or three times in cold water and allow to dry; you can help the drying along by placing petals on trays, covered with cheesecloth, in a well-ventilated, cool oven for a few minutes. Put the petals in a wide-necked bottle or bottles together with the following:

2 tbs. seedless raisins — *1 tsp. mace*
½ cup jasmine flowers (without stems) — *2 vanilla beans, or ¼ tsp. extract*
½ cup orange blossoms (without stems) — *3 or 4 cloves*
1 cinnamon stick — *1 qt. strong vodka*

Cork the bottle and shake well. Allow to rest in a warm, dark place for thirty days.

Then filter the liquid and add three and one-half cups of sugar dissolved in two cups of distilled water. If the liquid is not clear after the first time you filter it, filter again before adding sugar.

Bottle and cork tightly. Shake bottle vigorously every few hours for a couple of days before storing in a cool, dark place.
Do not use for at least six months.

— STRAWBERRY LIQUEUR —
(*Hypocras*)

This is a very old recipe from France.

2 qts. dry claret or rosé wine
2 cups aquavit, slivovitz, or strong vodka
1 stick cinnamon
1 cup fresh strawberries or raspberries, crushed
1⅔ cups sugar

Mix all the ingredients (sugar last) and allow to stand, covered, for twenty-four hours, shaking the bottle or jar every now and then, or turning it upside down every few hours. Then filter into the bottles. Cork tightly and store in a cool, dark place.
Do not use for at least one month.

— WALNUT LIQUEUR —

This is another European classic.

The walnuts you need here should be at the right point of unripeness around June. You must use them before the shell has hardened, so pierce the green covering with a sharp needle. If the needle goes through the nut without too much resistance, the inner shell is still soft.

When you have prepared thirty nuts, proceed as follows:

30 walnuts *4 cloves*
1½ qts. strong vodka *peel of 1 lemon, chopped*
2½ cups sugar *1½ cups water*
½ cinnamon stick *30 rose petals (optional)*

Quarter the nuts and place them in a large covered container, together with all the other ingredients. (If you choose to add the rose petals, these should have previously been dried slightly in the shade in a well-ventilated spot for at least one day.) Leave the corked bottle, which you will shake often, in a warm spot for forty days.

Strain first through a clean cloth, then once more through filter paper. Before you bottle it, taste it. If it seems too strong— and it may well be, depending on the quality of the walnuts— add one cup of water and let stand, shaking often, for a few more days.

This liqueur improves so much with time that you should not use it for at least one year.

• FRUITS IN SPIRITS •

There is no special process for making these delightful treats, which can be used as condiments for meat dishes or as desserts. The quality of the liquor you use, however, will be reflected in the final product.

— SPIRITED FRUITS —

This old German recipe is still widely used in this country. It is so easy to make and presents so many possibilities in its preparation that we are sure you'll want to try it.

Choose a large crock or jar with a wide mouth, one that can be covered tightly. As fruits come in season, pick a few fruits, ripe but not damaged (large fruits can be halved or quartered or not, pitted or not) and make layers in this jar, covering with sugar at the beginning and then vodka or brandy or any other liqueur you might have handy, provided it is 90 proof or thereabouts. Keep adding the fruit, sprinkling with sugar, and adding more liqueur, but in less quantity as you go along. The fruit should be just covered with it. Continue all summer, keeping the jar always covered. At the end of the summer, pour a large quantity of liqueur and seal tightly. Do not use for at least six weeks.

— BRANDIED DRIED FRUITS —

All dried fruits, especially figs, dates, apricots, peaches, and pears, can be brandied by placing them in jars and covering them with two parts of honey to one part of brandy. Fill jars completely, pressing the fruit down slightly, add the brandy and honey, cover tightly, and don't use for at least six or seven weeks.

271

— Blackberries or Mulberries in Rum —

Wash the berries, if needed, and drain thoroughly. Place in jars and cover with strong rum (90 proof, if possible) in which you will have dissolved one-half cup of sugar for each cup of rum. Seal tightly and store in a dark place. Do not use for at least one month if you have used blackberries, two months for mulberries.

— Cherries in Scotch —

3 lbs. dark cherries
1 qt. Scotch whisky (or brandy)
1 cup sugar
2–3 tbs. distilled water

The cherries should not be too ripe, but still rather firm. Put them in wide-necked jars, cover with the whisky or brandy, and seal tightly. Leave at least six weeks in a warm place. At the end of this time, strain out the liquid and mix with the sugar and two or three tablespoons of distilled water. Bring to a boil and boil for three or four minutes. Let cool, then pour over the cherries, seal tightly, and leave at least three months before eating. Turn the jars upside down for a few hours before you store them, so that the contents will be mixed.

— Chocolate-Coated Bourbon Cherries —

Use very large cherries, ripe but firm, together with their stems. Pack a quart of cherries fairly loose in jars, stems up, and pour over them the following syrup:

2 cups sugar
¾ cup honey (possibly dark and thick)
1 cup water
bourbon
chocolate

Boil the syrup for five minutes, allow to cool, and then add about one and one-half cups of good bourbon, stirring well. Add to the cherries, close the jar or jars tightly, and store for at least six months.

At the end of this period, drain the cherries and reserve the syrup (and don't forget to cover the jar, so that the alcohol will not evaporate). Melt two cups of bitter or semi-sweet chocolate (according to taste) in a small double boiler. Now dip the cherries, one by one, holding them by their stems, into the chocolate, then place them in a single layer on wax paper until the chocolate hardens and dries. When ready, store them in tin cans, placing a sheet of wax paper in between layers. Or, wrap individually in wax paper or aluminum foil. Store in a cool place, so that the chocolate will not melt.

The bourbon syrup can be used either in fruit salads or any other dessert; it is particularly excellent in parfaits of any kind.

— BRANDIED FRESH FIGS —

Choose about a quart of ripe, fresh figs, when they are still unopened at the bottom. Place in bowl and pour over them boiling water into which you have previously dissolved two tablespoons of bicarbonate of soda (baking soda) for each quart of water. Let stand five minutes, then rinse the figs in cold water, drain, and dry thoroughly in hot sun or slow oven. In the sun, allow about half a day, in the oven about two or three hours. They should just begin to wrinkle and ooze out a little of their internal juice.

Bring four cups of water and two cups of sugar to a boil and boil for five minutes. The proportion of water to sugar should be raised or lowered, according to the amount of figs you use. Add the figs and simmer for about thirty minutes. Remove the figs with a strainer and continue to boil the syrup until thick. Pour over the figs and let cool. After twelve hours, pack the figs into jars and add about one-fourth brandy to each one-pint jar. Seal tightly and store at least three months before using.

— GOOSEBERRIES IN GIN —

Clean the berries, leaving a small portion of the stem. Stick each fruit in several spots with a sharp needle, then place them in jars and cover with gin. Seal tightly and store in dark place.

Do not use for at least two months. You can then serve the fruits and liquor separately, or you can place one or two gooseberries in individual glasses and cover with gin.

273

— GRAPES IN VODKA —

Use the directions in the previous recipe with any very sweet grapes. Leave a portion of the stems and substitute vodka for gin.

— SPIRITED GRAPES —

2 lbs. grapes, seedless if possible, and large
1 cinnamon stick
4 cloves
grappa, aquavit, or slivovitz, at least 90 proof
½ lb. sugar
½ cup warm, distilled water

Snip each grape off the branch with scissors, leaving a piece of stem. Wash, then drain immediately and wipe dry with a clean cloth. Place them in jars about one-fourth from the top. Cut or break cinnamon and cloves, and using double or triple layers of cheesecloth, make one or more small bags, which you will tie with string after placing the spices into the bag. Place the bag in the jar, cover with grappa (or other liquor), seal jar, and let stand in a warm place for at least twenty days. At the end of this period some of the alcohol will have been absorbed by the grapes. Remove the bag with spices. Prepare a syrup made with the sugar and water. Let cool before pouring into jar. Seal tightly.

Let stand for at least three months before using.

— PEACHES IN VODKA —

2 lbs. peaches, not too ripe
¾ cup sugar
1 qt. water
12 cloves
1 cinnamon stick
strong vodka

Wipe peaches with a damp cloth, gently trying to remove some of their fuzz, though this is not essential. Pierce them in several spots with a sharp needle or toothpick. Dissolve the sugar in the water and boil the syrup for ten minutes. Then add the peaches and simmer ten minutes more after the syrup has returned to a boil. Remove from fire and allow the peaches to cool in the syrup for twelve hours, covered, then place in jars. At this point you may or may not remove the pits; we prefer leaving them, as they add flavor. Add cloves and cinnamon (divide if using more than one jar), and fill the jar or jars with the vodka. The proportion should be at least one-third vodka, or more if you like them strong. Seal tightly and place jar upside down for a few hours before storing in a dark place.

Store the jars for a minimum of three months before opening.

— PINEAPPLE IN WHISKY —

Peel, core, and slice pineapple in rounds about one-fourth inch thick. Prepare a syrup made with three cups of sugar for each four cups of water for each two pounds of cleaned fruit. Boil the syrup for five minutes, then add the pineapple and boil for ten minutes. Drain and place in jars wide enough to hold the slices horizontally. Cover them with rye or Scotch whisky. Seal tightly and place jars upside down for a few hours before storing.

— PLUMS IN CHERRY BRANDY —

Choose plums of a sweet variety, remove pits if you wish, and prick them with a needle in several spots. Place in a wide-mouthed jar but do not pack tightly. Cover them with a good-quality cherry brandy, using at least one-fourth of the jar capacity. Cover jar tightly. The next day, or two days later, add more of the liqueur, as the plums will have absorbed some. Continue to do so another couple of times, daily. Cover tightly for at least one month before serving. Add more cherry brandy as plums are eaten, and more plums (at the bottom of the jar) if you wish. We prefer packing them in medium or small-size jars and using them all at once.

— PLUMS IN SLIVOVITZ OR PRUNELLE —

Choose very ripe fruits, rather on the soft side. Peel them by plunging them in boiling water for about twenty seconds, then immediately soak them in ice water. You may try peeling them by hand as some varieties of plums, when ripe, peel easily. Leave a piece of stem if it's there. Put in jars and cover with liquor, using at least one-fourth for each jar. Seal tightly and place jar or jars upside down for a few hours before storing in a dark place. Allow to stand at least three months before using.

— TANGERINES IN VODKA —

Peel the fruit and remove the white filaments. With a very sharp knife, cut each tangerine horizontally into slices about one-half inch thick, removing the seeds as you go. Prepare a syrup in the proportion of two cups of sugar for each cup of distilled water for each pound of peeled fruit. Simmer the syrup for five minutes, add the tangerine slices, and simmer for another ten minutes. Drain and put in warm jars. Cover with one part syrup for every three parts vodka. Seal tightly.

— TANGERINES IN KIRSCH —

Prepare tangerines as in the recipe for tangerines in vodka, but when you are ready to store, cover them only with the liqueur, without adding the syrup.

You can also add Cointreau or Armagnac instead of kirsch. And you may wish to add some raisins to the jar.

— TANGERINES IN GIN —

Cut the fruit in halves or quarters and remove the seeds. Prepare the same syrup as for tangerines in vodka, but when you add the fruits, cook ten minutes longer. Drain and place in jars. Cover with a mixture of about one-fifth of the cooked syrup and gin.

CHEESES

The idea of making your own cheese will strike you as extraordinary, if you have considered it an art better left to the professionals. While this is true for many cheeses that need to be made and ripened under special conditions, there is a variety of cheeses you can easily make at home. All you need is some ingenuity and patience, and a keen eye for the correct moment at which to proceed with each stage of cheese-making.

According to a popular legend that has many versions, cheese was "discovered" accidentally a few thousand years ago by a Middle Eastern shepherd who, lacking a container in which to pour the milk he had just taken from his goat, placed the milk in the stomach of a freshly killed calf and hung it on the back of his mule while he was slowly traveling a long distance in the hot sun.

Actually, the primary condition for making cheese is a calf's stomach. In fact, the fourth stomach of a young calf contains in its lining high quantities of a powerful coagulant enzyme called rennin (more commonly referred to as rennet). This enzyme, also present to a lesser extent in the stomach of most domestic animals, is the substance still widely used to quicken the process of coagulation of the milk in making many cheeses. While in

277

many agricultural areas of the world the farmers and peasants still use the actual stomach of these animals when they make their own cheese, in this country rennet can be purchased in liquid or tablet form containing an infinitesimal amount of the stomach.

There are other effective coagulants that can be used in making cheese; many of these are extracted from various plants, and some American manufacturers have been experimenting with synthetic coagulants as well.

However, rennet is not used for all cheeses. Many fresh cheeses, such as cottage, farmer, cream, or ricotta, don't need rennet, but the coagulation process is helped by another "starter," such as buttermilk or lactic culture. And some cheeses turn out best if both a starter and a coagulant are used.

The primary aim in making cheese is to get the milk to separate into whey (the liquid portion) and curd (the solids). For most cheeses only the curd is used. But don't discard the whey. Whey can be used instead of water for soups, stews, or similar dishes, for baking, or just as a drink.

Cheeses are divided generally into just a few categories: fresh cheeses, which are usually soft and have to be consumed within a few days; mild or slightly ripened (meaning aged) cheeses, whose consistency is usually more solid and can keep for some time; and aged or cured cheeses, sharper in taste and usually harder. Some of these can keep for several months or even a couple of years and their taste actually improves with aging. Certain of these varieties require a special process of manufacturing and must be aged under strict temperature and conditions that would be next to impossible to reproduce at home. Many of these are cheeses that also need to be made in huge sizes, such as Parmesan or Swiss, and the sizes alone, aside from all the other requirements, are too much to handle in the average household.

But you'll be surprised to see how many cheeses you can actually make at home once you've mastered the basic principles, which don't vary too much from cheese to cheese. All you need to do is experiment with a few cheeses, the simple ones first; then you can use your imagination and a little daring, following the same general rules, and make up your own. After all, this is how all cheeses were originally invented, often by imaginative farmers and sometimes as the fortunate result of a mistake made during the manufacturing of another type of cheese.

So when you first attempt to make your own cheese, don't worry excessively about precise schedule, amount of starter or coagulant, or exact temperature. Your cheese may not come out exactly as it was supposed to, but unless you have really blundered, you may have invented a new cheese. And that's a good part of the fun. Every batch can be slightly different, and you can also experiment by adding herbs or spices, garlic, seeds, food coloring, or a little wine or brandy.

While we try to give you fairly precise instructions, some of the recipes are adapted from very vague guidelines given in books or pamphlets published fifty years ago or more. To give you an idea of how approximate these were, here is part of a recipe we found in an American cookbook from the middle of the nineteenth century:

"Strain the night's milk into the tub; in the morning stir in the cream and put a part of the milk over a fire in the kettle. Heat it enough to make the milk which is still into the tub quite warm but not hot; pour it back into the tub, and strain in the morning's milk."

All the utensils you use in making cheese should be kept scrupulously clean, not only while you make the first batch of cheese but even more so for your subsequent products, as the bacteria formed during this process tend to continue reproducing if not washed out completely, thereby affecting the taste and quality of your cheese.

You'll need very few things to make cheese. A dairy thermometer is essential, but before you buy one, check your candy thermometer to see if it registers lower temperatures than those needed for candy or jams; if it does, you will not need a special one.

Of course, you will need cheesecloth or muslin. Nowadays many types of fabric called cheesecloth are woven much more loosely than the original that gave cheesecloth its name and was used just for this purpose. If your cloth seems too thin, it's a good idea to fold it one or more times to reach the thickness of a

279

loosely woven muslin. Otherwise you are bound to lose some of the curd as you strain your cheese.

A larger double boiler is helpful but not essential. You probably have a large pot or kettle you can use for this purpose; keep in mind that you need room to work the curd while the whey is sloshing about.

While we recommend using your bare hands for stirring, there are times when you'll have to stir with a long wooden spoon or spatula. There is a special cheese stirrer that you may wish to buy, though it's not necessary. However, the spoon or spatula should be perforated, so as not to damage the curd.

To quicken the process of coagulation, it would be helpful for you to use either a commercial starter or fresh cultured buttermilk. And for many cheeses you'll also need a coagulant such as rennet, which can be purchased in specialized dairy stores or through commercial manufacturers, as can other non-animal coagulants. See list on page 326 for brand names and addresses.

Some cheeses are dyed different colors, primarily yellow to orange. We prefer leaving our cheeses natural, but if you want to use dyes you can use food coloring, or even licorice extract, or you can obtain cheese coloring from specialized dairy companies, also listed on page 326. The most common dye is a bright orange obtained from the seeds of a tropical tree called annatto (sometimes called achiote). This is harmless and you can use it without fear. Yellow coloring can be made by boiling saffron in water, or red coloring from beets. We suggest you make sure of the contents of other colorings before using them.

Another piece of equipment you will need is a cheese press. You can make your own, preferably out of wood, either square or cylindrical in shape. Or, you can use a plastic container, provided its width is the same on top as it is at the bottom. Or, easiest of all, you can use a very large sturdy can, perhaps one that contained fruit juice or coffee. Cut out top and bottom, taking care not to leave any rough edges, which may hurt not only your hands but the cheese as well. Obtain a plank of wood— thick plywood will be fine—and cut two pieces the exact size of the metal circles you have just cut out, or just right to fit snugly inside the can.

With the exception of the cheese press—which you'll use when the milk has already turned to cheese—it is recommended that all other utensils, especially the pot or kettle, be made of stainless steel and not of aluminum or galvanized metal. Earthenware is perhaps best.

The general directions for cheese-making precede the recipes because the basic steps are very similar for many cheeses. As you read the instructions for each type of cheese you'll either omit one of the steps mentioned here or you'll modify them according to the guidelines given in the specific recipe. So, as you make each cheese, please keep referring to this section.

The recipes given in this chapter have been arranged with the easiest first and become progressively more difficult. So, if you have never made cheese, we suggest you try the various cheeses in the order presented here.

The rules that follow deal for the most part with the more elaborate types of cheeses.

If you have unpasteurized milk, pasteurize it, and then cool it quickly by putting the pot in which you heated the milk into another container or basin filled with ice water, until the milk cools to 86 degrees Fahrenheit. At this point, don't let the temperature fall any lower, but replace the ice water with lukewarm water to keep the milk warm. If you started with pasteurized milk at refrigerator temperature, use lukewarm water in the outer basin to reach the same temperature, but *slowly*.

You are now ready to add the starter, which can be either a commercial lactic culture or cultured buttermilk. The buttermilk must be very fresh, and you'll usually need about twice the amount of the commercial starter. Or, instead of these starters, you could also add some milk that is in the process of turning sour. This is the way a lot of cheeses are still made in many countries, especially for home use, although the results may be quite uneven; using a starter that contains the right coagulating bacteria will give more consistent results.

Gently stir in the starter when the milk has reached the 86-degree mark or close to it, and maintain this temperature by adding a little warm water every now and then in the outer basin, if you are using this system. You could also heat the milk by putting the pot directly on an electric hot tray at the lowest temperature with a piece of cardboard under the pot; or near a radiator, with the pot wrapped in wool; or in any other way you can devise. If you have made yogurt (see Index), all you have to do is follow the same method. We find that the "double boiler" system is advisable because you can raise or lower the temperature easily by changing the temperature of the water in the outer container.

The milk should ripen in about forty minutes (or anywhere between half an hour and one hour).

The addition of rennet is not essential to all cheeses, but if the recipe calls for it, now is the time to use it. The amount is usually specified by the manufacturer, and it can vary so much according to the strength of the product that we would only confuse you if we gave you an exact amount here. Rennet can come in liquid or tablet form, the latter being more common, and should be diluted in a few tablespoons of cold water. You can, of course, use a vegetable coagulant or a synthetic one instead of the rennet, if you prefer.

Stir the rennet or other coagulant into the milk gently but thoroughly, after the milk has ripened. If you plan to color your cheese, this is the proper time to stir in the coloring as well. The stirring motion should be slow and constant, for about one minute. Cover the pot and let it rest completely undisturbed until the mixture coagulates, which should take about thirty minutes. If it takes less, it means you have used too much rennet. However, this will not affect the final results. Keep track of the amount of rennet you used so that next time you can adjust it according to this schedule, but make sure you use the same brand or you'll have to test it again.

The milk should be left undisturbed. Any vibrations nearby, or your moving or banging the pot, may cause the whey to ooze out of the curd before the allotted time, and while this may not totally ruin your cheese, it may get pretty close to it.

You are ready to cut the curd only after you have tested it for readiness. This can be done in either of two ways: (1) Insert the blade of a knife or spatula between the inner wall of the pot and the milk and gently pull it away; the space created by your pressure should fill with whey; (2) Insert your finger on a diagonal into the curd; if it comes out clear and the hole gets filled with whey, you are ready to cut the curd. The illustration below will help you visualize this very easy step. What you are trying to do is help the release of more whey, which is trapped inside the mass of curd. To do this you should cut the curd into chunks as even as possible in size and shape. The size is almost always specified in the recipe, and usually varies between one-fourth inch and one inch. Any handy gadget can be used, but make sure it's rustproof metal! With a long knife (preferably one with a blunted tip), cut the curd vertically first, in "slices" of the desired thickness, making sure you reach the bottom of the pot each time. This accomplished, give the pot half a turn and cut the curd again at the same distance. Then, since with a knife you will not be able to make perfectly horizontal cuts, slice the curd on a diagonal, first in one direction; then, giving the pot half a turn, in the opposite direction.

CUTTING THE CURD

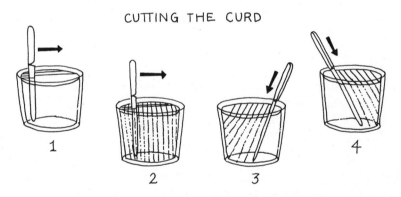

Cutting the curd should be done while the pot is still kept warm, as the temperature of 86 degrees Fahrenheit should be maintained throughout the process, from the time you started warming the milk.

A sufficient amount of whey should be released in fifteen minutes before you heat the curd and proceed. During this time gently stir the mass, especially at the bottom of the pot, where the curd may lump together after you cut it. Stir it two or three times, very carefully, so as not to damage the curd.

283

Sometimes heating the curd is referred to as "cooking" the curd, although you don't exactly cook it; in fact, you must constantly avoid reaching what is usually considered the cooking point. This is the most important step in successful cheese-making. The temperature should be raised *very slowly* to about 100 degrees Fahrenheit or a *little* higher. This again can be done by placing the pot into another pot or container half filled with warm water, and adding warmer water gradually until the desired temperature is reached, which must then be maintained. Any other ways you can devise to maintain this temperature are perfectly all right. Some people place their pot on or near the spot on their gas stove where the pilot light is burning; if they have an electric stove, they place the pot in the outer container on a burner kept at the lowest possible temperature. Others start their oven fairly high about twenty minutes before and place the pot on top of the stove, either switching off the oven or lowering it. Try the system that works best for you, but always make sure the temperature does not rise beyond the specified heat, give or take but a few degrees. And always make sure the curd reaches the desired warmth very slowly. It should take a minimum of thirty minutes for the curd to go from 86 to 100 degrees, so the first time you try, do it even more slowly than necessary. It doesn't matter if it takes a little longer, but it does matter if you try to shorten the time.

During the process of heating the curd, the chunks should be mixed every few minutes, especially those at the bottom. This is best done by using your hands, as you can easily gauge the inner temperature and you can move the bottom curds to the surface and those at the center of the pot to the sides, and vice versa, so as to warm them evenly. Should they lump together, gently separate them with your fingers.

Since more whey is released with the warmth, don't be surprised if the chunks you originally cut shrink in size. This is normal.

After a while, when you see and feel that the curds are becoming more solid, it is time to test their doneness. Take a piece of curd between your fingers, squeeze it, and release. It should break apart and be rather springy, not pasty. Or bite into one piece; if its consistency is that of thick gelatin and it squeaks under your teeth, it is ready. Test the curd a few times before you think the right moment is approaching. Try not to let it go beyond this point, or your cheese will come out too rubbery and hard. Since the curd will keep on "cooking" for a few minutes even after you begin cooling it, it is better to start cooling it just before it has reached the correct consistency.

Remove the pot from the fire or add a little cool water in the outer basin if you are using that heating system. Allow the curd to settle at the bottom for a few minutes, then scoop out most of the whey with a large ladle or a small pan, without disturbing or breaking the curd. Whatever is left can be poured off by stretching a muslin or double layer of cheesecloth on top of a strainer and gently pouring out both whey and curd. Allow the whey to drain for a couple of minutes or so, helping it by gently moving the curd with your hands and mixing it to make sure the curd does not lump together.

During this process the temperature should not fall below 86 degrees Fahrenheit, so act quickly and check it as you go.

Salting is better done a little at a time (the amount of salt varying according to the instructions in the specific recipe, or to taste). But, regardless of how much or how little salt you are adding, spread it evenly throughout the cheese. Sprinkle some on top, stir, then sprinkle on some more, stir again, and so on. Should you wish to add pepper, spices, seeds, and such, now is the time to do it.

Try to act quickly, so that the temperature will not fall below 86 degrees. If it should fall a little below, do not despair. This is the final step, and even if the cheese you are making needs pressing, the exact temperature is not as important now.

For hooping and pressing the cheese, unless you have an old-fashioned cheese hoop or are lucky enough to find one, you can, as mentioned before, make your own very easily. Prepare the lining beforehand, as the curd should be kept at the same 86-degree temperature until you fill the hoop.

Line the hoop or can with thin muslin or a double layer of cheesecloth, overlapping it slightly on the side (see drawing on page 286), and fold it at the bottom, leaving enough cloth so that the cheese won't be exposed and also leaving some cloth at the top of the can or hoop. The upper portion of cloth should be taped over the outer side of the can, or you can slide a rubber band to keep it in place while filling the container with cheese. Now fill the can with the curd, pressing the curd down with a wooden spoon or spatula as you fill it, to make sure you don't leave any air pockets, but don't press too hard; just fill the can evenly. When you reach the top, fold the edges of the cheesecloth over the cheese.

Now apply some weight on top of the can, either a clean stone or two, or a jar full of water, or anything else you might have handy. If you wish, you can put a wider surface, such as a flat plate, on the cheese if the weight you use is bigger than the hoop, but always check that the plate or flat surface rests completely on the followers, or your cheese won't get pressed. Add a third disk on top smaller than the diameter of the hoop. First add at least five pounds for about fifteen minutes. Then double or treble it. The amount of weight depends on the cheese you made and the length of time you are planning to cure it. Cheddar cheese, which is one of the pressed cheeses you can make at home, requires a weight of between twelve and fifteen pounds for the first ten minutes, then it should be increased to twenty-five or thirty pounds for another hour, and finally to thirty to forty pounds overnight or for about twenty hours, after the cheese has been "dressed" a second time (a step that is explained below).

Other cheeses will need less weight, and you can gauge the pressure yourself by experimentation and according to your taste. The heavier the weight and the longer you press the cheese, the harder the cheese. These are only general guidelines, and since one of the charms of home-made cheese is its slight difference from that you buy, pressing and aging are variable. Keep in mind, however, that both the weight and the length of time depend also on the amount of whey left in the curd, so press it more or less for a longer or shorter period of time, depending on the type of curd and the result you are aiming for. Remember also that too much weight too quickly can produce cracks in the cheese, which you most certainly don't want, especially if you plan to age it; these are like open wounds that will heal poorly if at all during the curing process. However, should any small cracks appear after you remove the cheese from the press, you can still dip it in warm water briefly and try to join the cracks together with your fingers.

When you "dress" the cheese, you smooth out the wrinkles from the cloth after the first stage of pressing. Sometimes this is repeated after the second stage, if needed. After pressing, the cheese will have shrunk as more whey is released by pressure, and so its "dress" will have become too big. Reduce the size of the cloth by pulling it closer to the cheese; again overlap it slightly on the side, fold it on top and bottom, and trim away the excess cloth. If you need to press the cheese some more, be gentle when putting it back into the hoop, then add the followers, and press it for another twenty hours or so, increasing the weight by a few more pounds than the previous time.

As you dress and re-dress the cheese, always check it for cracks and if you find any, dip it in warm water. Then squeeze the cracks together with your fingers, rebandage, and press it again for one hour, even if the cheese would normally not need any more pressing.

The process of aging is also called curing or ripening. Without "undressing" the cheese, but perhaps adjusting and smoothing the cloth a bit, you can put it back in either the can or hoop for a couple of days. Lay the can on one side so that the cheese can dry in the air; or, if it's firm enough to retain its shape, you can start the aging immediately. This should be done at a temperature of about 50 to 60 degrees Fahrenheit in a dry, well-ventilated place. The cheese should first be wiped with a clean, slightly damp cloth, then wiped dry. Place it on a clean wooden board or shelf, wipe it dry all over, and turn it upside down daily, also drying the board. After about one week the cheese should have formed its natural rind. You can then continue aging it in the same way. You don't need to wipe it daily any longer but should change the spot in which it rests and still turn it upside down every few days.

In fact, you will notice after a few days that the cheese will tend to become too dry on its surface. This can be counteracted by dampening it with a cloth ever so lightly. Using wine instead of water may improve the taste of the cheese. At the beginning, after the first week of drying, this dampening may have to be done daily or every other day. This is done primarily so that the rind won't dry so quickly that the inner portion of the cheese will not be permitted to age properly.

Should you prefer to omit this constant care of the cheese, you should treat your cheese in any of the following ways, after it has dried for about a week, and only after the rind has begun to form.

After you have dried the cheese for a week or so, brush the entire surface with melted paraffin, making sure it's not too hot. Repeat if you think the first coat was too thin.

You may choose instead to smoke certain cheeses (see Smoking chapter).

Among the other ways you can form a rind, the simplest is to rub the cheese with coarse salt all over, either a few days after it has dried on the shelf or even immediately. The salt draws out the inner moisture and at the same time quickens the drying process. If you apply salt the very first day, you may have to wipe the cheese dry after a few days and re-salt it.

Another method, very old-fashioned but perhaps the most effective not only in speeding up the drying process but also in promoting the curing, is that of rubbing the outer surface of the cheese with lime powder, finely ground and perfectly dry, or a mixture of lime powder and salt, about half and half.

Coating the cheese with lime not only quickens the formation of the rind but is very effective in preventing mold, which is one of the problems often encountered while aging cheese.

If you use this method, make sure you remove the rind when you eat the cheese, a precaution that is always advisable (with very few exceptions), even with commercially manufactured cheese sold in an outer wrapper. While lime does not affect the taste or quality of the cheese, the rind so treated is inedible.

— BUTTERMILK CHEESE —
(Petit Fromage)

Should you experiment in making butter, aside from using the buttermilk for other uses or as a starter for some of the cheeses described in the following pages, there is a very simple cheese you can make utilizing buttermilk exclusively. It comes from Switzerland, where it is sometimes called *petit fromage.*

Use only good buttermilk that you have obtained from very fresh heavy cream. Put it in a bowl or stainless-steel pot, covered, and let it rest at warm room temperature, undisturbed, for about twenty-four hours. Then raise the temperature slowly to 90 to 100 degrees Fahrenheit and maintain this temperature for several hours, or until the buttermilk has thickened considerably. Now skim the semi-solid portion and gently put it on a piece of folded muslin or cheesecloth (folded several times), which you will then hang to drip for several hours more, or until the cheese has become firm but not dry. Then remove it to a bowl, add a little fine salt and pepper, and work it well with a wooden spoon. Wrap it again in muslin or cheesecloth and put it in the press, or, simply line a small sieve with cloth and suspend the sieve until all the rest of the liquid has dripped out. If you use the press, don't add any weight; if you use a sieve, just cover it with the cloth. Either way, there is no need to press this cheese; just let it dry a second time.

Refrigerate and eat within a few days, as this cheese does not keep longer than that.

— CURDLED MILK —

You may or may not wish to call this a cheese, but it is an excellent and nutritious concoction that has been made all over the world for centuries. This international staple doesn't seem to have gained any special name except curdled milk. It is the easiest of all cheeses to make.

This is also a good way to put to use any milk you have that may be about to turn sour, or that has already curdled. But, of course, you can also make it with fresh milk.

There are two basic ways to make it:

For the first, put one quart of milk in an earthenware container or stainless-steel pot. Add the juice of three lemons, stir the juice in, cover, and allow to rest at a temperature of 60 degrees Fahrenheit or a little lower for about ten or twelve hours. Smear some butter on a loosely woven cloth (or two or three layers of cheesecloth) and pour the curdled milk on it, tying the ends of the cloth to make a little bag. Hang the bag to drip, with a bowl underneath. When it has stopped dripping, put the cheese, still in its bag, on a plate and place a flat surface on top (no metal, but another plate would do). Add a few pounds of weight on top. It is ready when it has become more solid and holds its shape.

Serve it in slices, with a little sugar, honey, or jam on top or, if you prefer, with salt, pepper, and a little oil of good quality.

For another kind of curdled milk, heat the milk quickly until almost (but not quite) at boiling point. Add two tablespoons of vinegar for each quart of milk (or lemon juice in the same amount, if you prefer). Allow to cool to lukewarm in the same pot, which should not be made of aluminum. If you use an aluminum pot, pour the milk into another container to cool. Then add a little salt, and proceed as in the previous recipe, hanging the container to dry without letting it rest.

You can make this little cheese from milk that has already curdled completely. Just start from the step at which you wrap it in cloth and hang to drip.

— RICOTTA —

This delicious, versatile cheese is so mild in taste that it is found palatable even by people who don't like cheese (including children).

There are two basic types of ricotta, and the one that is more popular for use in most familiar Italian dishes, such as lasagne, has probably never reached your table. This is Roman ricotta, which is used almost exclusively in Rome and southward, while the type we are familiar with in the United States is found almost exclusively north of Rome. In Italy it is called Piedmontese ricotta.

Roman ricotta is made from goat's milk, sheep's milk, or sometimes even from buffalo's milk, although this milk is more often used to make the old-fashioned (and more authentic) mozzarella. The ricotta made of goat's milk has a completely different taste and is firmer and not quite as creamy as the more common variety. To our palate it is much tastier, and most of the Italian dishes popular in this country are made with this kind of ricotta in Italy and are therefore more flavorsome and compact. If you can obtain goat's milk, there are two very simple ways to make ricotta. The first method is the easier, but the second comes closer to the real thing and has the added advantage of being one of the few cheeses for which you can actually use the whey you separated while making other cheeses. We therefore recommend you plan to make the second type of ricotta soon after you have made other cheeses, so that you'll have the whey it calls for.

To make what we shall call Ricotta I, for each quart of whole milk you'll need the juice of a small lemon (about one and one-half tablespoons) or the same amount of white vinegar. Mix the lemon juice or vinegar with the milk in a flame-proof earthenware container or heavy enamel pot (provided it has no chips inside), or any container that would retain the heat well. Bring it slowly to almost boiling point, when the milk will start to coagulate. Just before it boils, immediately remove from the fire and put the pot in another container filled with warm water, or cover the pot with woolen rags or blankets, or put near the radiator or on a hot tray at the lowest degree of heat, so that the milk keeps warm and doesn't cool below 80 degrees Fahrenheit. In about twelve hours you will have ricotta.

One quart of milk yields about half a pound of ricotta.

For Ricotta II, save a considerable amount of whey when making other cheeses. You can make the ricotta at the same time as the other cheese you've just finished is being pressed or is still draining. Or, you can refrigerate the whey. It will keep for about one week.

The recipe given here requires a half gallon of whey. Put it directly on the fire (without a double boiler) and heat it until a creamy substance rises to the top, at which point you will pour in fresh whole milk in the proportion of three cups for each half gallon of whey. Heat both to scalding point (do not boil). Immediately stir in three and one-half tablespoons vinegar or lemon juice and keep stirring vigorously until the curd floats, while the temperature is kept high but not quite at boiling point. If all the curd seems to float at the same time, drain it by pouring everything through a colander lined with a double layer of cheesecloth. If some of the curd has not risen yet, start skimming the curd that floats with a slotted spoon so that it won't overcook, then either continue to skim all the curd in this way or finish by draining.

Leave ricotta to drain thoroughly for about seven or eight hours in a fairly warm place (warm room temperature is sufficient). You can then mix in a little salt or leave it unsalted, as you prefer.

Refrigerate and use quickly, as ricotta does not keep more than a few days.

There is an infinity of ways to use ricotta that you may not be aware of. Aside from adding it to certain dishes you cook, which is probably the only use you put it to, it makes an excellent dessert. Just add sugar or honey to taste and brandy (Cointreau, or practically any other sweet liqueur, also to taste), and top it with chopped nuts; or add a tablespoon or two per pint of very strong coffee; or mix with a little coffee powder (ground fine), powdered chocolate, or carob, bits of fruit, etc.

— TOMME DE SAVOIE —

This little cheese is quite common in the Alpine regions where France, Italy, and Switzerland have common borders. In Italy it is called *Tomo* or *Tomino di Savoia*, since its origin is the region of Savoy, which is now French but which belonged to Italy before World War I.

It is a fresh cheese, very easy to make with the help of a coagulant. The amount of coagulant is not specified in our ancient Swiss recipe, as at that time it was still made by placing a piece of a calf's inner stomach on top of the milk, but we presume the amount should be fairly substantial, as the milk is supposed to coagulate in about ten minutes. The milk should be warmed up very gently to the usual temperature, when the coagulant is added. As soon as the milk curdles and the whey separates, stir, place in a basket (or double layer of cheesecloth), and let hang for twelve hours at room temperature, then turn upside down and allow to drip for another twelve hours. During this second drying period it can be gently pressed by putting a small weight on top, provided the cheese is placed in a container with rigid sides and perforated bottom.

In the refrigerator this cheese can keep for at least a week, but if you'd like to preserve it for a longer period of time and add a delicious taste, you can preserve it Italian style (see Index for cheese in oil). Should you decide to preserve it, make it in small shapes, and put one in each jar.

— CREAM CHEESE —

Next to ricotta, this is perhaps the easiest cheese to make and also rather economical, since a relatively small amount of whey is separated from the curd, yielding about two pounds of cheese for each gallon of milk used. Cream cheese is made with whole milk and needs no rennet, just a starter.

For one-half gallon of milk, you'll need to add a quarter cup of the professional starter or one-half cup of cultured buttermilk. Mix the starter in gently, trying to avoid the formation of bubbles, then allow to rest, covered and undisturbed, at a temperature of 86 degrees Fahrenheit for approximately ten hours.

Check the milk after about nine hours and keep an eye on it to see when it reaches the coagulating point. When the milk has coagulated, put the mass into a double layer of cheesecloth and hang it with a bowl underneath to allow the whey to drip out, or simply line a colander or sieve with muslin or cheesecloth (double layered) and place it over a container that will catch the whey. This draining process should take place at a temperature around 50 degrees, if possible. The refrigerator will do, though it's a little too cold. Let it drip until you think, by its looks and taste, that it has reached the right consistency. Stir in one teaspoon of fine salt and refrigerate it immediately if you don't want it to become too sour.

Your cream cheese is now ready to eat. It is usually creamier than the cheese you purchase in stores, but if you like you can make it stiffer by cutting the curd into chunks of about one-half inch, then letting more whey drain out by raising the temperature slowly to about 90 degrees for fifteen to thirty minutes, without mixing or stirring. Chill quickly.

— Cottage Cheese —

Contrary to popular belief, this cheese is a bit tricky to make, despite its humble appearance. It uses pasteurized, skimmed milk and the yield is approximately one pound of cheese from one gallon of milk.

For small-curd cottage cheese, no rennet is needed, but you must use a starter—either a commercial lactic culture or fresh cultured buttermilk. For one gallon of milk, the recommended proportion of starter is about one-quarter cup for lactic culture and one-half cup for buttermilk.

Raise the temperature of the milk to that of fairly warm room temperature, about 70 to 72 degrees Fahrenheit, and try to maintain the same warmth during the sixteen to twenty-four hours of incubation. When the desired temperature is reached mix in the starter very gently, cover the pot and leave undisturbed, but check it after about ten or twelve hours, because the milk may have reacted more quickly to the starter, or you may have used too much starter. At the end of this period the curd should be rather firm. Test it as suggested in the introduction to this chapter. When the curd is ready, cut it into one-quarter-inch chunks. Allow about fifteen or twenty minutes to elapse after cutting the curd, then start the "cooking" process by placing the pot in another larger pot, half filled with warm water, then putting both on a very low fire until the temperature has risen to about 115 degrees. Heat the water very slowly at first; it should take a minimum of thirty minutes to reach 100. Then you can raise the flame slightly, so that it will take another fifteen minutes for the curd to reach 115. During the entire cooking stage you should stir the curd gently with your hands or with a wooden spoon, but preferably with your hands as you can then feel the temperature easily and distribute the curd evenly. Be careful not to damage it as you move it about. Do this mixing every five or six minutes, or until the curd has become firm. Test a few pieces between your fingers; they should not break easily but should be slightly rubbery and spring back if you try to squeeze them gently. Do not let the curd overcook; it is preferable to undercook slightly, as the cooking process continues for a while even after you have removed the curd from the pot. On the other hand, if you have difficulties reaching the desired consistency within the time we specified, the temperature can be raised to 120 or a maximum of 130. If your hands can't take the heat at this point, use a wooden spoon for mixing.

Now the curd is ready to be drained. Do this quickly. Dip off as much of the whey as you can, holding back the curd with a flat strainer, then line a strainer or colander with a double layer of cheesecloth and let the curd drip for a few minutes. Now pull the curd up by joining the corners of the cheesecloth and immerse your bag in a bowl of cool water; lift it out, then submerge it again a few times. This cools the curd and washes away the excess acidity. Repeat rinsing in another basin filled with ice water, then drain it by placing it in a lined colander or suspending the bag for a few minutes. Now you can salt the curd and mix it, or you can refrigerate without salting it, though the salt cuts some of the sourness, so we suggest this addition.

Your cottage cheese is ready. Refrigerate it and enjoy it soon.

Large-curd cottage cheese is made in the same way as small-curd, except that rennet is added. Follow the manufacturer's instructions, or dissolve one-quarter tablet of rennet in a few table-spoons of cold water for an average-strength tablet. Add it to the milk together with the starter, after you have raised the temperature of the milk to 70 or 72 degrees. Then proceed exactly as in the previous recipe, but coagulation should take place sooner, in ten to fourteen hours. Cut the curd in larger pieces, about one inch in size.

You can cream either of the two types of cottage cheese. When you have finished making the cheese, stir in light or heavy cream, sour cream, or yogurt, in the proportion of three or more tablespoons for the amount given.

— NEUFCHATEL CHEESE —

This French classic is relatively easy to prepare and is similar to cottage cheese, but firmer and less sour. To make, assemble the following ingredients:

1 qt. pasteurized whole milk

½ cup buttermilk

¼ to ½ rennet tablet
(depending on brand),
dissolved in a few tbs. of water,
or as per manufacturer's instructions

Slowly raise the temperature of the milk to about 85 degrees Fahrenheit, then add the buttermilk and rennet. With a wooden spoon, stir very gently for about fifteen minutes, trying to "feel" the consistency of the milk change during the last few minutes. Stop stirring the minute you think the milk is setting.

Cover the pot and maintain the same temperature for several hours, or until the whey rises above the curd and the curd breaks clean. Cut the curd in one-inch chunks, then strain gently, using a colander lined with a double layer of cheesecloth or muslin. After most of the whey has dripped out, help it along by pressing the top of the cheese. Let drain a little longer, then put it in your press, if you have one, or fold over the corners of the cheesecloth, put a flat dish or plank of wood on top, and add about a two-pound weight. A jar filled with water or a few clean stones can do the job. Put the whey in the refrigerator in a bowl or wide-mouthed jar, covered. After a while you'll see that the cream floats to the surface and becomes harder. Skim it off and add to the cheese, working it in with your hands or with a wooden spoon. Continue kneading until the cheese has acquired firmness, then add salt to taste.

Refrigerate and use within a week.

— AMERICAN CHEESE —

This is relatively easy to make, and would be a good cheese for the beginner to experiment with. The yield is approximately one pound of cheese for each gallon of whole milk.

For this amount you'll need one cup of cultured buttermilk, or half a cup of the professional starter. Use a double boiler that will take more than one gallon, to allow yourself some room to work with inside the pot. Warm the milk slowly in the double boiler to a temperature of 86 degrees Fahrenheit, at which you will keep it for two hours. Now dissolve in about four tablespoons of cold water the amount of rennet called for in the instructions given with your product, depending upon the brand you use. Stir in the rennet gently but thoroughly and let stand at 86 degrees until coagulation occurs; this process should start about half an hour later. If you added too much rennet, it will start to coagulate sooner, so keep an eye on it the first time.

When the milk coagulates, cut the curd into about half-inch chunks. After another thirty minutes raise the temperature slowly by putting the pot in a double boiler over low heat. This is perhaps the trickiest step. The temperature should be raised ever so slowly, and it should take a *minimum* of thirty minutes for the curdled milk to reach 104 degrees. Wait a few minutes after you have reached this temperature, then wash your hands well, and start mixing the curd very gently without disturbing or breaking it too much. This is done to produce even heat, so that the best way is to bring the curd from the bottom and outer portion of the pot toward the center and vice versa. A scooping motion to raise the curd from the bottom to top is effective, but try not to crush or squeeze the curd, or you'll lose precious cheese. However, you should cut with a knife any curds that are considerably bigger than the rest, so that you'll have a fairly even size with the rest of the curds, which will shrink or have already shrunk as they expel the whey. The aim is not only to have curds that are even in size, but the chunks themselves should have the same texture inside as well as outside.

Maintain the 104-degree temperature for about one hour, mixing the curd with your hands every ten or fifteen minutes. If after about forty-five minutes the curds seem to be still quite far from the desired consistency, raise the temperature slightly, but not beyond 120. The correct consistency should be that of putty; if you sink the point of a knife into a chunk of curd, it should not stick to it and the chunks should not stick together. It is hard to describe the right stage at which the curd is ready, and you may go a little wrong the first time. Make notes of what you do and when, and these notes will help you when you make the next batch. Since the curd keeps "cooking" and tends to dry after the pot is removed from the fire, it is advisable to stop cooking it a little earlier than the exact moment of doneness, much as you would do when making jam. Overcooked curd makes a rubbery cheese, while slightly undercooked curd simply yields a softer cheese.

When the curds are ready, line a sieve with muslin or a double layer of cheesecloth, pour them into the sieve, and soak them in lukewarm water (slightly cooler than the cooking temperature). Lift the four corners of the cloth one at a time and allow the curd to roll to the bottom of the sieve so that the entire mass will be rinsed. Then drain, and when it has stopped dripping profusely, but before it has cooled and has drained completely, mix in one tablespoon of fine salt (a little more or a little less, to taste). Continue draining until the whey stops dripping. Then put the cheese into the hoop and press it, following the instructions given at the beginning of this chapter.

When you remove the cheese from the press, if you want mild American cheese, you can eat it immediately. If you prefer sharp cheese, age it. If you plan in advance to make the latter, you can either age it as is or, for a better-tasting cheese, increase the time of first incubation (before you add the rennet) from two hours to three. For cheese you want to age, follow the further instructions at the beginning of the chapter. It is recommended to paraffin or otherwise coat this cheese.

298

— CHEDDAR CHEESE —

Another American favorite, Cheddar cheese, requires some extra steps, and we suggest you try it only after you have made some of the simpler cheeses.

You start exactly as for American cheese, but add the rennet tablet or other coagulant about three hours after the temperature reaches 86 degrees Fahrenheit. The curds are softer and cut in smaller pieces than for American cheese, about half an inch, but the process of cooking and mixing continues in the same way.

At this point, however, the process changes. Strain the whey out by lining a sieve with folded cheesecloth but do not wash the curd. Put it instead into a clean pot, sprinkle one tablespoon of fine salt on it, and mix it with your hands without damaging the curd. Put in a double boiler, cover, and very slowly raise the temperature to about 100 degrees, but no higher than 105. Check the state of the curds and mix every ten minutes or so. They will probably gather in one lump. Should this happen, cut them with a knife or spatula to release more whey, which is then poured out. The curd should be rather firm and stringy before you remove it from the pot and rinse it in lukewarm water. Salt it again, after you have let the curd drain about halfway. Don't overdo it with the salting, but keep in mind that Cheddar cheese is supposed to be saltier than other cheeses. If you taste it at this point, don't be alarmed if it seems to be very sour; the taste will straighten itself out while the cheese is pressed, and even more while it is being aged. Finish draining as for American cheese, then follow the pressing instructions given at the beginning of this chapter.

Cheese connoisseurs rave about Cheddar cheese that has been ripened two or even three years; but if you are eager to taste your first attempt at making Cheddar cheese, age it for at least two or three months.

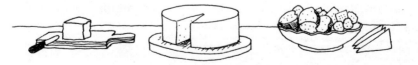

— ITALIAN CHEESE —

This is another basic method for making cheese. If we don't give it any specific name other than Italian, it is because, while this basic method is often used in Italy, the cheese obtained by following this recipe is a mixture of a few cheeses, not any specific one. It bears a vague resemblance to provolone, but we cannot call it that as it is softer and not quite as tasty. If you have goat's milk, though, use it for this cheese and the result will be a closer relative to provolone.

Follow the guidelines already given in the previous two recipes, as well as the instructions at the beginning of this chapter. For one gallon of whole milk, after warming it to 86 degrees Fahrenheit and without using a starter, immediately add a high dosage of rennet or other coagulant, about three times the amount used to make American cheese. Wait for coagulation (it may take about forty-five minutes). When the curd breaks clean, cut it in large chunks, then cook it by raising the temperature very slowly to about 130. Even more so than with other cheeses, it is recommended that you use your hands rather than any kitchen implement, because the mass of curd for this cheese must be gathered together into one rather hard lump. When you succeed in doing this, the cooking has reached the proper stage. Now pull out the ball of curd and wrap it in muslin or a double layer of cheesecloth. Remove the pot of whey from the outer pot of water and raise its temperature almost to scalding point (but do not boil) and submerge the wrapped curd in the liquid, immediately removing the pot from the fire. Cover and allow to cool. Then suspend the cheese in the bag and let it drip for about twenty-four hours in a dry, warm place.

Your cheese is now ready to eat. Or, you can smoke it, as this cheese lends itself particularly well to that process. Age it at least a few months before eating it. If you don't smoke it, allow it to dry, suspended, for at least one week before coating the outer portion. It should form a rather dry crust naturally, though, so you may omit any other step.

— Home-Style German Cheese —
(*Potato Cheese*)

This cheese is still made very frequently in the north of Germany, as well as in other German regions.

Choose five pounds of potatoes of a mealy variety, scrub them, and boil them in their jackets until they are very well done, then peel and mash them. Add a little salt and knead briefly into a thick paste. Add one quart of clabbered milk a little at a time and knead the paste again until you obtain a homogeneous paste. To clabber milk, bring it to scalding point, add one and one-half tablespoons of white vinegar or lemon juice, and stir vigorously until the milk separates. Allow to cool a bit, then knead.

Put the paste into a jar and cover it, letting it rest at warm room temperature for four or five days. Now take out the paste, knead it again, line a wooden tub (preferably) or wide-mouthed earthenware jar with muslin or a double layer of cheesecloth large enough to fold over on top, stuff the cheese in it without leaving any air pockets, fold the corners of the cloth over it, and place the container in a well-ventilated spot, away from the sun. After four or five days, or when the surface of the cheese seems to have become considerably drier, pull out the cheese, holding it by the ends of the cloth, wipe the inside of the container if any liquid has gathered, open up the cheesecloth and place the cheese in it upside down, then insert it once again inside the jar or tub and allow the other end to dry a few more days. The drying period should take about fifteen days, and the two ends of the cheese should be exposed twice, so pull out and upturn the cheese every few days.

The wooden tub or box is preferred because the cheese can dry more thoroughly and has to be turned only once; if you used a crock or glass jar, it may have to dry longer. The wooden container is also a better choice because at the end of the drying period the cheese stored in it will continue to age, if put in a dry, cool, ventilated place.

This is an excellent cheese, and can be eaten either immediately after the drying period or later, after it has aged. It can also be aged outside its container. In this case, provided it is solid enough not to lose its shape, pull it out and leave it in its cloth wrapper for a few more days, turning it every day and wiping the spot in which it has rested, then "undress" it and paraffin it.

— HOME-STYLE COOKED CHEESE —

The recipe for this very unusual, rich cheese comes from Switzerland, where this cheese is still made at home, especially in the Alps with its abundance of dairy products.

3 qts. clabbered milk
6 or 7 tbs. butter
salt and pepper to taste
1 egg yolk

If your milk is not clabbered, follow the instructions in the previous recipe.

Put the clabbered milk in a pot and raise its temperature to about 68 degrees Fahrenheit, then leave undisturbed for two hours, or until curd and whey are well separated but before the

curd hardens. Now drain the curd and suspend it wrapped in a jelly bag or a bag you make yourself out of folded cheesecloth or muslin. Drain it sufficiently but don't allow it to become too dry. Then crumble the curd with your hands, making fairly even, small chunks. Cover the bowl or crock with several layers of muslin or cheesecloth resting directly on the cheese, and let it rest at a temperature of 65 to 68 degrees for about three or four days, or until the mass has become yellowish in color and begins to smell like cheese. Now set aside two tablespoons of the cheese. Slowly melt the butter in a pot large enough to contain the cheese, which you will add together with salt and pepper, as soon as the butter has melted, and stir constantly with a wooden spoon, working the paste so that it becomes homogeneous. Continue to simmer until the mixture looks oily; it doesn't matter if it starts boiling, but keep the flame as low as possible. Mix the egg yolk with the cheese you have set aside, then add it to the rest of the cheese and mix well, turning off the heat. Pour the cheese into small, warm jars, wide-mouthed so that it will be easy to remove the cheese. Allow to cool before sealing. Store in a cool place.

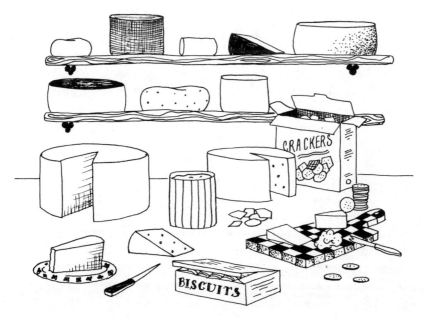

SAUSAGES

Sausages are an excellent means of processing certain kinds of meat. They can be smoked or simply dried before cooking and last indefinitely without refrigeration.

One of the problems here is putting in a supply of sausage casings. Most ordinary markets, at least those we checked in the Northeast, don't carry them. A number of specialty meat markets and meat wholesalers do, however, and in a medium-sized Connecticut town we found a meat wholesaler who was delighted to sell sausage casings to private individuals. And we were just as pleased to hear him speak of selling them by "the hank." A "hank" is a bunch of skins that will accommodate about one hundred pounds of sausage-meat.

The skins are, of course, the large intestines of the pig, that most entirely usable of farm animals, although the cow's intestines are often used too. Stuffed derma, a feature of many a Jewish wedding feast, on the other hand, is also a kind of sausage, but the casing in this specialty is usually not the intestine of any animal but instead the skin of a chicken's or turkey's neck, available wherever poultry is sold.

— Basic Sausage —

To make two pounds of sausage, chop coarsely or pass through a meat grinder one and three-quarter pounds of any type of pork meat (preferably the shoulder) and one cup of unsalted lard. To make good sausage, the meat must be of very good quality, without too many nerves. Add about two tablespoons of coarse salt (the salt used for curing), half a tablespoon of freshly ground pepper, and half a tablespoon of powdered saltpeter. Mix all ingredients thoroughly. (Herbs and other spices can be added to the mixture, if desired.)

To prepare the casings, cut a few yards and wash thoroughly in running cold water, allowing water to run inside as well, but making sure you don't break the casings. Then submerge in luke-warm water for about half an hour to soften further.

To stuff the sausage you can use a funnel with a wide neck, then place it inside the casings and gather the skin accordion-like around the neck of the funnel. The entire length of the casing should be bunched up. Tie the far end securely with string, then start inserting the meat (without breaking the skins) a little at a time. A small stick can be helpful in stuffing. As you press down the meat, gently squeeze the casings to push the stuffing toward the bottom. Repeat this often, or it will be more difficult to stuff the rest of the meat. Your hand should become like an extension of the funnel in helping the meat get properly stuffed, and you can keep squeezing the casings gently as you insert the meat. This sounds more complicated than it actually is. But it is very easy, once you get the hang of it. In case you rupture the casing, simply tie the sausage just below and again just above the hole and continue stuffing. At the end, remove the funnel, give a final push to stuff the last of the meat, and tie this end. Cut the casing if you have some left over. Now tie your sausages very tightly at intervals of about four or five inches. Stick them with a needle a few times and hang in a warm place for a few days. Then store them hanging in a cool place for at least a week before eating.

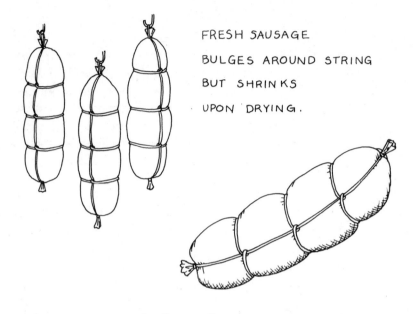

FRESH SAUSAGE
BULGES AROUND STRING
BUT SHRINKS
UPON DRYING.

— Liver Sausage —

To make two pounds of sausage, chop coarsely (or pass through a meat grinder) one and three-quarters pounds of pork liver and one cup of unsalted lard. Add two tablespoons of coarse salt, one-half tablespoon of freshly ground pepper, one and one-half table-spoons of seedless raisins, and two teaspoons of thinly peeled orange rind, chopped finely. Stuff as for basic sausages.

— Luganega Sausage —

To make this Italian favorite, chop coarsely or pass through a meat grinder two pounds of shoulder of pork and two cups of unsalted lard. Place mixture in a bowl, add one cup grated Parmesan cheese, two teaspoons of ground white pepper, one teaspoon of mixed spices, and one-half cup of meat stock. Mix all ingredients thoroughly, then stuff as for sausages. The casings for this sausage should be of a smaller diameter than those for sausages, if possible. Before you tie into sausages, prick the outer skin with a large needle, to make sure all air and excess liquid are expelled.

— Coppa —
(*Pig's Head*)

You can make this delicious *coppa* only if you or somebody you know has just butchered a pig, or if you can obtain a pig's head from a nearby sausage factory.

You'll need half a pig's head, cut lengthwise. Remove the eyes and brain and scoop out the fat portion in the cheeks. Immerse the head in clear water for at least half an hour, then wash it thoroughly in running water so that all the particles of coagulated blood are washed away. Then boil it in a large pot with enough water to cover, until the meat can easily be removed from the bone. If you prefer a leaner *coppa,* add to the head other pieces of pork meat, such as muscles from the shoulder or from other parts of the pig. Separate the meat from the bones very carefully, making sure no pieces of bone are left in the meat. Then chop it coarsely and for each two pounds of meat add the following seasoning: three and one-half tablespoons of salt, one teaspoon of freshly ground pepper, and one teaspoon of mixed spices. While the meat is still hot, mix all ingredients.

You'll need about one yard of large casings (cow's intestines) at least three inches in diameter, which you will wash as for other sausages. Tie one end of the casing with strong string, leaving one end of the string very long. Stuff as for other sausages, pricking frequently with a large sharp needle to remove air and excess liquid. When you finish stuffing, pull the long end of the string over and use it to tie the finished other end of the *coppa.* Then tie like an old-fashioned salami, using the longitudinal string and passing it through in the other direction, pulling enough to make the meat in between bulge about one inch. Secure the entire *coppa* by repeating at intervals of a few inches, using the same length of string, and making a loop at one end for hanging. Prick with needle a few more times as you tie the *coppa.* This process is important, because it helps compress the meat, which tastes not unlike Philadelphia scrapple.

Hang the *coppa* to dry and finish cooling. When cool, wipe with a clean cloth and hang again in a cool place. Do not eat for at least three days.

This *coppa* can keep for a few months. In the summer, if your storage place is not sufficiently cool, refrigerate.

— COTICHINO —

Following are two recipes to make *cotichino*, a sausage that is later cooked. In Italy they can be bought, so that all you have to do is cook them, but since they are almost impossible to find here, try making them yourself.

Chop coarsely about five and one-half pounds of the pig's neck and shoulders and two and one-half pounds of pig's skin. Then pass it through the meat grinder twice, or until finely chopped. For this amount of meat you'll need:

¾ cup coarse salt	*3 tsp. freshly ground pepper*
1½ tsp. saltpeter	*2 tsp. cayenne pepper*
2 tbs. ground nutmeg	*grated Parmesan cheese*
2 tbs. ground cinnamon	*to taste (6 tbs. or more)*

Mix all ingredients, together with some water previously boiled and allowed to cool partially, making a fairly loose paste. Stuff in pig's or cow's casings (if you use cow's intestines, choose them rather small), using the same method as for sausages (see recipe at the beginning of this section). Make these sausages about eight inches long, either cutting them so that you make them separately or like sausages, but allowing about one-half inch of empty skin in between a double tying, so that they can be cut loose later. Hang them to dry for at least three days in a warm, well-ventilated place.

Or, for another kind of *cotichino*, you can use rather large pig's intestines as casing and wash thoroughly, as for all previous recipes. Drain and pat dry, then immerse in a bowl with white wine for one hour. Now stuff them as for sausages using one and one-half pounds of lean pig's meat from neck and shoulder, and about three-quarters pound of fresh pig's skin, to which you have added one-half pound unsalted lard or bacon, three table-spoons coarse salt, one-eighth teaspoon saltpeter, and one teaspoon of mixed spices. The meat and pig's skin should be ground very fine before adding the other ingredients.

Proceed with stuffing and tying as in previous recipe. To finish curing the *cotichini,* use any method that will provide a dry temperature of about 75 degrees Fahrenheit or a little higher. They should be left at this temperature for about thirty hours. If kept longer they will last longer, but don't leave them more than two or three days. Hang them about three feet above a stove or heater and hang a thermometer beside the *cotichini.* A stick or wire should be placed at this height, horizontally, so that the *cotichini* can hang from their loops. Make sure they don't touch.

After you have dried them, hang them in a cool, dry place. Either kind of *cotichino* should be boiled before eating and can be preserved up to two months.

— Zampone and/or Zampino —

Zampone means large paw, and *zampino* small paw, so the only difference between these two sausages is one of size. As the name implies, these are encased in the lower portion of a pig's foreleg, which is a bit tricky to prepare but well worth the trouble. *Zampone* is very similar to *cotichino*, except that it is not quite as fatty. The stuffing can be very similar to that used for *cotichino.*

Try to obtain a pig's leg that has been cut rather high, so that you'll be able to use more stuffing and make a bigger *zampone.* Make sure that the leg you get has not been pierced by the butcher's hooks, or you will not be able to use it. Scrub the outside of the leg with a stiff brush and a little warm water, but do not soak in water. Rinse it by wiping it with a damp cloth and again wipe dry with a clean cloth. Starting from the higher portion of the leg, begin "peeling" off the skin by opening it inside out, as if it were a stocking. Proceed very carefully, with a small sharp knife, to cut the tendons and separate the bone from the skin, then remove the bone until you reach the actual hoof, which you will leave attached. Make sure you don't pierce the skin with your knife as you work to separate the skin from the flesh. Now rub the skin with coarse salt inside and out and sprinkle it with freshly ground pepper, then put it on a platter or shallow pan and cover with a weight. Let stand for ten days in a cool place. At the end of this time, rinse with one cup white wine and leave it in the wine while you prepare the stuffing, for which you will need:

1½ lbs. lean pork (shoulder or neck or both)
⅓ lb. fresh pork skin
2 tbs. coarse salt
1 tsp. mixed spices
⅛ tsp. saltpeter

The stuffing for *zampone* should be rather lean, but if the meat you have seems to be excessively lean, add about three table-spoons of chopped, unsalted lard. Chop or pass through a grinder the pork skin first by itself, as it is often rather tough, then pass it through the grinder once more with the meat. Mix all ingredients thoroughly with your hands, until the whole mass is evenly seasoned. Wipe the leg casing dry inside and out, then stuff it, pressing it down as you fill it, and pressing again at the end, making sure there are no empty spaces. You can stuff it tightly by pushing in your fingers and fist. When you have finished stuffing the leg, take a large needle and strong thread and sew the top portion using a basting stitch. Pull gently at the end, so that the skin will gather a bit, then secure the end by sewing a couple of stitches backward and out.

This sausage should also be cooked before eating, after aging it at least a week.

· SALAMI ·

— GENOVESE SALAMI —

Make a mixture of meat that is half lean veal and half pork, the pork half being two parts lean meat to three parts fat. Put the meat through your grinder with a few garlic cloves (peeled), about two cloves to the pound of meat. Then spice it strongly, using one tablespoon to the pound of meat if either mixed sausage spices or equal quantities of salt, peppercorns (or pepper), or powdered clove, cayenne pepper, and saltpeter. (The salt-peter will help in both preserving and hardening the meat; if you don't have any on hand, let the alcohol in your favorite red wine or liqueur do the job.) The choice and proportion of spices are a matter of taste, though you should not underdo them, both for preservation and faithfulness to the Genovese way. Now stuff your casing as for a solid, closely packed sausage. Tie the salami securely at both ends, leaving the string very long on one side, then use it to tie the salami at few-inch intervals as if for making a bulky package, and pull each time to squeeze the sausage so that it will bulge (later on the bulge will disappear as the salami dries). End with a loop by which you'll hang it in the usual cool place.

The salami should remain hanging at least two months before eating, but not much longer than six months or it may dry out too much.

Salami of any type (provided it is not the commercially made kind that has plastic casings) that has dried and aged a bit may be coated with beaten egg whites all over. When the egg white is dry, hang it again in the same cool place. This should preserve it longer. Or, you can age it for a year or so under ashes.

— PHILADELPHIA SCRAPPLE —

1 fresh pig's head, eyes and teeth removed	pepper
1 pinch each: sage, thyme, marjoram	buckwheat flour
	yellow cornmeal
salt	

Scrub the head well, cut off ears, and scrub inside. Put head and ears into pot with enough water to cover by a few inches. Boil until the meat separates easily from the bones. Remove and chop very fine, discarding the bones, then put meat back into the liquid in which it was cooked, and add the seasonings. Mix buckwheat and cornmeal in equal parts with a little cold water. The proportions should be one cup meal for each three cups liquid (including the water), plus three cups chopped meat. Cook over medium fire, stirring constantly, until you have a thick mush. Allow to cool completely, then slice and fry it until golden brown.

Scrapple will keep in a cool place for several weeks.

{ BUTTERS AND SAUCES }

• BUTTERS •

— ANCHOVY BUTTER —

Remove the spines of the anchovies, if necessary, and mash them with more than twice their amount of sweet butter. Put in small jars and close tightly. Store in a cool place. If the jars are full, it will keep well.

It is frequently used as a base for canapés, or alone as a spread, but you can also add it to certain bland vegetables as you cook them. Or, dot your steaks with it as they come out of the broiler. Just remember not to add any salt to your dishes if you plan to use it. If you think the taste of this anchovy butter is too strong, try curry butter.

— CURRY BUTTER —

1 cup clarified butter
1½ tsp. curry powder
¼ tsp. ground pepper
¼ tsp. paprika
dash cayenne pepper (optional)
1 tbs. brandy or vodka

Mix all ingredients well until thoroughly blended, leaving brandy or vodka for last. Stuff the butter in small jars, fill completely, seal, and store in cool place.

Use as sandwich spread or serve on meat or fish, especially broiled. By substituting other spices or herbs for the curry, or by mixing it with other sauces, such as Worcestershire sauce (in this chapter), you can vary the taste and make your own version of any "butter."

Or, you can prepare in advance and store the following basic butters.

— HERB BUTTER I —
(for Use on Meats)

4 tbs. chopped parsley	2 tbs. port, sherry, or madeira
4 tbs. chopped chives	1 cup clarified butter
1 tsp. salt	2 tsp. prepared mustard
2 tsp. powdered sage or powdered bay leaf	½ tsp. freshly ground pepper

If you use fresh parsley and chives, double the amount of salt. If you use dry parsley and chives, cut their amount in half, and soak them, together with the sage or bay leaf, in the wine for half an hour before blending them into the butter and other ingredients. Preserve in sealed jars in a cool place.

— HERB BUTTER II —
(for Vegetables)

1 cup clarified butter	½ tbs. fresh tarragon
1 tbs. lemon juice	1 tsp. fresh basil
2 tbs. fresh chives	1 tsp. salt
½ tbs. fresh dill	ground pepper to taste
	pinch bicarbonate of soda

This sauce must be made with fresh herbs to give the right tang to vegetables. Should you have only some of the fresh herbs indicated above, soak the dried crushed herbs in the lemon juice for at least fifteen minutes before mixing the other ingredients. The fresh herbs should be chopped when you are ready to make the sauce and not before. Add the bicarbonate of soda last, mixing it well into the rest of the paste. This sauce may not last very long, only a few weeks perhaps, and you may wish to refrigerate it. It is excellent on practically all fresh vegetables which you previously steam or boil. Remove the hot, drained vegetable to a skillet, add some of the sauce, and heat up together briefly on a high flame, stirring. Serve hot.

— PEANUT BUTTER —

Your own peanut butter will keep in a cool place longer than your family will allow it, and will be free of the dangerous preservatives some commercial varieties contain.

A pound of peanuts in the shell makes about two cups of peanut butter, with the addition of about one-quarter cup of your favorite vegetable oil. Just shell the nuts and pour them into your grinder or blender, and add portions of nuts and oil alternately until they are all ground up. Stop the blender when the consistency, chunky or creamy, pleases you. Then taste and add salt, if needed. Remove to jars and seal tightly.

— APPLE BUTTER —

Use tart cooking apples. Peel and quarter, and measure about three pecks. To two gallons of water add nine pounds of brown sugar and bring to a boil. Add the apples and, when the mixture returns to a boil, stir constantly until most of the liquid is absorbed and it seems the right consistency. Then add cinnamon and nutmeg to your taste.

An even richer product can be obtained if in place of the water you use sweet apple cider, which you have boiled to reduce to half.

· SAUCE BASES ·

The following recipes are essences or extracts from which delicious sauces can be made. They are easy to store and will keep indefinitely in sealed jars.

— Seasoning Essence —

2 cups dry white wine	4 cloves
2 tbs. white vinegar	2 tbs. chopped mushrooms
2 tbs. salt	1 tbs. chopped parsley
10 crushed shallots or 20 chives	6 sprigs chervil
	2 sprigs tarragon
1 medium onion, chopped fine	2 sprigs thyme
1 tbs. peppercorns	4 bay leaves
4 slices medium carrot	1 tsp. coriander
2 stalks from heart of celery	pinch ground nutmeg

Place all ingredients in a pot and cover tightly. Bring to a boil and simmer for a few minutes. Then place a flame-resistant pad under the pot, or use a double boiler, and simmer very slowly for seven or eight hours. Let cool and strain through muslin or cheesecloth. Pour into small jars, close tightly, and store.

Use a very small amount of this essence to add flavor to sauces, soups, stews, casseroles, and many other dishes.

— Meatless "Meat" Base —

Our vegetarian readers may find this preparation excellent and use it as a base for most dishes that call for a meat base, such as meat sauce, croquettes, ravioli, etc. It comes from a French vegetarian friend. Of course, when eggplant is in season, you can use the same recipe and prepare whatever dish you are planning immediately. But you can also preserve this delicious base.

Peel and cube any amount of eggplant you have, sprinkle the cubes with fine salt, mix them so that the salt reaches everywhere, spread them on a flat sieve for half an hour, then fry them in good oil. Remove them when golden-brown and mash or blend them with one-third their amount of chopped walnuts (chopped almonds can be used instead, but walnuts are better). Then fill warm, sterilized jars with the mixture, pressing down as you fill them so that no air pockets are formed. Close the jars, and boil in canner for twenty minutes. Allow to cool, then store in a cool place.

315

— Mushroom Extract I —

A classic extract from France, the land of gourmet sauces, is the mushroom extract we are now sharing with you. It can be added to any dish, but especially to sauces that must remain smooth and free of chunks of mushrooms. It is powerful, so use sparingly.

Chop any quantity of mushrooms and put them in a pot with just enough water for them to start cooking without sticking to the bottom of the pot—just a few drops. Simmer, covered, and when they give out their juice, pour it into a smaller pot, which you will keep covered. Put the mushrooms back on the fire, adding boiling water in the same quantity as the juice you have just removed, and simmer again. Repeat several times until, tasting the juice, you think it has lost flavor. At this point discard the mushrooms and simmer all the juice you have obtained until it thickens to the consistency of a syrup. Remove to warm jars and seal tightly.

— Mushroom Extract II —

A spicier variation comes to us from Switzerland.

Put mushrooms in a bowl, sprinkle them with salt, mix, and sprinkle them again. Cover the bowl and let stand twelve hours. Then press the mushrooms with a wooden spoon as much as you can, and boil the juice they gave out, adding a little ground pepper and a few spices (of your choice) to the juice. Skim the foam occasionally, if necessary. When no more foam is rising to the top, strain and pour the juice into very small jars; this extract is rather potent (so that you'll need a small amount) and should be used fairly quickly after the jar has been opened or the aroma will evaporate.

— Onion Extract I —

Here are two ways to make a delicious extract you can use as is on bread whenever you'd like a tasty snack, or that you can add to meats, fish, poultry, or any other dish. The first is an old American recipe and the second is of European origin.

Put five pounds of onions into a heavy-duty pot and cover them with water. Bring to a boil, turn the heat down to a bare simmer, cover the pot, and simmer for twenty-four hours. Check it every two hours or so, and stir and add a little water if the contents threaten to "burn on." After a day and a night you will have a dark-brown, gooey concentrate with some lumps in it. Stir it into a uniform sauce, add salt to taste, and let it simmer, this time uncovered, until the remaining liquid is cooked off. Seal into jars.

— ONION EXTRACT II —

3 lbs. onions	3 tsp. honey
1 cup good oil	1 spice bag
1 tbs. vinegar	2 tbs. soy sauce
1 tbs. sugar	6 tbs. brown coloring

Slice the onions and sauté in oil until they are almost dissolved but not burned. Add vinegar, sugar, honey, and spices, and stir. Strain the sauce through a fine sieve or muslin and add the soy sauce and coloring. Taste and add salt if necessary. Put back on a very low fire, covered, until the sauce thickens. Pour into jars and seal well.

— DRIED TOMATO PASTE —

Wash and quarter or cut very ripe tomatoes, sprinkle them with salt on all sides, and allow to drain and ferment a little by placing them, spread out, on a flat sieve or by stretching cheesecloth on top of a large bowl and securing it with tape or a rubber band around the bowl. After seven or eight hours, boil the tomatoes, uncovered, for two hours, stirring often. Now pass them through a fine sieve to remove seeds and peel, then place again in pot and cook on a low flame, stirring, until they have become like a dense sauce. Spread in a thin layer on a slightly oiled baking tray, scoring the paste with a knife in all directions to speed up concentration. Put in a slow oven, stirring with a wooden spoon every now and then; or in strong sun, covered with cheesecloth.

When sufficiently dry but not crusty, remove to cool shallow pans and let stand, covered with muslin or thin cloth, for about four days. Cut into squares and form into little balls the size of

317

small eggs, by working them with your hands, which you will have previously oiled slightly. Now dip the balls into olive oil or very good, dense oil and put them in jars, which you will seal tightly. It is a good idea to place a piece of cloth or paper towel soaked in oil at the top of the jars, before closing them.

This concentrate can be used as a base for tomato sauce for pasta, or can be diluted with a very small amount of boiling water and added to soups, stews, and many other dishes whenever a recipe calls for tomato sauce. It will keep indefinitely in a cool place.

· SAUCES ·

The following miscellaneous section is devoted to various favorite recipes for sauces that keep particularly well and that have the additional advantage of preserving certain kinds of vegetables and herbs that you may have in some quantity.

— CHESTNUT PURÉE —

Chestnut purée stuffing, combined with other ingredients, is one of the Christmas favorites for goose or duck in Scandinavian countries, and a fine accompaniment to some vegetable dishes, poultry, and meat, especially game.

For every two pounds of chestnuts you will need the following ingredients:

2 cups meat stock	*½ tsp. salt*
6 or 8 small center celery stalks	*⅓ cup heavy cream*
2 stalks fresh fennel (finocchio) or ½ tsp. ground or powdered anise seeds	*2 tbs. dry Madeira or sherry*
	¼ cup butter

Shell the nuts and then skin them by immersing them briefly in boiling water and paring with a knife. Cover them with stock and bring to a boil. Add celery, fennel, and salt, reduce heat to a simmer and cook until the liquid has been entirely absorbed and the chestnuts are soft and crumbling. Discard the celery (and fennel, if you used the fresh vegetable) and put through a strainer. Dry the mixture out in a saucepan over medium heat, stirring. When no liquid is left, blend in the cream, wine, and

318

butter. Remove to warm jars, seal, and store in a cool place. The purée will keep for about two months, longer if refrigerated.

If you wish to use this purée for desserts or as a sauce for puddings, ice creams, parfaits, etc., use clear water instead of meat stock and omit the celery. A touch of vanilla extract can be added.

— Green Sauce Florentine —

6 tbs. good-quality oil	1 clove garlic
2 tbs. lemon juice	3 tbs. parsley
2 tbs. capers	3 fresh sage leaves
1 medium onion	or ½ tsp. powdered sage

Chop very fine all ingredients except the first two, and mix the oil and lemon with a fork or wire whisk vigorously. (If you use a blender, all the ingredients can be put in together.) Put mixture on a high fire and remove as soon as you bring it to a quick boil, stirring constantly. Remove immediately to a warm jar, which should be almost full. Fill up the remaining space with oil.

This is an excellent sauce for any type of boiled meat, hot or cold, roasts, and a very good sandwich spread.

Do not use for at least one week. It will keep a few months.

— Red Sauce Milanese —

This sauce is made with red beets. For each medium-size beet, you'll need:

1 tbs. finely chopped parsley

1 clove of garlic, chopped or crushed

1 anchovy, chopped fine (or 1 tsp. soy sauce,
or Worchestershire sauce)

Bake washed and gently scraped beets in the oven, leaving about one inch of the top and without cutting the tip. Slice the beets very thin when cooked, and press into a jar with alternating layers of the above mixture plus good oil and vinegar, salt, and pepper. Cover with about one-half inch of oil on top.

Seal jar, and do not use the sauce for at least one week. It will keep for months.

— HERB SAUCE —

A Spanish vegetarian friend uses this sauce on boiled or baked potatoes or other boiled vegetables, as a filling for hard-boiled eggs (in which case she includes the crushed yolks at the last moment), or as a spread on crackers. But you can also use it on boiled or roasted meats, as well as on boiled fish.

2 tbs. pine nuts or peeled almonds	pinch salt
1 tbs. crushed capers	pinch freshly ground pepper
1 yolk of a hard-boiled egg	pinch grated nutmeg
1 tbs. chopped parsley	pulp of bread the size of an egg, soaked in vinegar, then squeezed
3 pitted, green olives (drained from their brine)	5 tbs. good-quality oil
1 tsp. fresh basil leaves or ¼ tsp. dry basil	juice of 1 lemon

Mix all ingredients except the last two, chop them and pass through a sieve (or mix all ingredients in blender). If you chopped them by hand, the oil and lemon should be mixed vigorously with a fork or wire whisk before you fold in the mixture.

Put in jars, seal, and store in a cool place. It will keep for months.

— PESTO SAUCE —

(*Green Sauce for Spaghetti*)

An outstanding sauce for spaghetti, linguine, fettuccine, or any other long and thin pasta, pesto is a specialty from Genoa, and must be made with fresh basil, so do not attempt it if you only have dried basil. If properly prepared, it will keep for months and months, so it's a good idea to make a large amount in the spring, or when your basil plants have reached about medium growth. The right moment to pick them is when the leaves are not so young that they have not yet developed their full aroma and not so old that they will have become tough and their taste has almost left them or is difficult to extract. Collect youngish

leaves and have ready for every cup of fresh basil leaves the following ingredients:

6 fresh cloves garlic	*3 walnuts or 1 tbs. pine nuts*
½ cup Romano, feta, or any goat or sheep cheese	*(optional)*
	2 cups olive oil
½ cup grated Parmesan cheese	*1 tsp. salt*

You can reduce the amount of garlic if you think it may be too strong for you, but remember that this sauce must have at least some garlic, which is also a preservative that will lengthen the storage time.

This sauce is usually made by pounding the ingredients in a mortar until you have a thick paste. You can use a blender, but if you do you are going to have to leave part of your sauce in the machine, as it is difficult to scrape out; and if you use the blender, select a slow speed.

Some people don't add any cheese to the sauce and prefer to sprinkle the grated cheese directly on the pasta when it is served. The sauce will keep either way, so you can follow either of the two methods; or you can add some cheese to the sauce and more when you are ready to eat your pasta.

Put your sauce in jars, seal well, and store in a cool, dark place. It is a good idea to really stuff the sauce into the jars and add a little olive oil on top.

It will keep for about a year, until you have more fresh basil to make a new batch.

When ready to use the sauce, drain the pasta well, place in a bowl, and mix in a small amount of sauce without heating it. Pesto sauce has a very unique but strong flavor, so use about one-fourth the amount you would use of regular tomato or meat sauce. Melted butter or margarine or (preferably) olive oil is usually added to the sauce and the pasta when mixing it before serving.

You can also add a small quantity of this sauce to a minestrone soup or any other vegetable soup that lacks zest.

— Tomato Catsup —

Make your own at home. It will keep practically forever on the pantry shelf.

Cut up and cook until soft a gallon of ripe red tomatoes, then pass them through a medium sieve. Add:

2 cups cider or wine vinegar
1 tsp. red pepper
3 tbs. sugar
½ cup salt

Then tie into a bag two tablespoons each of black peppercorns, cloves, and dry mustard; three tablespoons cinnamon; and one-half tablespoon mace.

Boil about four hours, remove the spice bag, and bottle while still hot.

Although catsup is most often made from tomatoes, you can substitute for the tomatoes any number of other fruits, berries, or vegetables, and follow more or less the above procedure. Modify the spices to go with the different taste of apples, gooseberries, cucumbers, mushrooms, or cranberries. They are all delicious.

— Catsup from Beer and Wine —

2 qts. strong flat beer
1 qt. white wine
¼ lb. anchovies
3 ginger roots, sliced
6 tbs. peeled shallots, chopped
1 tbs. ground mace or ½ tbs. ground nutmeg

Cook all ingredients except shallots and mace or nutmeg over moderate heat until one-third reduced. Cool, add shallots and mace or nutmeg, pass through sieve, and bottle it.

It will keep many years without refrigeration.

— "Store" Sauce —

2 tbs. grated horseradish 1 tbs. salt
1 tbs. allspice 1 tbs. sugar
½ tsp. nutmeg, grated pinch cayenne pepper
3 lbs. pickled onions, 1 qt. vinegar
minced fine
24 black peppercorns

Mix all the spices together and crush them. Pour the vinegar over and let stand two weeks in a cool place, covered. Then bring to a boil, strain, and set aside a day or so to cool and settle. Bottle and seal tightly.

This sauce is an excellent gravy, sauce, or stew base.

— Tomato and Mushroom Sauce —

You can serve this Italian specialty with spaghetti or any other kind of pasta, as well as other dishes.

2 large onions 2 lbs. very ripe tomatoes
2 medium-size carrots 3 tsp. chopped parsley
1 medium-size celery stalk 5 leaves fresh basil
3 tbs. butter (or 2 tsp. dry)
1 tbs. oil (olive oil preferred) pinch salicylic acid
1 cup chopped mushrooms

Chop one onion, carrots, and celery, and simmer, covered, with a little water for two hours. Pass through sieve. Slice the other onion very thin and sauté lightly in the butter and oil, then add mushrooms. After a few minutes add the tomatoes and cook one hour. Add parsley and basil and simmer ten more minutes. Allow to cool some, add salicylic acid, mix well, and put in jars, well sealed.

— "Worcestershire" Sauce —

This is as close to Worcestershire sauce as the well-guarded secret of the original manufacturers would allow us to come. It tastes very much like it and is certainly better than most of the various steak sauces commercially available in this country.

Another added attraction is that you are making it yourself and you know that none of the ingredients is going to harm you.

½ cup molasses	_1 tsp. black pepper_
3 tbs. onions, finely chopped	_½ tsp. fenugreek_
3 tbs. coarse salt	_½ tsp. ginger powder_
3 tbs. dry mustard	_½ tsp. cinnamon powder_
1 tsp. paprika	_½ tsp. cloves_
¼ tsp. cayenne pepper	_¼ tsp. cardamom seeds_
1 clove garlic, crushed	_few drops Tabasco_
1 anchovy fillet, finely chopped, or ½ tsp. anchovy extract	_1 cup dry white wine_
6 tbs. fresh tamarind, or 1 tbs. tamarind extract	_2 cups vinegar (preferably aromatic)_
	2 tsp. burnt sugar coloring

Grind very fine or pound in mortar all the above spices that are not in powder form. Place in pot with the rest of the ingredients except the wine, one cup of the vinegar, and coloring. Bring to a boil and simmer on a very low flame (or double boiler) for one hour, adding the rest of the vinegar a little at a time, when it evaporates. Remove from fire, add the wine, and let stand, covered, for eight days. At the end of this period, filter the sauce through fine muslin or cheesecloth folded several times. Add brown coloring, bottle, and seal.

Do not use for at least one month, and shake the bottle before using. It can be preserved for years, especially if stored in a cool place.

— Mock "Worcestershire Sauce" —

A variation of the previous sauce, especially for those of you who don't happen to have a fresh crop of tamarinds or who cannot find tamarind extract, this is also a very good steak sauce.

2 tbs. strained catsup
3 finely minced shallots
2 finely chopped anchovy fillets or 1 tsp. anchovy extract
½ tsp. powdered cloves
1 qt. strong vinegar

Combine all ingredients in a small pot, place in another pot containing boiling water, and continue boiling the water until the sauce in the inner pot is well heated but not yet boiling. Remove from fire, cover, and let stand two days, then strain finely and bottle.

It will keep for years in a cool place.

SOURCES

Anything in this book that you don't grow or make yourself, you can buy in your local market, hardware store, pharmacy, butcher shop, health-food emporium, or other specialty shop. We also suggest that you explore the rich store of written material available from the U.S. Department of Agriculture and other government agencies. For a catalogue of U.S. Government publications, write to the Superintendent of Documents, U.S. Government Printing Office, Washington, D.C. 20402. The local extension services of the Department of Agriculture in your own state can also be extremely helpful in directing you to the specialized companies and stores in your area.

But just in case you have problems obtaining information or material, here are some addresses of companies from which you can order by mail:

General Information

American Cultured Dairy Products Institute
910 17th Street
Washington, D.C. 20006

National Frozen Foods Association
1 Chocolate Avenue
Hershey, Pennsylvania 17033

326

National Preservers Association
25 Chestnut Street
Chicago, Illinois 60611

Home Smokers and Other Specialized Equipment

Colonial Garden Kitchens
270 West Merrick Road
Valley Stream, New York 11582

Hammacher Schlemmer
147 East 57th Street
New York, New York 10022

R. H. Macy & Company
1 Herald Square
New York, New York 10001

The Original Vermont Country Store, Inc.
Weston, Vermont 05161

The Oster Corporation
5055 North Lydell Avenue
Milwaukee, Wisconsin 53217

Smoker Products, Inc.
P.O. Box 26469
San Francisco, California 94126

The Vermont Country Store
Rockingham, Vermont 05101

Sausage Casings

Esposito's
500 Ninth Avenue
New York, New York 10018

I. Klayman
5701 Tacony Street
Philadelphia, Pennsylvania 19131

Omaha Beef Company
9 Maple Avenue
Danbury, Connecticut 06810

Cheese- and Yogurt-Making Ingredients

Hansen's Laboratory Inc.
9015 West Maple Street
Milwaukee, Wisconsin 53214

International Yogurt Company
628 North Dohemy Drive
Los Angeles, California 90069
or
1000 Bedard Boulevard
Chambly, Quebec, Canada

Mid-America Dairymen, Inc.
2424 Territorial Road
St. Paul, Minnesota 55114

New Jersey Dairy Laboratories
P.O. Box 748
New Brunswick, New Jersey 08903

Pfizer Inc.
4215 N. Pt. Washington Avenue
Milwaukee, Wisconsin 53212

Pfizer Inc. is the only company, at this writing, that has developed a very good vegetable rennet, called "sure-curd."

Salada Foods Inc.
Woburn, Massachusetts 01801

Wagner Products, Division of Wagner Mfg. Co.
Box 405
Hustisford, Wisconsin 53034

Uncommon Herbs and Spices and Other Exotica

Aloupis Company
916 Ninth Street N.W.
Washington, D.C. 20001

American Tea, Coffee & Spice Company
1511 Champa Street
Denver, Colorado 90202

Antone's Import Foods
2605 S. Sheridan
Tulsa, Oklahoma 74129

Barzizza Brothers
351-353 S. Front Street
Memphis, Tennessee 38103

Big Tea Party Store
1928 Packard
Ann Arbor, Michigan 48104

C. & K. Import Company
2771 West Pico Boulevard
Los Angeles, California 90006

Capello's Imported Foods
5328 Lemmon Avenue
Dallas, Texas 75209

Central Grocery
923 Decatur
New Orleans, Louisiana 70116

Columbus Food Market
2604 Lawrence Avenue
Chicago, Illinois 60625

De Laurenti's Italian Delicatessen
Lower Pike Place Market
Seattle, Washington 98101

Dimyan's Market
116 Elm Street
Danbury, Connecticut 06810

T. Eaton Co.
190 Yonge Street, Dept. 579
Toronto, Ontario, Canada

S. Enskin Inc.
1201 St. Lawrence Blvd.
Montreal 129, Quebec, Canada

Euphrates Grocery
101 Shawmut Avenue
Boston, Massachusetts 02118

Gourmet Appetizers Inc.
203 Houston Street
New York, N.Y. 10002

India Spice House
126 Lexington Avenue
New York, N.Y. 10016

International House
712 Washington Avenue, S.E.
Minneapolis, Minnesota 55414

International House of Foods
440 West Gorham Street
Madison, Wisconsin 53703

Joseph's Imported Food Co.
621 Fields Avenue
Jacksonville, Florida 32202

K. Kalustyan
123 Lexington Avenue
New York, New York 10016

Kassos Brothers
570 Ninth Avenue
New York, New York 10036

Persia Imports
347 Grant Avenue
San Francisco, California 94108

Purity Importing Company
4507 Swiss Avenue
Dallas, Texas 75204

Quality Imported Foods
717 N. Sixth Street
St. Louis, Missouri 63101

The Top Banana Ltd.
62 William Street
Ottawa 2, Ontario, Canada

·INDEX·

331